THE
POSITIVE HABIT

**6 STEPS for TRANSFORMING NEGATIVE
THOUGHTS to POSITIVE EMOTIONS**

Fiona Brennan

GILL BOOKS

Gill Books
Hume Avenue
Park West
Dublin 12

www.gillbooks.ie

Gill Books is an imprint of M.H. Gill and Co.

© Fiona Brennan 2019

978 07171 8330 2

Designed by www.grahamthew.com

Edited by Susan McKeever

Proofread by Jane Rogers

Printed by Scandbook AB, Sweden

This book is typeset in Alda Regular, 10 on 16 pt .

A CIP catalogue record for this book is available from
the British Library.

15 14 13

The identities of the case studies in this book, both who have
told their own stories and those I have told, have been changed
to protect the privacy of these individuals.

This book is not intended as a substitute for the medical advice
of a physician. The reader should consult a doctor or mental
health professional if they feel it necessary.

For Ciaran and Luca
Our three hearts beat as one – always.

Access the **FREE AUDIO HYPNOTHERAPIES** at www.thepositivehabit.com by entering the password **HABIT**.

INTRODUCTION

*'The secret of change is to focus all
of your energy, not on fighting the old,
but on building the new.'*

SOCRATES

Imagine we are together in a room that is cosy, bright and calming. It is your first consultation and perhaps you came to see me because you have recently been feeling more anxious or stressed than is comfortable, or perhaps you feel overwhelmed with work and too many responsibilities. Maybe you feel nervous speaking in public or at meetings and are worried about the impact this will have on your career. You might have been getting angry with the people you love – your partner, your children – and you feel ashamed about this. Maybe you are worried about your health because you are eating too much and/or drinking too much to escape from difficult emotions. It could be a combination of all these reasons. Either way, you have doubted yourself and your mind is racing with negative thoughts.

It is also possible, even highly likely, that you have no idea why you are here; you've had an uneasy, niggling feeling for a while that there has to be more to life, that you have the potential to be happier, to have a more positive outlook. Whatever your situation is, I want you to imagine that I am sitting across from you now and I want nothing more than to help you.

You are explaining to me how you feel, and I am listening attentively to you. I ask some questions that make you think I have an idea of how you feel. I tell you that I will give you 100 per cent commitment to help you to feel better. I empathise with how hard it is to find time for yourself in a busy world. You may feel a little self-conscious; after all, how do you know I can really help? Is this a waste of your time and money? How can you trust me? Maybe you feel it is self-indulgent to talk about yourself. You feel like a character in a Woody Allen film; it makes you uneasy to talk about yourself, you feel weak and vulnerable, you 'should' be able to 'fix this' yourself, yet at the same time it is a relief to speak to someone who seems to genuinely want to help and is not there to judge you. You may even be fighting back tears and asking yourself what is wrong with you; you promised yourself you wouldn't cry and that you would be positive! You may want to run, but you don't.

I explain that the way you feel is not your fault – it is an evolutionary habit, it's part of being human and the negative emotions you feel are there for a reason. While negative emotions are an unfortunate habit that you have learned unconsciously there are also many people, just like you, who have consciously cultivated six, super-emotional, positive habits that I will share with you. Each habit is like a rung on a ladder. Each step brings you closer to happiness. Either way, emotions are not there to be judged but accepted and through this acceptance and the power of your mind and love you can move beyond the doubts that drain your precious energy.

You start to feel a little more relaxed: the feeling that you are not alone gives you hope. I explain that it is important we work together to understand the roots of any negative and limiting beliefs that you may have from your childhood, so that we can embrace the six new habits that will help you to flourish. I ask you to work with me and I explain that, at the end of the day, all therapy is self-therapy – *you* are the person who makes the changes and takes control. My desire to help you is worth nothing without your own determination to help yourself. However, we are very much in this together. I won't tell you what you 'should' do to develop the mindset that positive people have, but I will clearly and kindly show you *how* to do so. Fundamentally, this is about moving from a state of fear to one of love. This is the beginning and the end of everything.

You are starting to feel that if you keep an open mind and commit to make time for yourself this could work. I explain that the transformation works on two levels, conscious and subconscious, which is why the six positive habits approach is so effective and can produce transformative results relatively quickly. I tell you that the first seven minutes when you wake and the last seven minutes before you sleep contain the most powerful potential for change as this is when your subconscious is most relaxed and therefore suggestible. I explain that I will make it really simple for you and provide you with a seven-minute recording to listen to first thing in the morning as you wake and a 24-minute one last thing at night as you drift towards sleep. Many people fall asleep within the first seven minutes and during this time your conscious and subconscious merge. I tell you that clients who have suffered from poor sleep for years now enjoy a peaceful eight hours' sleep each night. The sleep time hypnotherapy you will listen to each night will programme your subconscious mind with the six positive emotional habits as you drift off. Your subconscious never sleeps, so you can relax and let me do all the work on that level. *It is essential that you listen to them every night: their efficacy is based on consistency.*

Think about it: is your mental health worth 14 conscious minutes a day?

I ask, 'Do you want to sleep deeply and peacefully with no medication but the power of your own mind to guide you to sleep? Do you want to wake up happy and grateful, to feel calm and confident in all that you do?' You nod in anticipation; it seems too good to be true, until I say, 'I also need your conscious effort and commitment to the process. There will be some hard moments as you begin to understand your current emotional habits better and I may need you to confront memories from the past, not to upset you but to strengthen you so that you can truly let them go.' Positive people make time for themselves, not as a luxury but as a necessity.

'I believe you can do this but it's up to you,' I say. 'Are you prepared to make time to commit to yourself? You will need to be patient and not rush; I don't want to add pressure to your life but to relieve it. So, can you take a leap of faith that allows you to believe in yourself?' What answer do you hear yourself give?

You have only just met me, but we end the session with a hug. You feel tired but relieved and you have hope in your heart. You go home and at bedtime you put on your positive habit sleep time hypnotherapy and you sleep better than you have done in a long time. The next day you wake up and it surprises you to notice that you automatically seek out your seven-minute morning ritual. Already you feel just a little bit better than you did yesterday. You have a plan, a strategy, something to hold on to and you are going to stick to it. Finally, you feel that you are in control of your own life.

 THE POSITIVE HABIT EMOTIONS QUIZ # 1

Your next step is to take the quiz on the next page. This will help to evaluate your current emotional health. It's interesting to note that the word 'health' is derived from the word 'wholeness'. How complete or whole do you feel at this moment?

Answer each question with the <u>first</u> answer that comes to mind. Be honest, don't debate your response, do it quickly without overthinking. That answer is usually the most truthful one.

Please answer 'Yes' or 'No' to each question. Allocate a point for each 'Yes' answer that you give and also write down the answer.

1 Do you feel present most of the time?

2 Do you make time to care for your mind each day?

3 Do you love yourself?

4 Do you believe you are a compassionate person?

5 Are you able not to take anything other people do or say personally?

6 If you feel stress or anxiety, do you use your breath to calm your mind?

7 Do you protect your mind from negative information, people and places, for example having regular digital breaks/avoiding people who drain your energy?

8 Do you feel confident to speak your mind and feel equal to others?

9 Are you kind to yourself if you make a mistake?

10 Do you feel grateful each day?

11 Do you let go of grudges from the past?

12 Do you visualise a bright future?

13 Do you feel you are living your life purpose?

14 Do you take care of your physical needs, such as getting eight hours' sleep, exercising and eating a balanced diet?

15 Do you feel that you are good enough as a person?

16 Do you trust that no matter what happens you will be able to cope?

You will take this same quiz at the beginning of each of the six emotional habit chapters. Take a note of your score each time you do the quiz – that way you will be able to see your progress. I will remind you to do this.

Can you see which areas need more of your attention? The 'no' answers are as important as the 'yes' ones; it is from these that you will really learn where to put your focus.

Score =   /16

+ + +

Explaining the Positive Habit

'Watch your thoughts; they become words. Watch your words; they become actions; watch your actions; they become habits; watch your habits; they become your character. Watch your character; it becomes your destiny.'

LAO TZU

YOUR LIFE IS A MIRACLE to be celebrated, honoured, loved and lived to the full. I hope that you already know this, and the fact that you are reading this book means you do 'know' it, but perhaps you no longer *feel* it? There's a word for this – 'anhedonia' is the absence of being able to feel positive emotions or pleasure and is one of the most common symptoms of depression and anxiety. If you have felt like this, you will know all about the black hole that swallows your heart, mind and soul. If you are suffering from this I will help you to fill this void using the technique of mindfulness to self-generate the six positive emotional habits that will leave any feelings of apathy where they belong – in the past.

We have become a society which is afraid of feeling, especially of feeling negative emotions. However, each emotion, whether it is positive or negative, is valid and it is there to guide you and help you.

According to the World Health Organisation[1] one in four of us suffer from some form of mental health issue at some point in our lives. This is a startling statistic and with most people not getting the help they deserve, the time has arrived for each individual to help change this. We must aim to prevent poor mental health habits developing rather than trying to cure them. We must equip ourselves and our children with the tangible skills that teach emotional intelligence, resilience and how to take control of our hearts and minds.

We are in the grip of an anxiety epidemic, with many people living in a chronic state of unnecessary fear. The latest findings[2] show that approximately 9 per cent of the global population suffer from anxiety. Women come out as the most vulnerable at any age but experience peaks in the 15–24 age group (5 per cent), and again in the 40–49 group (6 per cent). In men the figure is 3 per cent across all ages with a slow decline in the over-sixties. I imagine the actual number of men suffering anxiety is higher, but many men would not come forward and admit to a mental health issue – they are conditioned to suffer in silence.

Why are so many of us suffering now? Anxiety is not new; it was always part of being human. The word 'anxiety' is derived from the Latin *angō*, meaning 'I cause physical pain' and for many a severe anxiety attack does indeed manifest with physical symptoms, such as a stomach ache. One of the main reasons for the rise in anxiety is that as the world becomes busier, many of us have forgotten to value simply being alive. The digital age conditions us to always want more: more success, more information, more power, more money, more followers on social media platforms. Previous generations may have had fewer material things, but it appears they had more of what matters – peace of mind. In the West we live in a post-Christian society and have lost faith, not only in God, but also in ourselves. We have lost our faith in the divine and replaced it with technology and, as a result, we are suffering spiritually. This lack leaves a gaping emptiness in our souls that we try in vain to fill with things like status, property and shopping.

For many, every day becomes a struggle and feelings of being overwhelmed result in anxiety and stress. It is helpful to remember that the human race is adaptable and survives even in the most hostile of circumstances – you are stronger than you think you are. You must ensure that you become a master of the digital age and not a slave to it. As society evolves, so must we. The root of modern anxiety is not technology or its use; this simply exacerbates an underlying condition that is part of our biological makeup.

In the midst of this rather bleak picture of mass anxiety there are rare people who seem to be authentically happy and nauseatingly positive! How do they do it? Are they genuinely positive or are they putting on an act? The truth is that positive people are not really happy all the time but they are not acting either: they have simply made a choice to view the world through a lens that aids rather than hinders them. Positive people are not naive and unrealistic but are strong, optimistic, resourceful and resilient. In short, they choose to bring out their best selves, not their worst.

Positivity is pragmatism, it is worthwhile, it is resilience, it is a choice.

Being positive is not about denying the negative but embracing it courageously. Positive people are intelligent people who choose to live fully in the moment. They live without unnecessary fear; they constantly create and make things happen. Being in their company is exciting and exhilarating. You already have all of these attributes, but perhaps they just haven't been unearthed yet. You too can live and love, fully present to the immense possibilities of life.

Following the steps in this book will enable you to reconnect with your true, positive self and feel an energy that desires only to love and be loved. You will feel this love in your heart first thing every morning and sense it last thing at night before you drift into a peaceful, restorative sleep. You will become habituated, through the power of presence and self-knowledge, to what I refer to as 'The Now Habit' which is feeling loved, calm, confident, grateful, hopeful and happy. These six positive emotional habits will be the energy that guides your thoughts and actions and become the driving force that shapes your character and destiny. Each habit is designed to build on the last and amalgamated together they are 'The Positive Habit', the master habit that incorporates all six.

The Positive Habit works. I say this because I know it works; I have had the privilege of seeing positive transformations in many of my clients who courageously and consistently changed old emotional habits of fear and anxiety into the six new ones. They join the ranks of the rare but growing breed of truly positive, conscious people who are fully awake to all the wonders of life.

On a personal level, I too have reaped the rewards of the empowering brain-training methods that I teach: my brain is much fitter, stronger and happier than it was ten years ago. If I were to undergo an MRI brain scan my left prefrontal cortex (the part of the brain that is activated by positive emotions) would light up, indicating a positive and resilient outlook.

Most of us spend more time unloading the dishwasher and doing laundry than we do tending to our mental health. While this is undoubtedly part of the problem, I want you to focus on the solution. The seven-minute morning ritual audio that you will listen to is one of the simplest and most effective ways of making time for yourself a daily habit. Starting the day with a positive mindset allows everything to flow from a strong and productive start. The sleep time hypnotherapy audio will transform your thoughts as you sleep; lasting change comes from an authentic desire within the subconscious mind to care for and love yourself.

The Positive Habit is based on years of research on the science of habits and happiness, positive psychology and neuroscience.

Habits have three components (see page 52). Once you understand how these work you will be able to apply them to both your emotional and behavioural habit loops. It's not wishful thinking – you will *scientifically* be turning negative emotional habits into positive ones. William James (1842–1910), an American philosopher and psychologist known as the 'father of psychology', described humans as a 'mere bundle of habits',[3] most of them existing below our conscious awareness. James believed that if we can automate positive habits we can free the mind from the constant battle of trying to change negative habits. This battle is what I refer to as 'inner conflict' and I have seen so many of my clients struggle with this exhausting and damaging practice. They want to change a negative mindset to a positive one, they want to get healthier, fitter, slimmer and happier but feel they self-sabotage each attempt to do so. In this book I will look at why we do this, why it is not our fault and what we can do to change it.

More than 40 per cent of what you do each day is a habit and many of these, as James pointed out, are subconscious and automatic.[4] Some of them are clearly useful, like brushing your teeth, reading a bedtime story to your child or driving a familiar route to work, but others, like smoking, eating or drinking too much, are clearly harmful. We generally tend to think of habits as 'bad,' as a behaviour that we need to change. What if you discovered that you are also engaged in habits for the remaining 60 per cent of your day and that many of those habits are often not so healthy either?

Thinking is a habit that most of us are unconsciously addicted to.

Being seemingly unable to 'switch off' your mind is an unfortunate and nasty side-effect of evolution and in the digital age it is mirrored by the lack of ability to switch off technology. This keeps the mind permanently switched to ON, which is exhausting and a major factor in sleep issues. I will analyse this more thoroughly later, but for now consider that negative thoughts fuel your emotions to become negative and when you are flooded with toxic emotions you use up all your energy simply to survive.

Do you ever wonder why you fly off the handle at seemingly insignificant things? For example, always having to put out the rubbish or clear up after others or having a partner who never puts away their shoes? Surprisingly, it's not the shoes or the bins that are the real problem, although, I admit, nobody likes tripping up or dealing with smelly rubbish! What is happening here is that you are more than likely being triggered by an old, subconscious belief, for example, the need for order (the shoes left strewn) or a memory from childhood that life is 'not fair' (putting out the rubbish).

Understanding yourself better and dispelling some of these subconscious beliefs will reduce the power they have over you in creating toxic emotional feelings. I do not advocate rumination on the past or bringing up past traumas unnecessarily, nor do I believe in ignoring the past, hoping it will go away, but in order to progress we do need to be aware of how past events, beliefs and patterns of behaviour have shaped who we have become. People with a positive mindset have often taken a long and hard look at their past and have spent time learning to understand their personal history.

Once you understand your own childhood and take the time and courage to work through your memories, you become genuinely ready to let go of the negative, live peacefully in the present and bring all your positive insights into the future. If you feel you have issues from your past that are too traumatic for this book alone to help you with I strongly suggest you consider seeking help from a mental health professional. Please also continue to read and engage with the book, though.

Whatever therapeutic work you have already done on yourself will be complemented by reading this book. Please don't view the exercises I set you in forthcoming chapters as daunting but more as a spring clean for the mind; it takes initial effort, but it is so worth it. Afterwards, you can start to enjoy things without negative, unconscious thoughts dictating your life. You will then consciously create positive emotions with the power of your thoughts and imagination. When your mind is clearer and calmer you are more able to rationalise your behaviour and to start becoming more emotionally resilient and happy.

+ + +

Tools for Change

NIALL BRESLIN, one of Ireland's leading mental health ambassadors and campaigners for change, has suffered from both acute and chronic anxiety and has spoken openly about his journey. In doing so, he has empowered others to step out of the darkness of shame and stigma. A Lust for Life, his mental health charity, has provided millions of people with a safe platform to share their stories and insights and to learn from mental health professionals. Breslin has attended many seminars where speakers tell people that they have to change their mindsets, but don't equip them with the tools of *how* to do it. He said, 'it is pointless, we know we need to change, we just don't know how.'[5] This therefore is my mission – to give you the tools.

The Wisdom
of Ancient Greece

ANCIENT GREEK PHILOSOPHERS such as Aristotle, Socrates and Epicurus offer us timeless wisdom on how to be human, how to live the good life, how to do the right thing and find meaning in a world that can be overwhelming at best and tragic at worst. They teach us how to bring peace to our inner and outer worlds, stressing that happiness is not a passive goal but an active pursuit in which we employ the services of the rational mind. Their message is eternal and it echoes throughout the pages of this book.

The ancient Greeks were world leaders in the fields of architecture, art, science and philosophy. They endlessly sought to improve their knowledge and to make sense of their world, which led them to create mythical gods. In following this book, you will use the same power of imagination, but rather than creating gods, you will create six inner, positive, emotional habits that, like columns of a Greek temple, are built to last. Once the initial building work is complete you can then rely on it for shelter and feelings of safety and wellbeing. When you experience the reward of emotional resilience you will maintain it with love and care.

Classical Greek structures were built with strong foundations and solid pillars that support the roof and keep the building stable. Iconic buildings such as the Parthenon in Athens (the temple to Athena, the goddess of wisdom) represents resilience in its highest form: this temple still stands, powerful and robust, after almost 2,500 years.

In his 1996 book, *Emotional Intelligence*[6] (EQ), psychologist Daniel Goleman argued that EQ is more important than IQ. Leaders who are emotionally intelligent will create happier staff and higher profits. Goleman outlines the five principles of EQ:

1 **Self-awareness** – understanding what drives your emotions.

2 **Self-regulation** – feeling autonomy over your emotions, pausing before reacting.

3 **Internal motivation** – knowing your life purpose.

4 **Empathy** – having compassion for others, seeing things from their point of view and not taking things personally.

5 **Social skills** – confidence, communication, building rapport, leading by example.

Together, in this book, we will examine all of these.

At the Temple of Apollo in Delphi the words inscribed over the forecourt are 'know thyself'. EQ boils down to self-knowledge, which, in essence, is self-awareness and an understanding of why we do what we do. Understanding begets compassion and compassion cultivates self-love that creates an inner peace which in turn creates a collective higher consciousness.

In short, the more self-aware we are, the less conflict there is both internally and externally. Those with a high EQ have taken the time and developed the mettle to uncover and deal with subconscious negative emotional habits. As a result, positive people take responsibility for their actions and have compassion, both towards themselves and towards others. It is their default state.

The Master Habit of Positivity

I WILL REFER to this master habit throughout this book as the Positive Habit because it encapsulates the six positive emotional habits that create your best self on a spiritual level. Cultivating positivity will put you at the top of the EQ class. The Dalai Lama believes that 'happiness is not a luxury but a human necessity,' and that a positive mindset can change the world. He therefore encourages us to cultivate positive mental states and reduce negative ones so that we can literally 'feed on joy'.[7] Initially, this takes courage; to feed on the positive we need first to weed out the negative until the rewards of a positive mindset start to replace the perceived protection that the negative seems to provide. Many people hold on to negative emotional habits as they are familiar and provide what psychologists term 'secondary benefits'. An example of this could be an elderly aunt who has psychosomatic pains every day – this means her family visit her regularly. But what if the pain went away? Would they still visit her as often? Her pains are a subconscious response to her dread of loneliness.

Miriam Kerins Hussey was a practising pharmacist for ten years and now works as an integrated wellness and nutritional coach. She became disillusioned by the standard medical practice of dispensing medicines via prescription when she saw many patients become prescription-dependent and get progressively sicker rather than better. 'Every disease has an emotional beginning' she points out, 'an emotion that is suppressed will, with time, manifest physically in the form of pain and illness.'[8] Numbing suppressed emotions with medication is ignoring the warning signals rather than tackling the emotion behind the condition.

Positive emotional habits naturally lead to positive behavioural habits.

Have you ever noticed in the most heightened, happy moments that you feel a twinge of sadness? A new mother looks adoringly at her baby, but, at the same time worries about the day the child grows up and leaves her. The niggling thought, 'this is wonderful *but* how long will it last?' creeps in like an unwanted shadow.

Many of us are constantly bemused by the speed at which time passes. When we see a child we haven't seen in a while, we 'can't believe' how big they have become, as though we expect them to remain frozen in time, like the baby in *The Simpsons*, never getting any older. We have a deep-rooted fear of change because change brings uncertainty. Therefore, many of us are more comfortable living our lives half asleep, letting fear dictate our decisions (whether we are consciously aware of this or not). How can we 'feed on joy' if we are asleep to life and its boundless possibilities? Where is the 'comfort' in fear?

I will help you to wake up fully to your life without fearing change and uncertainty. Becoming comfortable with being uncomfortable is, in fact, very comforting the more often you embrace it.

The best place to start is to pause and take some time to understand your emotional habits as they are now. Why do you think what you think? Why do you feel what you feel? Why do you do what you do? These are some of the basic questions you will find answers to in the following chapters.

+ + +

The Positive/Negative Sundial

THE POSITIVE HABIT is a practical and powerful formula that you can apply to your daily life. Each of the six positive habits is designed to help you face any challenge, both personal and professional. For example, if you are feeling stressed because of a difficult boss or relative, applying the techniques in the Calmness Habit will help you to move forward. As you progress you will quickly draw upon the habit you need most.

Whatever state your emotional health is right now, it is not stuck, it is not fixed and can change. I will explain this on a neuroscientific level in the next chapter but for now take comfort in the fact that positivity is a habit that can be learned and practised like any other.

Take a moment to consider your mental health up to this point – there will have been periods when it was in better shape than others; we all have good and bad days: it is a sliding scale. We all move up and down this scale depending on what is going on in our lives. Knowing where you are now on the scale will help you to measure progress as you follow this book.

In Ancient Greece, people measured time using a sundial which told the hour depending on the shadow of the sun on the dial. In order for you to measure how 'sunny' you feel, look at the image on the next page and circle the number that indicates how positive your emotional health is right now (12 is feeling really positive, peaceful, content and happy and 0 is feeling negative, anxious, overwhelmed, irritable and sad).

Be honest with yourself and choose the first number that comes to mind without analysing it. In general, the busier your mind the more likely you are to be lower on the dial. Conversely the calmer your mind and the slower your thoughts, the happier, lighter and closer to peak sunshine you will generally be. We will refer back to the sundial at the end of each chapter as a very simple and visual way of monitoring your progress.

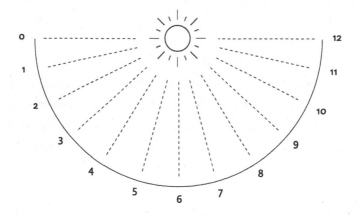

Wherever you are now on this scale is perfectly okay, it's where you are. This is where you need to be right now.

+ **0–5:** This is low, but don't worry; any negative feelings are there for a reason. Embrace and accept them without judgement. You will get so much from the Positive Habit and there is only one way for you to go and that is up!

+ **5–7:** This is where many people come in and it may seem 'not too bad', but is 'not too bad' good enough for you? Not in my opinion.

+ **8–10:** If you already have a generally positive mindset that is wonderful. This book will help you to not only maintain it but also to continue to progress.

+ **10–12:** Put this book down, you don't need me! Actually, not the case. It will help you to have more 12 out of 12 days. There is no reason why most of us cannot live up in the joyous heights of 12 out of 12 most days.

+ + +

Inner, not Outer Goals

Many people who read self-help literature are hoping that by doing so they will finally achieve 'success'; become an affluent entrepreneur, travel the world, meet the 'perfect' partner, be acknowledged as a world expert. While these may all be exciting pursuits, they are also external goals, which ultimately can't make you happy. Stoicism, a school of philosophy founded in Ancient Greece, taught its followers that eternal happiness is contained in our inner worlds which are accessible to us now in this life, in this moment. When you place your sense of self-worth on what you achieve or what you do, you live in a constant state of striving and once one of these goals is realised you tend to quickly look to the next one and are thus never truly content. You are not living in the moment but always projecting to the future.

Striving and dissatisfaction rarely lead to inner peace, which is the only success worth cultivating.

Shawn Achor, author of *The Happiness Advantage,* whose TED talk 'The Happy Secret to Better Work'[9] has more than 16 million views, argues that if we believe success will make us happy we need to flip it the other way: if we become happy first, success will follow. Internal goals have nothing to do with fast cars, losing weight or getting promoted and everything to do with feelings of inner peace, calmness and resilience that help us to feel strong no matter what challenges we face.

Take a moment now to ask yourself which of the six habits that shape a positive person you feel you really need the most right now? Take a deep breath, put your hand on your heart and let your instinct guide you. Is it ...

Habit # 1 – Love?
Habit # 2 – Calmness?
Habit # 3 – Confidence?
Habit # 4 – Gratitude?
Habit # 5 – Hope?
Habit # 6 – Happiness?

Whichever one you choose, let that be your inner goal. Personally, the one I need to return to most is calmness. Be aware that the habit you need to draw upon most today can change depending on your circumstances and the particular challenges you may be facing on any given day. For example, if you have an interview coming up, perhaps habit number three, the Confidence Habit, needs more attention. On the other hand, if you or a loved one is ill you may focus on habit number five, the Hope Habit. Knowing which habit to draw upon at any given moment is a key component in the makeup of an emotionally resilient person.

When you place your attention and intention on a creating a positive inner emotional state as your goal as opposed to an external representation of your achievement you will be amazed as a myriad of abundant opportunities flow into your life. Each of these supreme positive emotions will lead naturally to the creation of successful outcomes as they become the perk of feeling positive and not the goal; when we love ourselves, we will meet the right partner for us, when we feel confident we will become a successful entrepreneur, when we feel calm we will have the courage to travel the world.

+ + +

How to Follow the Book

THE FOLLOWING SYMBOLS are used throughout the book and act as a simple guide to keep you on track.

THE LADDER TO HAPPINESS

> 'You cannot push anyone up the ladder unless he be willing to climb a little himself.'
>
> ANDREW CARNAGIE

You will see the ladder at the beginning of each of the chapters. Each rung represents a habit you are cultivating. The work you do in Part 1 is the preparatory groundwork for the creation of your ladder to happiness. It is fundamental before you even begin to climb the ladder that you are fully prepared and understand how to cultivate a positive mindset, how to embrace the negative and how to live in the now. Then the habits of Love, Calmness, Confidence, Gratitude and Hope all build towards the final step, the Happiness Habit. Each chapter leads to the next and is built on the previous one. They are interconnected and inter-dependable, but they must be read in the order in which they come. Please do not skip forward or you could lose your balance on the ladder and fall down!

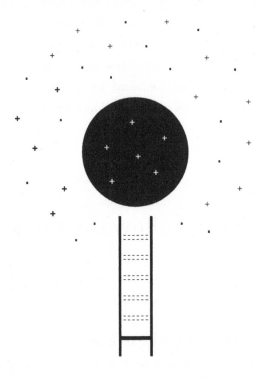

Rather than spending all your time and energy climbing the career or property ladder, focus your effort and attention on climbing the ladder to happiness as this inner state will create abundance in all areas of your life. Take your time; you are creating the most important habit of your life. Don't rush the process. Read slowly, listen to the morning and sleep time audios for at least 66 days and read the book in no less than 21 days. The slower the better: the brain needs time to adjust and change negative thought patterns to positive ones.

 NOTEBOOK
SYMBOL

Find or buy a notebook for yourself, perhaps a nice hardback one. This is essential for our work together as I will ask you to use it at many points throughout the book. Mark it PRIVATE and keep it beside this book. You will see this symbol when you have an exercise to do. This notebook is your journal, your private space, and it can be used both as a mechanism to release toxic emotions and for acknowledging progress and expressing gratitude. Don't let the fear of other people reading your journal stop you. If it helps, hide it in a place that only you know about.

 AUDIO MEDITATION
SYMBOL

Thomas Edison once said, 'Never go to sleep without a request to your subconscious.' As you now know, the first seven minutes of your waking day and the last seven are when your subconscious is most malleable and open to change and therefore you need to listen to your seven-minute morning ritual and sleep time hypnotherapy audio *every day*. The sleep time hypnotherapy is around 24 minutes long, yet you are only actively listening to it with the conscious mind for seven minutes or less. Many people drop off very quickly, but however long it takes you is just right for you. The perk is that either way it does not require you to find any extra time in your day as you listen to it while you fall asleep.

Creating the habit of listening to these recordings is critical to the success of transforming your mindset from negative to positive.

I cannot emphasise enough how important the habit of listening to the recordings is – this is where the 'magic' happens.

They form the positive habit on a subconscious level and consolidate all the therapeutic work you are doing in the reading and exercises. As you progress through the book you will really begin to understand why listening every day is so crucial.

Start to listen to the recordings today. You will find them on www.thepositivehabit.com by entering the password HABIT. If you are listening on a phone, turn it to 'do not disturb'. It is a good idea to keep your phone close to this book and notebook when you go to bed at night. This is your opportunity to make technology work for you and not against you.

If you do not have a smartphone, congratulations; I admire you! You can of course still access the audios on a computer or tablet. If you prefer to listen on a CD it is possible to burn the recording to a CD from your computer. The three main audios to cultivate the six habits of positive people are:

1 **Seven-minute morning ritual** – Set your alarm seven minutes earlier than you normally do and listen to the audio as soon as you wake; you can be lying down or sitting up in bed. Please make sure to use the phone *only* for this purpose and have it switched to do not disturb and/or have all your notifications switched off. Do not get caught up with checking emails or social media until you have finished listening, had your break-fast, shower, etc. and your working day has started. Most people grasp for their phone before their eyes have fully opened. Do you want to be like most people? Make this change today.

2 **Sleep time hypnotherapy** – Listen to this last thing at night and if possible without headphones; if you sleep alone this is easy but if you are with your partner you can encourage them to listen if they are open to it. If not, that's fine, the earphones will fall out during the night.

3 **Meditation visualisations** – These empowering, mindfulness meditation visualisations are designed to help you deal with an emotional block or to help you experience a shift from negative to positive thoughts. You will find them with the morning and night time audios organised by chapter on www.thepositivehabit.com. Most of them are about five minutes long.

THE QUIZ SYMBOL

This is the quiz you have just taken and you will do so again at the beginning of each of the six positive emotional habit chapters. At the end of the book you can then compare your scores so that you can measure your progress. You will also take the quiz, 'How present are you?' at the beginning of How to Create Peaceful Presence and again in the Conclusion.

 IMAGINEERING SYMBOL

This is an exercise that asks you to tap into your imagination at certain times so that I can illustrate a point. Einstein once said: 'Imagination is more important than knowledge and the preview of life's coming attractions' and his 'thought experiments' were the basis of his discoveries. Please go with this, open your mind and try your very best with these exercises; the most direct route to your subconscious is through the power of your imagination.

 AFFIRMATIONAL TOOTH BRUSHING SYMBOL

Each of the six habits has three affirmations that you repeat silently to yourself while you are brushing your teeth in the morning and at night.

> **When you tie a new habit into an existing, established habit you are more likely to remember it.**

What do you usually think about when you brush your teeth? You may just see it as a means to an end, but using this time to consciously programme your mind for positivity is both resourceful and powerful. A crucial aspect of using affirmations is that they must be felt in the heart; simply repeating them without attaching an emotion is ineffective and is the prime reason many people quickly stop using them. As you repeat the affirmation you need to generate the required feeling and let the positive emotions be absorbed into your subconscious.

MINDFUL SHOWER SYMBOL

When you are in the shower, where are you really? Who else is in there with you? Your boss? Your mother? Your adolescent daughter? Most people spend this time worrying and planning the day, what will happen, what they will say, going over endless to-do lists or ruminating on something from the past. My own mind is quick to hop to planning mode; what I will do after the shower, and after that, and after that. You can see how exhausting this can become. I now observe my mind doing this, smile and bring my attention back to the sensation of the water on my skin, focusing on my breathing and simply being in the shower with no agenda! I would love you to also spend these precious minutes being present, calm and conscious. Imagine the warm water is cleansing not only your body but also your mind.

HOW TO CREATE THE HABIT SYMBOL

This symbol denotes mindful daily techniques, tips and suggestions on how to make the emotions into habits at the end of each emotional habit chapter. These are designed to be incorporated into your daily practice and don't require any extra time.

ACKNOWLEDGE
PROGRESS SYMBOL

Most of us neglect to give ourselves credit when it is due. If you do not acknowledge progress, you will not continue to make it. Simple.

At the beginning of each of the chapters dealing with the positive emotions:

You will take a positive habit emotions quiz, similar to the one you took at the start of the book. Please answer honestly and note your last score beside your current one in the space provided, which will enable you to keep an eye on your progress and highlight areas that need your attention.

At the end of each chapter:

1   Write the three emotional habit affirmations you have been saying as you brush your teeth and also identify and write down the concrete evidence that change is occurring. For example, 'I love myself, just the way I am.' Concrete evidence: 'Today I cringed less when I looked in the mirror and I felt a little more comfortable saying, "I love you".' This ensures that these affirmations do not remain as just aspirations: they are bringing about positive change and the concrete evidence supports this.

2   Identify your level of positivity on the sundial (0–12) and compare it to the previous chapter.

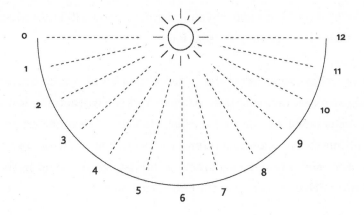

+ + +

How Much Time Does It Take?

THE JURY IS still out on how long it scientifically takes to create a new habit; for a long time it was believed to be 21 days and then more recently it has become widely accepted to be an average of 66 days. However, in one recent study the period was anywhere from 18 days to 254 days.[10] Because it is so subjective it is probably best not to put a number on it. It is more important that you take your time, get it right and establish the habit than rush it. I imagine the last thing you need in your life is more deadlines? Therefore, you should move through the book at your own pace. However, to reiterate, it is *very important* not to go too quickly and so I recommend the **minimum** timeframe below:

+ **21 days** to read the book.

+ **66 days** to listen to the recordings and apply the mindfulness exercises.

Mark 66 days from today in your calendar so you will know when you have been listening for that long.

Many of the exercises require patience in order for you to benefit fully, so please take your time. After 66 days you will automatically be accustomed to listening to the audios and I recommend you continue this in order to reinforce the habit. You could also listen to other audio resources online – a full list can be found in the Further Reading section at the end of this book.

Hold yourself accountable by ticking the days that you have listened to the morning and sleep time rituals. There is a grid at the end of the conclusion that provides a space for you to keep a note of how often you listen. Mark at the top of the grid 66 days from the first day you start to listen. This is not to put pressure on you for the days you may have missed or to make you feel guilty but rather to proudly acknowledge the days you have listened and been present.

+ + +

Our Promise to Each Other

Take a look at the two statements below:

> *I promise to help you to the best of my ability. I promise*
> *that all of the material in this book has been researched*
> *and designed for your greater good. I believe 100 per cent*
> *in the power of The Positive Habit and I am here with you*
> *every step of the way.*

Signed: *Fiona Brennan*

> *I promise to read the book in the order it is written and in*
> *no less than three weeks' time. I will get myself a notebook*
> *and do the exercises to the best of my ability, listen to the*
> *recordings outlined every day for 66 days and if I miss a*
> *day or two, I will not become frustrated or annoyed with*
> *myself or give up. Instead, I will smile kindly to myself,*
> *focus on how well I am doing and keep going.*

If you agree with the above statement, please sign below. These
are our promises to each other.

Signed: ....

Remember:

BEFORE moving to the next chapter:

+ **Get yourself a notebook,** write the word PRIVATE on it
  and/or put it somewhere you feel it will not be read by
  anyone else unintentionally or otherwise; you need to feel
  secure that it is for your eyes only.

+ **Listen** to the seven-minute morning and the sleep time
  hypnotherapies starting today. To access them log onto
  www.thepositivehabit.com and enter HABIT. If you are on a
  mobile device save The Positive Habit to your home screen
  when prompted for ease of access. I really hope you enjoy
  listening to the audios. They are a crucial part of the process
  and to feel the positive transformation you must listen to
  them every day.

 NOTEBOOK
SHARE WITH ME

Your first journal exercise!

Go back to the imaginary consultation scenario at the start of the Intro-
duction (page 3). Take a moment and journal what you think you would
have said to me. No faffing. Do this exercise before reading on and don't
hold back; offload all the thoughts and feelings you would have brought
up in the consultation. The following questions might help you:

+ Why did you buy the book?

+ What do you fear most in life?

+ What is your hope for yourself?

+ Are you worried about anything in particular?

+ Are you sleeping well at night?

+ Do you have recurring negative thoughts? If so, what are some of the most common ones?

+ Do you believe you can learn The Positive Habit?

The fact that you bought this book and have started reading it already shows that you do care about yourself and the world around you – the seeds of your positive soul are germinating and being brought to life where they can blossom. Remember, I am here throughout this journey supporting you every step of the way.

 **MEDITATIONS**

+ Morning ritual

+ Sleep time hypnotherapy

PART ONE

HOW TO
CULTIVATE A
POSITIVE MINDSET

*'If we are what we repeatedly do, excellence
is then not an act but a habit.'*

ARISTOTLE

ARISTOTLE TAUGHT US that virtues are indeed habits; his hypothesis is that the mind is a *tabula rasa*, or blank slate, when we are born and our living and social conditions shape our characters for better or worse. This theory remained buried for many years, until John Locke, the seventeenth-century philosopher and enlightened thinker known as the 'father of liberalism', revived it. Since then, the idea has met with much opposition and to this day the 'nature versus nurture' debate rages on. However, there is growing empirical evidence to suggest that the mind is indeed largely shaped by our environment and most positive psychology scientists take the view that we have 40 per cent control over our own happiness, with 50 per cent the result of genetics over which we have little control, and the remaining 10 per cent coming from the life circumstances you were born into.[11] The empowering news is that habits are malleable and once learned they become automatic and reliable. This is something that is highly evident to positive people.

In this chapter, we will examine the science of neuroplasticity (the flexible, plastic nature of the brain) and also the three components of habit which will allow you to identify your own habit loops. You will create your very own personal trigger list to help dispel old, negative habits of behaviour.

Every habit has a beginning – the first time we felt anxious, the first cigarette we smoked, the first time we felt we were not worthy. Knowing why the habit formed in the first place is integral to changing it because this helps to disempower the trigger feeling at its root. For example, if you started smoking as a teenager in order to be 'cool', you can very quickly see that this is no longer a valid reason to continue smoking – the reverse has become true as many smokers now carry social shame for smoking rather than kudos.

Much of our thinking, as well as our emotional and mental habits, stems from early conditioned belief systems and very often these are out of date, negative and need to be changed.

Developing the six positive habits explained in Part II as your default state does not mean denying the negative; in fact the opposite is true. If you are able to identify negative emotional habits and thought processes, thereby embracing your full emotional range, you will know which thoughts are helpful and which you can and should discard.

The six emotional habits explored in this book have been carefully selected and put in a specific order. We cannot fast-forward to happiness without taking the time to climb each step and generate each of the positive emotions that must precede it. Positive emotions are often subtle and can slip through your brain like flour through a sieve, so listening to your morning and sleep time audios every day reinforces the development of the habit and embeds the six emotions into your mind effortlessly.

+ + +

Why Do We Have Positive Emotions?

BARBARA FREDRICKSON, a professor at the University of North Carolina, is the author of *Positivity* and a leader in the science of happiness. She developed the 'broaden and build' theory in 1998. It has since become a key component in explaining why we have positive emotions.[12] Negative emotions and positive emotions *both* play a significant role in keeping us alive; when we feel positive we expand our awareness and this gives us the opportunity to find solutions to problems we can't see if we are steeped in negativity. As you have probably experienced, trying to solve a problem at work when you are feeling anxious is difficult and frustrating to say the least whereas when you are feeling more positive such problems are often solved more quickly and more importantly without the accompanying discontent.

Positive emotions also help us recover faster from negative ones; you may remember a time when you found something funny in the middle of a heated argument with the result that the tension immediately evaporated. It would appear that a generous dose of positive emotions broadens our awareness of risks, allows us to excel socially and to creatively solve problems in addition to making life worth living.

Fredrickson has conducted hundreds of randomised, controlled studies to illustrate her 'broaden and build' theory. 'When you inject people with positivity, their outlook expands. They see the big picture. When we inject them with negativity or neutrality, their peripheral vision shrinks. There are no dots to connect.' Negativity keeps us small, hence the phrase 'narrow-minded'.

+ + +

Positive Neuroplasticity – Your Flexible Brain

THERE IS A STORY of an old Native American chief who was walking beside a river with his young grandson. Wishing to impart some wisdom to the young boy he looked at the river for inspiration and compared the river to his mind, ever flowing, but with different currents. Turning to his grandson he said, 'I have two wolves in my heart, one that is full of love and peace and which sees the best in me and everyone else, and another which is full of anger and jealousy so that it is often sad, irritable and lonely.' 'Really? Which wolf will win?' asked the boy. 'The one that I feed,' said the sage old chief.

The old chief on the riverbank did not realise that he was practising self-directed neuroplasticity, but that is exactly what he was doing. This long word refers to the fact that the brain is plastic and malleable, proved by incredible research over the last 40 years or so. This malleability is also called cortical remapping.[13]

Neurons that fire together, wire together – our thoughts create synaptic transmissions that mesh together through a neurochemical that is released from one brain cell and absorbed by another.

Think of this as similar to a spider weaving a web, delicately connecting threads together. Neuroscientists have identified two areas in the adult brain where neurogenesis – the birth of new neurons – occurs: the hippocampus, located in the emotional brain, is the home of long-term memory; and the cerebrum, which is responsible for coordination and muscle memory.[14] The brain is like a muscle: it grows and becomes stronger when actively engaged. The 'old' model of the brain was based on the belief that after childhood the brain was largely set and unchangeable and crucially this included negative behavioural patterns such as worry, anxiety and depression. Advances in neuroscience have now proved this is not true and that, in fact, our brains *can* be rewired.

You can 'shape' your brain according to your desires, a process that MRI scans now conclusively demonstrate.

When I give a workshop, I will often ask for a show of hands to see how many people have heard the term, 'neuroplasticity' and it is usually fewer than 5 per cent of the group. On this widespread lack of awareness, Ruby Wax, author of *How to Be Human*, says 'It's like we have this Ferrari on top of our head but no one gave us the keys. It's amazing to me this information isn't shouted from the rooftops and on every headline of all newspapers.'[15] If we can change our brains why don't more people know about it? Perhaps you are already aware of neuroplasticity, but being aware is one thing and choosing to train your brain for positivity is quite another. It's a bit like being a member of a gym that you never use or having a beautiful singing voice but being too self-conscious to sing. It's a waste of your potential and a missed opportunity.

Michael Merzenich, Professor Emeritus of Neuroscience at the University of California, is the world's leading researcher on brain plasticity. He writes, 'Your brain, every brain is a work in progress. It is "plastic" from the day we're born to the day we die, it revises and remodels, improving or slowly declining as a function of how we use it.'[16]

Merzenich has identified two critical periods of plasticity:

+ The first is when we are children and the brain wires itself for the first time. This is the period when the brain's plasticity is at its highest.

+ The second is when we are adults and the brain has the continuing capacity to rewire itself with new stimuli.

 IMAGINEERING

Imagine a farmer walking down a path to feed his cattle. Every day he opens the gate and walks down the same path to the field. This action becomes an automatic and well-established habit. Imagine that this path represents negative or limited thinking. One day, the farmer decides to walk a different route – let's imagine the new path represents positive or open thinking. When he first starts walking on the new path he will have to remind himself each time he does this of his decision. After some time and a lot of determination, though, the new path will become his automatic route.

Your neural paths are no different from the farmer's pathways and the more often you choose to think in a positive way, the easier it becomes to establish the neural connections that make the new path an automatic habit. A key component of neuroplastic success is based on repetition, a little like when you first learned your times-tables, which is why I strongly recommend the daily practice of your seven-minute morning ritual and sleep time hypnotherapy audio, the affirmational tooth brushing and the other mindful visualisations you will find throughout the course of this book. You employ the mind to change your brain – literally.

Neuroplasticity, in combination with neurogenesis, means that you can literally change and grow your brain. This is the catalyst for positive change in your life now, not tomorrow or next week. From this moment you can start to change the structure of your brain through the power of your thoughts.

Believe you can succeed and you will.

When I was growing up, dismissive phrases such as 'he is a born worrier,' or 'she has always suffered from her nerves' were commonly used and it was believed that poor mental health was entirely genetic and/or the result of a chemical imbalance that could only be managed with medication. Unfortunately, these beliefs still prevail to a large extent. It's become my life's work to dispel them, replacing them with the discoveries of neuroscience and sharing these with the world in a highly accessible way.

+ + +

The Science of Positive Emotions

'Habits of thinking need not be forever. One of the most significant findings in psychology in the last twenty years is that individuals can choose how they think.'[17]

MARTIN SELIGMAN

BEFORE THE BIRTH of the positive psychology movement, psychology had mainly concerned itself with 'fixing' what was wrong with the human psyche. The bar for mental health was set pretty low with an emphasis on survival and staying sane. Thriving and flourishing were just not on the agenda. In the mid-twentieth century, psychologists such as Carl Rogers and Abraham Maslow expressed an interest in improving an individual's self-image or self-actualisation (the things that make them feel worthwhile), but they did not have the neuroscientific evidence we have today. Martin Seligman, regarded by many as the father of positive psychology, started the first serious scientific studies on happiness and transformed the study of psychology. Ironically, it was his initial theory of 'learned helplessness' (where a person feels they have no control over their situation) developed in the sixties and seventies to help depressed people, that led him to look at 'learned optimism'. If we could learn through our conditioning to feel helpless, he wondered, couldn't we also learn the opposite?

In both cases, it is the *belief* that matters; if we learned helplessness and are depressed, we give up hope. By the same token, if we believe that there is something we can do to change, we learn optimism. Thus, Seligman became highly motivated to help people overcome what he terms 'languishing', a state, he believes, in which most people habitually reside: neither happy nor depressed but just coasting through life, feeling indifferent and accepting that life is hard and will always be a struggle. Like the Native American chief referred to earlier, Seligman promotes the power of choice.

Are you languishing or flourishing right now?

Positive people make the choice about how they think, feel and behave. They make this a habit and so can you. By reading this book and following its powerful formulas you are learning to be a happier person with all that entails.

Shortly, I will introduce you to a powerful and practical mindfulness technique, the four-second positive pause, which will help you to flourish.

+ + +

Positive Epigenetics

THERE IS A GROWING body of scientific research into the area of epigenetics – the study of what influences genes. *Epi* comes from the Greek meaning 'above', so in this case, a force that is above our genes; our genes are NOT predetermined, but are, in fact, formed by external or environmental factors such as diet, stress and our connection to others. As far back as 1998, John Cairns, a leading molecular biologist, conducted an experiment to illustrate that organisms can evolve 'consciously' as DNA changes its response to the environment. He demonstrated that we are not 'victims' of our genetic coding but that everything, from what we eat to our feelings and emotions, has an impact on our genes, be it positive or negative.[18]

Bruce Lipton, a leading cellular biologist and author of *The Biology of Belief,* states that simply being told to 'think positive' does not work, as most of our brain power is subconscious.[19] The well-known placebo effect demonstrates how many people get better after receiving so-called medication (in reality, a sugar pill). In such cases the belief, not the substance taken, fuels recovery. Epigenetics takes the placebo effect to another level and explores the 'nocebo' effect which can occur with people who have a history of mental or physical illness in their families and because of this believe that they will end up in the same health situation as their mother or father. By thinking this way they literally start to create the genes that lead to the illness! Believing that illness is their fate creates a self-fulfilling prophecy.

Your daily emotional habits shape your brain and have the greatest effect on the health of your genes.

Oliver James, British psychologist and author of the highly controversial book *Not in Your Genes*, is convinced that it is time to hang up the nature versus nurture debate as there is no conclusive scientific evidence to support the conjecture that mental illness or psychological traits are passed on to us by our parents.[20] He discounts the many famous studies of twins as manufactured media hype, stories twisted to suit scientists who still struggle to find the concrete evidence they need to prove their theories.[21] James states, 'Mental illnesses run in families because of nurture, not genes. If unhappy patterns are broken, they will not be passed to the next generation.' He quotes one of the world's leading gene psychologists, Professor Robert Plomin, who when asked in 2014 about the current evidence that supports the premise that our characters are passed to us by our parents, told *The Guardian* newspaper, 'I've been looking for these genes for 15 years and I don't have any.'[22]

Personally, I don't think the debate is over; it is only beginning. The revolutionary scientific theories of neuroplasticity and epigenetics do help us greatly and information really is power; we can choose to make positive decisions to enable us to live as the best version of ourselves. Our generation is the first in history that can validly question the commonly held beliefs that we are simply victims of our genetic coding. We now know that habits can be learned and also, mercifully, unlearned!

Understanding the Habit Loop

'First you make your habits and then your habits make you.'

JOHN DRYDEN

IN ORDER TO create the six positive habits it is necessary to understand the neurological process that makes a habit and to take conscious control of what is fundamentally a subconscious pattern.

In his bestselling book *The Power of Habit*, Charles Duhigg identifies three components of any habit and shows that negative habits can be transformed into positive ones.[23] The three components are:

1 Trigger

2 Routine/behaviour

3 Reward

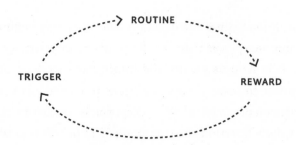

We are creatures of habit because we are highly programmed to seek rewards. The neurotransmitter dopamine is released when we experience a reward, making our habits automatic and often subconscious.

In most unwanted habits, such as eating too much chocolate, being too quick to anger, drinking too much wine or gambling, it is the perceived 'reward' that overrides the desire to change the behaviour. The inner conflict, previously discussed, is ignited; imagine someone who is trying not to drink alcohol, whose inner voice (the conscious mind) tells them as they reach the bar to 'order water' but the other voice (the powerful subconscious) contradicts this completely so that they hear themselves order 'a glass of pinot grigio please'. Part of them is elated and justifies the behaviour immediately: 'Everyone else is having one, it will be just the one.' Sound familiar? You will have had your own internal civil wars, no doubt.

The conscious and subconscious continue to wrestle until the need to escape and the associated noise of the mind results in the person ordering a second glass. Round two of this battle commences next morning when they, like many others, feel 'the fear' and the anxiety that goes with it. If you suffer from anxiety, drinking too much alcohol is the cruellest thing you can do to yourself; it is impossible to feel calm and confident when suffering from the come-down from alcohol – or any other drug for that matter.

If you want to get fit, eat less chocolate, give up or reduce your level of alcohol consumption or feel good enough as a person, you need to understand *why* you developed the negative habit in the first place. As you now know, we have both emotional and behavioural habits. They are interlinked and both can be positive or negative. For example, the positive emotional habit of believing in yourself will lead to behaviour such as seeking a promotion, whereas the negative habit of self-doubt will hold you back from progressing with your life.

+ + +

How to Change Habits

Duhigg argues that the golden rule of how to change habits lies in identifying the three components and then keeping the trigger and the reward the same but changing the routine.

1 **The first component** of a habit is the *trigger*, also known as the cue. In a moment I will ask you to make your own trigger list, so make sure your notebook is within easy reach. Making this list is fundamental to the process so whatever you do, **don't skip this step**. The trigger stays the same for now but in time the negative triggers will diminish and with them the habit.

2 **The second component** of a habit is the actual behaviour, the *routine* itself. This is the part we need to change.

3 **The third component** is the *reward* and is the reason you keep repeating a behaviour or emotion that you no longer consciously wish to do. This part also stays the same.

To clarify, let's take a look at a behavioural habit first and after that we will address an emotional one.

Tom is a 35-year-old ambitious, single man who works long hours, in a competitive corporate environment.

1 Tom's **trigger** is the time of the week: On Friday evenings after work, Tom is stressed, tired and relieved it is the weekend.

2   His **routine** is going to the pub: He goes with colleagues straight after work, doesn't eat dinner, binge-drinks and usually doesn't recall what time he gets home. The rest of the weekend he spends mainly alone, recovering, anxious and plagued with demons about what happened on Friday.

3   Tom's **reward** is socialising with other people: He avoids the loneliness of going back to an empty apartment and feels he has let off steam and relaxed at the end of a hard week.

At first glance this doesn't look too bad a situation for Tom except for the fact that he spends the rest of every weekend recovering from his Friday night binge. But added to this he feels anxious, down and lethargic. He worries about how he behaved when he was drunk. Did he try it on with the receptionist again?! So it is clear Tom needs help: he deserves to be rewarded for working hard all week, he needs to socialise and connect with people but what he does not need is to run his physical and mental health into the ground. Poor Tom!

Now have a look at this new habit loop where the trigger and reward are the same but the routine changes.

1   Tom's **trigger** remains the time of the week: On Friday evenings after work, Tom is stressed, tired and relieved it is the weekend.

2   His **routine** changes: After leaving the office, Tom has an early dinner, goes to play tag rugby with a new group of people, has two sociable drinks afterwards then goes home and has the rest of the weekend to enjoy himself, see his family, go to the cinema, etc. On Monday morning, Tom is mentally and

physically in better shape and has the energy he needs for facing into the week's work.

3 Tom's **reward** remains socialising with other people: He avoids the loneliness of going back to an empty apartment and feels he has let off steam and relaxed at the end of a hard week.

Clearly, the second habit loop is better for Tom and allows him to flourish and feel he is in control of his life.

Here's another sample emotional habit loop.

Martha is 45 years old, separated with three children, and works full-time.

1 Martha's **trigger** is the time of day: First thing in the morning she is stressed, getting ready herself and getting the kids ready for school.

2 Her **routine** is shouting at the kids: She shouts at them to hurry up when they can't find their shoes, schoolbags, etc.

3 Her **reward** is to feel momentary relief from stress when the kids are dropped off at school.

In this example, Martha feels she needs to shout to get the reward – the kids safely dropped off at school. Yet who really wants to start their day shouting? Each time she gets annoyed she releases cortisol into her system and leaves for work in a state of high stress and shortly after shouting she feels bad about herself and questions what kind of mother she is. She then goes on to doubt herself and finds it hard to focus at work.

The more often Martha feels bad about herself the more likely she is to continue to shout and get irritable. When we feel bad about ourselves we behave in ways that support that belief and a negative emotional loop is formed.

Now have a look at this new habit loop where the trigger and reward are the same but the routine changes.

1 Martha's **trigger** remains as the time of day: First thing in the morning she is stressed, getting ready herself and getting the kids ready for school.

2 Her **routine** changes: Martha delegates responsibility to the kids to ensure they have their schoolbags and shoes in the hall ready the night before. She then checks herself that they have actually done this!

3 Her **reward** remains feeling relief from stress when the kids are dropped off at school. And once they see that the morning shouting has stopped, the kids will also feel the relief and the family can start their day free from stress.

For emotional habits, the triggers are often things outside our control such as other people and situations. However, if a trigger is a thought or a feeling, we have complete control and with time it will disappear along with the habit. The perk of cleaning up your emotional habits leads to all the other habits in your life improving: when you feel positive and good about yourself you make healthy choices, you desire to eat well, you sleep well and you want to exercise.

NOTEBOOK
PERSONAL TRIGGERS

Now it's time to write your own personal trigger list. This list is really important, so please do give it proper consideration and the time it deserves. This is your list of everything, and I mean everything, that has the potential to cause you to have negative feelings, so it includes, for example, being stressed or overwhelmed, feeling anxious, having low moods or low self-esteem, feeling angry, jealous or irritable and/or having self-doubt.

Use the categories below to brainstorm and note it all down in your notebook. Remember, this is not static and can be added to as you progress through the book; the more aware you become the more you will notice your own triggers.

+ + +

Self-Knowledge is Self-Power

In order to help you, common triggers have been divided into nine categories: the first six concern external triggers and the last three internal ones. Keep in mind that you can change internal triggers but you may not be able to change the external ones. Nevertheless, you can start to change *your response* to the trigger, which is ultimately the same thing. As Wayne Dyer, the American philosopher and self-help guru once remarked, 'when you change the way you look at things the things you look at change'.

Completing this list means that you have to observe yourself and examine your answers. Knowing what your triggers are in advance is like seeing a warning sign on a winding road – it gives you time to respond and avoid catastrophe.

Here is Martha's full trigger list as an example.

1. TIMES OF DAY THAT TRIGGER YOU:

'Mornings, getting the kids ready for school, feeling I will be late for work. Afternoons when I feel tired and so reach out for chocolate to perk up my energy levels. At night when I am trying to sleep and feel tightness in my chest.'

2. TIMES OF THE WEEK THAT TRIGGER YOU:

'Sunday nights, when feelings of dread surface about work on Monday morning. Saturday mornings when I feel like I have no time for myself as it's all about the kids' sports.'

3. TIMES OF THE MONTH THAT TRIGGER YOU:

'Just before my period I suffer from PMT and I am worried about the menopause.'

4. TIMES OF THE YEAR THAT TRIGGER YOU:

'At Christmas I miss my mum not being here any more. On family holidays, I struggle to enjoy them and stress about the kids when I should be relaxed. I always feel more depressed in January – doesn't everyone?'

5. PEOPLE WHO TRIGGER YOU:

'My boss at work when he bursts into my office. Friends telling me I should try internet dating. My sister, who makes comments about my weight. My father, in whose company I sometimes feel like a child. I also feel guilty that I don't visit him enough even though I go as often as I possibly can.'

6. PLACES THAT TRIGGER YOU:

'My kitchen – it is always a mess. Visiting my friend's house that always seems perfect – how does she do it? Hospitals and visits to the dentist.'

7. NEGATIVE THOUGHTS THAT TRIGGER YOU

'I can't cope. I hate my body. I hate myself. I'm never going to do anything exciting with my life. What will happen if I get sick? I'm a bad mother for shouting at my kids.'

8. BELIEFS ABOUT YOURSELF THAT TRIGGER YOU:

'I'm not good enough. Why would anyone love me? I'm selfish and bad-tempered.'

9. EMOTIONS THAT TRIGGER YOU:

'Feeling hurt. If someone I love is dishonest. I can't stand lies. I don't trust others.'

If you met Martha, you would be very surprised because, like many people, on the surface she comes across as confident and calm and displays all the outward signs of success. She would also be the first person to help you despite her belief that she is selfish.

If you harbour any negative thoughts and beliefs (and most of us have at least some, if not a cascade), then let's work together to dispel them.

Noticing yourself is hugely valuable.

If writing this list leaves you feeling a bit low, remember that focusing on what annoys you is unlikely to generate positive emotions. However, this is where you need to be for now so please work with me on this! Optimistic people are positive for a reason – they know their limits and boundaries so that they don't leave themselves exposed to the whims of the world and instead respond calmly to difficulties.

This initial list is an essential reference point for our work together. As you progress you will also make trigger lists for each of the six positive habits, the purpose being to trigger positive emotional states rather than to avoid negative ones.

NOTEBOOK STRESS/NEGATIVE TRIGGERS

Using your notebook, choose one of your stress/negative triggers and analyse your default emotional habit loop. How do you respond in a behavioural sense to the trigger? Do you get angry or quietly sulk and ruminate on things, or do you find yourself reaching for a second glass of wine or comfort eating? Be entirely honest with yourself and note it all down.

Remember, you need to keep the trigger and reward the same but change the behaviour. Let your instinct guide you on selecting alternative behaviours. For example, it could be that you used to snap at your mother when she made negative or hurtful comments but now you choose to take seven deep belly breaths or use humour to defuse the situation. Work through as many triggers as you can.

This technique is highly effective in transforming both behaviour-based and emotional habits. Understanding your habit loop and *then* using the following practical technique is vital to the success of your overall positive habit. Let me show you *what* to do when you are being triggered – how to break the negative habit and start to create the Positive Habit.

THE FOUR-SECOND POSITIVE PAUSE TECHNIQUE (2 MINUTES)

'Between stimulus and response there is a space. In that space is our power to choose our response. In our response lies our growth and our freedom.'

VIKTOR FRANKL

My most treasured mindfulness technique, inspired by Austrian psychiatrist Viktor Frankl (see page 228), is the four-second positive pause which will move you from a reactive to a responsive mode and transform how you live, how you feel and how you communicate. It is instant, it is empowering, and you can use it anywhere at any time.

The concept behind the technique is that you *choose* your response to any situation.

In the small yet dynamic space that exists between stimulus and response, between trigger and habit, lies the power of choice.

The best way to practise this is to use the audio clip that you will find on www.thepositivehabit.com. Practise it until it becomes an automatic habit, so much so that you won't even notice you are doing it. You are programming your brain to pause before responding to negative triggers and you are taking control of situations that used to control you.

Before you listen, choose one of the triggers that you find most difficult and keep this in mind as you practise.

Please note in your journal the moments when you used this technique successfully. This process acknowledges progress and cements positive shifts in your neural pathways (remember the farmer and his field).

+ + +

No Time to Be Busy

THE STANDARD ANSWER to the question, 'how are you?' is no longer, 'fine' or even 'good', but 'busy!' It seems that everyone is 'busy,' that 'things have been hectic' and that being 'up the walls' has become the new badge of honour. If you say you are busy people will nod understandingly and then proceed to tell you how much busier they are than you! The message is clear – being busy is a competitive sport and it is time to get busier! The 'humble brag' is a modern phenomenon, most commonly seen in WhatsApp messages and on social media where it is used as a means of boasting, of making sure everyone knows how successful and popular you are. A common example goes something like this:

'Thanks so much for the invite, would love to go but it's been mental and I'm exhausted. We were at John's award ceremony last night and today I've to pick up Laura from her tennis as she won the cup for her club. I'm totally wiped and we have a party tonight … I've nothing to wear …'

One of the most common negative beliefs people have is that they are 'not good enough.' This is a reason why people engage in 'humble bragging'; the busier they are the more important they feel. The insecurity of overemphasising how busy they are is an attempt to prove their own worth to themselves. If they feel that they are not 'good enough' at their work, as a husband/wife, mother/father, this feeling of lack can also transfer into feeling they don't have enough time, money, sleep, exercise, fun or friends.

We have become a society of lack, no matter how much abundance we have.

When you are busy, negativity, self-doubt, and anxiety have plenty of opportunities to plant their seeds in your subconscious mind and because you are 'so busy' you don't even notice it happening. The Love Habit looks in depth at the role of self-love, but let's look now at the concept of self-care. There is growing realisation that self-care is not selfish but is actually the opposite: it is selfless.

What if I told you that you don't have time to be busy? Quite literally, being so busy and neglecting yourself leads to physical and mental burnout. In all this busyness, where is the time for *you*? Do you even feature on your own to-do list? Where is the time to connect inwards, to realign yourself with your true purpose and values? This is the purpose of your seven-minute morning ritual and the sleep time hypnotherapy.

Positive people are often busy people so that old phrase of 'if you want something done, ask a busy person' has some truth in it. Having a positive mindset allows you to achieve more in less time as you are not wasting energy on negativity and stress. But many people are 'busy' yet unproductive, as they are wasting time and energy complaining, worrying and resisting the world which is mentally draining.

Positive people make self-care a non-negotiable habit, they own their lives with authority and love. In just 14 minutes of your waking day you can create the six positive habits of positive people and if you feel you can't give yourself this amount of time then the hard question you need to ask yourself is, why? You owe this to yourself regardless of your circumstances and it will help you reap the rewards. When the Dalai Lama was asked what surprises him most about humanity, he answered,

'Man ... because he sacrifices his health in order to make money. Then he sacrifices money to recuperate his health. And then he is so anxious about the future that he does not enjoy the present; the result being that he does not live in the present or the future; he lives as if he is never going to die, and then dies having never really lived.'

The next time someone asks you how you are, please say anything else but 'busy'! Try 'great!'

When you neglect your mind, heart and soul you pay the price; likewise, when you care for yourself with tenderness and compassion you flourish internally no matter what chaos exists outside. In the next chapter we will examine why so many of us suffer from anxiety and stress, and more important, why it is not our fault.

THREE KEY TAKEAWAYS FROM THIS CHAPTER

1 Neuroplasticity – your brain is flexible and can change by using the brain-training techniques in this book.

2 Habits have three components – trigger, routine and reward. To change a habit we keep the trigger and reward and change the routine – i.e. the behaviour.

3 Self-knowledge is self-power. Keep your personal trigger list handy and use it.

MINDFUL SHOWERING

Imagine the water cleansing both your mind and body. Feel the water on your skin and continue to bring your mind back to the sensation each time your mind goes into planning mode.

ACKNOWLEDGE PROGRESS

Now mark how you are feeling on the positivity sundial below. How are you doing compared to the first one that you did on page 22?

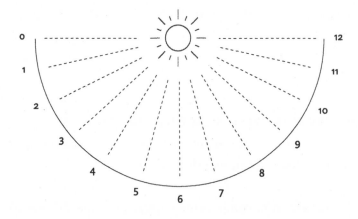

Remember to keep listening to your seven-minute morning and your sleep time hypnotherapy. Tick the days so far that you have listened at the back of the book in your 66 day grid. Be proud of the times you have listened and don't give yourself a hard time if you have missed one or two days; that is okay – keep going!

 # MEDITATIONS

+ Morning ritual

+ Sleep time hypnotherapy

+ The four-second positive pause

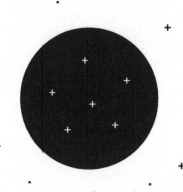

HOW TO
EMBRACE THE
NEGATIVE

'Dogs bark at what they don't understand.'
HERACLITUS

CAN YOU REALLY change the way you think while you sleep?

Yes, you can. Jack Canfield, motivational speaker, corporate trainer and bestselling co-author of the *Chicken Soup for the Soul* series said: 'Whatever goal you give to your subconscious it will work night and day to achieve.' Your subconscious mind is continuously absorbing stimuli, even while you sleep. Knowing the power of your subconscious and making it a habit to shape it according to your desires allows you to join the ranks of the supremely positive people in this world. Your subconscious has been recording your life from the moment you were born until this very moment. That is a significant amount of data and in order to process this, the mind uses filters which are the result of our childhood and cultural conditioning. Identifying your personal filters will help you change how you see the world; you will be able to realise opportunities that you haven't previously seen because of the prevalence of negative filters. As a result, your life will become richer, brighter and happier.

The beauty of changing negative filters to positive ones while you fall asleep is that it is effortless!

As you develop the habit of listening to the morning and sleep time audios, your feelings and behaviour organically become more positive: it is a well-acknowledged fact that repetition and practice begets success. As this effortless transition is at a subconscious level you may be pleasantly surprised to notice that your behaviour changes to reflect your growing positivity levels. For example, you may find yourself feeling more confident and volunteering to do things that you would usually have avoided, such as giving a speech or booking a holiday to somewhere new.

You may find yourself feeling calmer in situations that caused you stress in the past and finding that you have more patience with people you find challenging.

One of my clients had been consistently listening to one of my positive suggestion recordings every night as she went to sleep and told me that her husband started to quote from my audio almost word for word. When she pointed this out to him, he had no idea what she was talking about and was completely oblivious to his new-found positive mindset. He had, in fact, absorbed the positive vibes from her listening to the audio and as a result was in great form, his business was booming and the couple were growing together, becoming closer and more compassionate towards one another. All of this from simply going to sleep while the recording played!

Matthew Walker, author of the bestseller *Why We Sleep*, is the leading expert on sleep science today. He explains how crucial it is for the brain to have a full eight hours of sleep each night; the less sleep you get, the shorter you live. Many people 'get by' on as little as five or six hours a night and Walker clearly outlines the risks involved in such an approach:

'The leading causes of disease and death in developed nations – diseases that are crippling health care systems, such as heart disease, obesity, dementia, diabetes and cancer – all have recognised causal links to a lack of sleep.'[24]

When you put it like this, it seems fairly black and white. Not surprisingly, sleep deprivation also has a major impact on our mental health. REM (rapid eye movement) sleep is when we dream, and dreaming provides us with nature's most potent self-therapy programme.

As Matthew Walker states: 'The best bridge between despair and hope is a good night's sleep.'

Can you identify with that feeling of going to bed feeling anxious but when you wake the feeling has softened and it does not have the same intense rawness to it?

This is no coincidence: it is not just the passing of time that has helped, it's the fact that the anxiety-inducing neurochemical, norepinephrine, is shut off while we dream. In any 24-hour period, REM sleep is often the only time we have had a break from the 'fight-or-flight' neurotransmitter and the stress hormone of cortisol circulating in our bodies. This 'golden' window provides the brain with a calm and safe time in which to process some of the complicated and frightening thoughts and events that have occurred during our waking hours. Simply put, a good night's sleep is essential for your emotional and physical wellbeing. Listening to positive suggestions will help you to drift off to sleep more easily and even if you have disturbing dreams, don't be alarmed, be grateful and do your best to learn from them – your subconscious is healing your mind so that you can be at your best the next day.

Studies have indicated that many patients, either under anaesthetic on the operating table or in a coma, can hear and understand conversations around them, even if they appear to be unconscious.[25] The American anaesthesiologist George Mashour writes, 'the unconscious mind is not this black sea of nothingness [but an] active and dynamic place; one might imagine the anesthetized mind as a concert hall in which the conductor is missing but the orchestra still performs.'[26] This is why both doctors and families need to be careful of what they say in the presence of patients who appear to be unaware or even unconscious.

The same applies to children, who are far too often exposed to conversations that leave them anxious and confused. Choose to bring conscious control to what you say when children are present, even if they appear not to be listening; your words have an impact and are absorbed into their malleable minds.

'Crystallised intelligence' is the term that Joshua Waitzkin, former chess prodigy and tai chi world champion, uses to explain how he utilises the first ten minutes of his morning to tap into his subconscious power rather than to check his smartphone.[27] He finds a quiet place, meditates and then writes whatever comes to mind in his journal. This is a good time for being creative. Many world leaders and influential people are acutely aware of the transformative potential of the early hours.

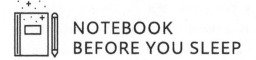

NOTEBOOK BEFORE YOU SLEEP

A habit for success in all that you do is to write down any questions you have before you go to sleep. Whether you are struggling to make a decision or are seeking a solution to a problem, this technique is invaluable. By writing down your conundrum you are cleansing your mind before you sleep, freeing it from the pressure to solve the situation and putting your faith in the full power of your subconscious mind. Read your questions first thing in the morning and see what answers organically occur to you; as you were sleeping peacefully your subconscious was doing all the hard work for you and will present you with answers. The old adage, 'never make an important decision without first having had a good night's sleep,' is true. The clarity morning brings is a gift you receive every 24 hours, so use it!

+ + +

Your Subconscious Power

AS PREVIOUSLY POINTED OUT, your subconscious mind is highly suggestible; it takes everything literally and has no sense of humour or irony. Like a child, it craves love, attention and a feeling of safety. It has a vivid imagination and if left to its own devices can conjure up all sorts of wonders and, unfortunately more frequently, catastrophes; this is due to the brain's negativity bias, which I will explain later in this chapter. However, the prime objective of the six habits is to coach your subconscious to visualise what you desire and not what you fear.

The conscious mind is the gatekeeper to the subconscious. Hypnotherapy and positive visualisations are transformative as they are the most direct avenue to quieting the conscious mind and accessing the subconscious.

The electrical pulses that connect the millions of neurons in the brain are brain waves and are measured in the unit of frequency, hertz, defined as one cycle per second. The slower your brain waves are, the more open your subconscious becomes. The faster they are, the more on high alert and anxious you may be and just like the waves in the sea, we feel safer when they are calmer. These electrical pulses are created via your thoughts and emotions, so slowing your thinking mind will create inner calmness. While we experience different brain waves every day, the goal is to be able to generate and maintain the ones that best serve you and those in your world.

The five brain wave states are:

1 **Gamma**: (38–42 Hz) These fastest brain waves also have the slowest amplitude, making them rather special. We produce them when we feel bliss and happiness and interestingly they are present in the brains of monks and people who meditate a lot. Gamma waves allow the brain to operate at its peak of performance with high cognitive functioning and sharper memories. People who experience high levels of gamma brain waves are usually calm and happy and display high levels of emotional intelligence. The absence or lack of gamma brain waves is often associated with depression. Meditation, hypnotherapy and visualisation produce gamma wave states, particularly when we focus on feelings of love and being at one with the world. Listening to the morning ritual audio and the loving kindness meditation from the Happiness Habit, will help you to produce lots of happy gamma waves.

2 **Beta**: (12–38 Hz) These fast brain waves dominate our waking state of consciousness when attention is directed towards cognitive tasks and the outside world, allowing us to be alert, attentive, engaged in problem solving, judgement, decision making or focused mental activity. 'High' beta states occur when the mind is racing and create a constant drip of the stress hormone cortisol into your system, which can hinder sleep and impair focus, decision making and the building of positive relationships.

3   **Alpha:** (8Hz–12Hz) These slower brain waves occur when we feel calm and relaxed. They are good for learning and for feeling 'present'. Alpha is the resting state for the brain. Alpha waves aid overall mental coordination, calmness, alertness, mind/body integration and learning. The simple act of closing your eyes will bring you down from beta to alpha, which is a good place to be in during your waking hours.

4   **Theta:** (3H–8Hz) These even slower brain waves occur most often in sleep but are also dominant during deep meditation. Theta is our gateway to learning, memory and intuition. In theta, our senses are withdrawn from the external world and focused on signals originating from within. This is the place where I want to bring you in the sleep time audio and where you naturally are in those first few minutes of the morning. When the conscious mind hasn't yet engaged is the magic gap between sleep and wakefulness. Random thoughts enter your mind, you access your intuition easily and creativity increases. You are in the perfect state for a positive change as the subconscious mind absorbs everything.

5   **Delta:** (0.5 Hz–3 Hz) These slowest of brain waves are generated in deepest meditation and dreamless sleep. In this state your body has a chance to repair itself and boost your immune system, and that is why deep restorative sleep is so essential to the healing process. Without this deep and slow brain wave activity we simply cannot survive.

Ciara Cronin, a deeply spiritual mindfulness-based psychotherapist, yoga teacher and trainer, told me a story about one of her student teachers who also happened to be a scientist and was interested in finding out what brain waves people had in 'asana'

– a movement state of yoga.[28] He discovered that while most of the students went from beta to alpha, some of the teachers, who had been yoga practitioners for years, went into the theta state almost immediately. It appears that the more accustomed you get to slowing down your brain, the quicker your brain accesses the healing state of theta, even when you are upright.

+ + +

Making the Unconscious Conscious

UNCONSCIOUS EMOTIONAL and thinking habits need to be cleared in order for you to glide down to the transformational theta state or indeed to elevate your mind to the blissful gamma state. Emotions are the language of the body and when we ignore, suppress or fear them they remain trapped and have the potential to make us ill as well as unhappy.

Take a moment to recall how your body felt the last time you experienced conflict: was there muscle tension in your shoulders and back? Knots in your stomach? Did your chest and throat feel tight? It is possible that the experience even gave rise to a cold or a sore throat. Negative emotions take their toll on the body, leaving us exhausted and drained and also challenging the immune system.

The Latin root of the word 'emotion' is *emovere* and it means to move, or agitate. I cannot empathise enough that positive people are, above all, emotionally intelligent people; they allow their emotions, both negative and positive, to move through their minds and bodies. If you want positive mental health you must do the same.

Being controlled by negative emotions alone is debilitating; turning towards them with love and courage while at the same time self-generating positive emotions is empowering.

Freud's theories about the unconscious and subconscious mind transformed our understanding of the human mind and form the basis for much of present-day psychology and therapy; terms such as 'ego', 'anal repression', 'Freudian slip' and 'neurotic' are all now part of the everyday lexicon of mental health.

Comparing the mind to the three levels of an iceberg, Freud postulated that only 10 per cent of the totality of the mind is on the conscious level.[29] This is the part that most people identify with even though it represents a tiny fraction of who we are. Fears, habits and belief systems reside in the unconscious mind and if they remain hidden they can have a controlling impact on your life. This is why writing down your dreams first thing in the morning is a fruitful way to access the subconscious and even though you won't necessarily immediately understand the dreams and their hidden meanings, simply being aware of their content may allow their significance to unfold itself to you.

In the 1910 *Titanic* catastrophe the approaching iceberg was **not** seen in time and the consequences were devastating. Ignoring the iceberg of unconscious fears has the potential to cause chaos in your life. Having the courage to understand the deepest and darkest parts of yourself often reveals that the fear of the fear far surmounts anything you may find. You can literally steer your mind to safety when you become aware and by doing so, bring the subconscious to the surface of the conscious mind.

Gradually turning on the lights for a child who is terrified of the dark will show them that all is well and that there is nothing to be afraid of. Similarly, dealing with the past will allow you the freedom to live in the present. The alternative of allowing your past to unconsciously dictate your present keeps you forever a hostage of history.

A common coping mechanism many people employ is to only focus on the present, avoiding dealing with the past. While this may indeed appear to be a positive solution, it is about as effective as sticking a Band-Aid on a broken leg. Freud once said, 'Most people do not really want freedom, because freedom involves responsibility, and most people are frightened of responsibility.' Are you afraid of responsibility? If so, you are not alone – many people shy away from it – but in order to live in harmony with yourself it is essential to take responsibility for your past with honesty and compassion. This is an ongoing process that never finishes; when we are confronted by new challenges we need to look again at the roots of our reactions. For example, if/when you become a parent your perspective on your own parents may change; you may understand their plight more compassionately or you may, in fact, feel more aggrieved when you compare their parenting skills to yours.

Negative Emotional Habits
Are not Your Fault

CONSIDER THE FOLLOWING scenario:

Dan (fictional name) was very dedicated to his family and did his best to contribute to society. He was a senior member of staff in a financial firm and the main breadwinner of his family, with four children and a wife to support. A trustworthy person, he was kind and carried the weight of his responsibilities with grace. The company he worked for became involved in a major corporate fraud and unbeknownst to him his bosses embezzled millions. He had in no way been suspicious of any illegal activity and if he had been, he would have reported it. While he had always worked honestly and diligently and never questioned authority, his bosses were masters of secrecy. When the scandal over the fraud broke he was accused along with the rest of the senior staff and everybody believed that, even if he was not guilty, he must have been aware of what was going on. As a result, his staff no longer trusted him and he felt that even his family and friends were suspicious and critical. Although he hadn't committed any crime he could not forgive himself for being so stupid, blind and gullible. He became cloaked in shame and the stress left him deeply paranoid.

Financially ruined by the collapse of the company, publicly humiliated and with a big, young family to support, one spring morning he drove his children to school, returned home and hung himself in the family garage. The shame of the scandal, his loss of reputation and his financial concerns were simply too much to bear.

This sad and sorry waste of life occurred because he blamed himself for something that was not his fault. If he was guilty of anything it was not questioning authority. This man was the father of a friend of mine when I was a teenager and I have never forgotten the impact his sudden, tragic death had on his family and the community.

I constantly tell my clients who are mentally beating themselves up from shame, guilt and negative emotional habits to understand that these unwanted feelings are not their fault. As in this heartbreaking story, much of the shame we carry is never ours in the first place. This is not to suggest that we deny responsibility for our behaviour – instead we should shine the light of understanding on why the behaviour is there in the first place. Ignorance is not actually bliss. It is essential to educate yourself about yourself and your behaviour so that you can progress. Learning how to manage your mental health by using techniques, such as the four-second positive pause (see page 62) will enable you to do just that.

+ + +

Understanding Your Brain

IT'S IRONIC that many of us understand how highly complex machines work but we have very little knowledge about how the brain works. The simplest way to describe it is to think of it in three parts: the old brain, the emotional brain and the new brain. This 'triune' brain model was first developed in the 1960s by the American physician and neuroscientist Paul D. MacLean.

The **old brain** is the smallest and oldest part – it evolved hundreds of millions of years ago. It is known as the reptilian brain as it is similar in structure to that found in reptiles. It is reactive in nature and programmed to pick up on any potential threat. This is the part of the brain that gives the command to fight, flee or freeze. It is situated at top of the brain stem leading from the spine, and is responsible for the body's vital functions such as heart rate, breathing and balancing temperature. When people lash out and attack others they are usually relying on this old part of the brain This is not to say that the reptilian brain does not have a useful function; its main concern is to protect, which is, of course, essential to our survival under *genuine* threat.

The **emotional brain**, also perhaps better known as the mammalian brain or limbic system, is a series of interconnected structures that records experiences and memories and decides whether we like or dislike something or someone. It has no concept of time or logic, is located in the centre of the brain and is home to the amygdala, which is the fear centre of the brain and acts as an alarm: if danger is perceived it will warn the 'old brain' to prepare for threat. The hippocampus also resides in this area and is the home to both our short- and long-term memories. This is the part that holds post-traumatic stress disorder and can replay old memories as if they happened yesterday. It's also responsible for rumination and catastrophising – the two most toxic habits of anxiety that I will expand on later. However, its other functions are focused on mating and connecting, seeking pleasure and avoiding pain, particularly emotional pain.

The **new brain** is the neocortex, which gives us the power of conscious choice. At only 359 million years old it is the most recent addition in the evolution of the mammalian brain. This period in our evolution marked a cognitive revolution as we developed the power of language and the ability to work and live together in large communities. This is the largest part of the brain, comprising about 76 per cent of brain matter, and is located in the frontal lobes in six layers of deeply grooved tissue. Consciousness, logic and higher-thinking skills are its contributions to the development of brain function. The left area of the neocortex is more active when we feel compassion and happiness. It fires neurons throughout our lives and if we use it properly it is powerful as it is 'plastic' and it allows us to change our habits. If we don't look after it or use it properly we lose its true capabilities; racing thoughts and negativity cause us to give away the gift of consciousness and slip into negative, emotional habits (the emotional brain) and reactive behaviour (the old brain).

All three parts of the brain work closely together with a strong neural network between the emotional brain and the new brain. Using these connections we can build a superhighway of positivity, love and understanding.

+ + +

The Negativity Bias

HAVE YOU EVER had an appraisal at work after which you focused on the one piece of 'constructive criticism' rather than the five good things your manager mentioned? Can you recall a time when you were at a party having great fun and someone made a negative comment that you couldn't let go of? Can you remember searching for a parking space in a busy area and saying, 'We'll never get one'? These reactions are not your fault, they are all part of the negativity bias that is 'protecting' you. Of course, often it does the opposite: at best, you don't get a parking space; at worst, over time, you erode your self-esteem and live in a state of high stress.

The negativity bias is part of our 'old' mammalian brain and a lamentable hangover from our evolution. It has us wired to scan everything and everyone for threats. Humans jumped to the top of the food chain in a relatively short period of time; Yuval Noah Harari, Professor of History at the Hebrew University of Jerusalem and author of *Sapiens – A Brief History of Mankind*, writes, 'Having so recently been one of the underdogs of the savannah, we are full of anxieties and fears over our position.'[30] The 'hasty jump' we made to become king of the jungle did not give our fearful brains time to evolve to our heightened status.

The negativity bias might be useful if you live in a jungle or a war zone or even if you are walking home alone in the dark from a nightclub; otherwise, it can be very debilitating and can lead to chronic anxiety and paranoia. When I share this information with clients it can elicit responses like, 'how depressing' and 'I knew it, I'm doomed to be anxious', which is simply not the case.

Knowledge and practical application have the power to transform the negativity bias.

For example, if your partner or family member is late coming home, rather than allowing the negativity bias to jump to the worst-case scenario, let's say a car accident, breathe deeply, use the four-second pause technique on page 62 to give yourself space rather than just reacting immediately to the emotion. Instead, imagine that all is well, that your partner/family member is most likely just held up and is safely on their way home. In fact, you should visualise them coming through the door before they actually do, which is more than likely what will happen. You have the power **not** to let the negativity bias rule your responses and damage you emotionally.

Rick Hanson, psychologist and *New York Times* bestselling author, coined the phrase:

> **'The brain is like Velcro for negativity and Teflon for positivity.'**

This refers to how quickly we respond to the negative in order to survive and how easily positivity sifts through our brain. Hanson explains that when our brains are wired in a negativity bias habit loop, 'the effects include: a growing sensitivity to stress, upset and other negative experiences; a tendency towards pessimism, regret, and resentment; and long shadows cast by old pain'.[31] This clearly needs our love and attention.

Living in a state of high vigilance and reactivity can be seen everywhere today, for example in road-rage incidents when those involved often release floods of pent-up fear and negativity in the face of perceived danger. If you are on the receiving end of such an outburst it is important not to take it personally, although admittedly this can be a challenge. Remember that the rage is being triggered by the innate negativity bias and that it is not really the perpetrator's fault; they have yet to train their brains in the same way as you are doing now.

I was fortunate enough to study positive neuroplasticity under Hanson and the most important thing I learned was that by toning down the negative and dialling up the positive we can physically change the brain for the better. It is, however, important to recognise the critical role that negative emotions play in our lives.

+ + +

Negativity Is Necessary

NIALL BRESLIN has said, 'If you do not feel anxiety or sadness, you are either dead or a robot.' It is important that you feel negative emotions and do not try to outrun or avoid them as they will always catch up with you when you least expect it. Deal with emotions as they arise; think of it as a form of housekeeping – little and often prevents chaos from ensuing.

Negative emotions, like challenging people, are our greatest teachers.

Many people are unintentionally living the six habits of negative people, which all have fear at their root:

1 **Anxiety** – fear of uncertainty and danger
2 **Anger** – fear of injustice
3 **Hatred** – fear of the self and others
4 **Jealousy** – fear of not being loved
5 **Resistance** – fear of what is
6 **Hopelessness** – fear for the future

There are two principal types of fear:

1 **Genuine fear** usually arises in dangerous situations. It is important to be vigilant and listen to the warning systems of the 'new' brain in order to assess the real level of threat. For example, passing through a war zone or driving alone at night on unfamiliar and twisty roads are clearly dangerous activities and it is important that you listen to the fear that your mind generates if you are to survive.

2 **Unnecessary fear** is an overreaction to a situation that is not a threat. Most anxiety is actually unnecessary; it is a case of suffering from the fear of the fear. In such situations, if you lash out with irritability or anger your 'old' brain is reacting to a perceived threat that may not really exist. It's is simply doing what it has been programmed to do and that is to keep you alive. But running out of the house in a panic because the smoke alarm has gone off when you burned a piece of toast is clearly irrational and this is something that you employ the rational mind to clarify. Can you imagine a life without unnecessary fear? Getting specific on the difference between necessary and unnecessary fear and putting this into practice will liberate you from anxiety. Often, the confusion caused in failing to understand why we feel an emotion leads us into a downward spiral of negativity.

> **The hardest negative feelings are the ones we cannot label; they leave us with a general unease that is very hard to sit with.**

Having emotional clarity leads to self-regulation which means you do not allow yourself to become hijacked by toxic emotions.

The following exercise will help you to find the courage to sit with an uncomfortable emotion and the more often you practise this the better you will become at distinguishing between genuine and unnecessary fears.

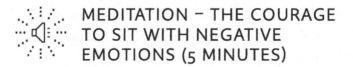

MEDITATION – THE COURAGE TO SIT WITH NEGATIVE EMOTIONS (5 MINUTES)

Do this exercise whenever you feel a negative emotion and/or you feel uneasy but you are not sure what is causing it. It will teach you not to follow old patterns of avoiding negative emotions, but instead to identify the emotion and then turn towards it, sit with it and accept it. Being with yourself in this tender and attentive way is the ultimate expression of self-love.

*First of all, you need to identify **where in the body** the negative emotion resides and then you can start to separate your thoughts from the emotion, meaning that you do not fuel it with more negative thoughts that serve only to intensify and prolong it. You go directly to the heart of the emotion by letting the thoughts sift away and focusing only on the physical sensations within your body. You may be amazed at how this technique provides you with a sudden clarity as to why you feel a certain negative emotion and this clarity provides you with an immediate sense of relief and an ability to move on.*

Even if you feel fine at the moment, take some time now to practise this as it will help you to prepare for a time when you really need it. You can access the audio on www.thepositivehabit.com.

Running from Rumination

TWO ZEN MONKS, a young one and an old one, were on a long journey between two monasteries. The strict order they belonged to forbade them to make any contact with women. On this journey they approached a choppy river and found a beautiful but distraught woman who did not have the courage to cross the river. The older monk, without talking to her, simply picked her up and carried her to the other side, put her down and carried on with his journey. The younger monk was shocked that the older man who 'should' know better could behave in a way that went against their teachings and philosophy and for the next few hours he raved and ranted. Eventually, the older monk turned towards the novice and calmly said, 'Why are you still carrying the woman? I put her down hours ago.'

Rumination is one of the biggest curses of the thinking mind.

Most people find it really hard to let things go, especially if they feel they have been wronged. Think of how many families have been affected by an issue, often related to a will or property, that keeps them estranged, unable to let go of a grudge. It is sad to see once-close families allow fear to conquer their love for one another. If you hear yourself, either mentally or out loud, ruminating on a past event or repeating a negative story, think of the monk and literally put the story down. You have crossed the river, you got wet, it may not have been pleasant but it is now over. Move on, don't get stuck.

Practising the exercise, 'the courage to sit with negative emotions' will help you let go of rumination on the story (the thought process) and to focus instead on the emotion it brings. By doing this you put yourself in a strong position to walk towards freedom in mind, body and spirit.

NOTEBOOK
UNNECESSARY
NEGATIVITY

Are you holding on to unnecessary negativity?

Take a moment to note honestly the answers to the following questions in your journal:

1 How much of your negativity is gratuitous?

2 Are you holding on to things from the past that cause yourself and others harm?

3 Is there anything that you can choose to let go of?

+ + +

Catastrophising is Crippling

THE IMAGINATION IS a powerful thing. This is especially true in someone suffering from anxiety and/or stress, who is bound to predict the worst possible outcomes in every situation. Catastrophising is one of our most common negative habits. As Mark Twain said, 'I've had a lot of worries in my life, most of which have never happened.' Catastrophising usually has two steps, both of which are not grounded in fact: the first involves dismissing positive outcomes and the second involves believing that even *if* something positive happens, it will turn into a negative. An example of this might be a person who wants to change job because they are stuck in a rut but also fears change. In this situation the catastrophiser will predict that they will never get a job and even if they *did* get a new job it would probably be worse anyway. Another example might be a person seeking a new relationship who will not go on dates because they believe there is no point, that they will never meet anyone nice and even *if* they did it wouldn't work out.

Catastrophising plays a nasty trick on us as it produces an illusionary veneer of self-protection but it often is, in reality, a major contributing factor to anxiety. It is a habit that can leak into all areas of your life, from fearing that your flight will be delayed and probably crash to social anxiety – that if you speak your mind nobody will listen to you and even if they did, you would be judged and therefore it seems safer to stay at home and stay quiet.

Remember that your subconscious mind does not know the difference between imagination and reality, so if you catastrophise, it will start to create the toxic emotions as if the worst-case scenario were true.

> **Catastrophising is crippling, it burns a hole deep in your sense of self and it causes continuous self-doubt.**

However, if you are prone to this, even on a small scale, the news is positive! The power of your imagination can be turned a full

180 degrees by visualising everything working out just the way you want it to. Many of us have a fear that if we hope for the best we are inviting disappointment into our lives. While this is totally understandable it is also totally unnecessary; the mechanism at play here is similar to that outlined in the Introduction: the inbuilt fear of positivity does not protect us – it actually keeps us stuck.

Observe yourself in the coming days to see if you have made it a habit to catastrophise. Also observe others to see the process at work. What impact does it have on the decisions they make? Do you feel they are unleashing their full potential?

+ + +

The Positivity Offset

BARBARA FREDRICKSON'S 'broaden and build' theory, discussed in the last chapter, clearly indicates that positive emotions are paramount to our survival. As we evolve and the world changes, the need for positive emotions has perhaps become greater than ever; the negativity bias that developed to protect the species now has the potential to destroy us.

In moving from a state of fear to one of love we become proactive in seeking peace, living in harmony with ourselves and looking after the planet and one another.

One of the most direct and immediate methods positive people use is to diminish unnecessary negativity by turning the neutral into the positive, a process known as the 'positivity offset'. Social neuroscientist John T. Cacioppo discovered that our ability to interpret neutral events positively diminished depression and anxiety.[32] For example, much of what you do every day may be considered mundane, tasks such as unloading the dishwasher, brushing your teeth, sweeping the floor, making the kids' lunches, not to mention the administration involved in your professional work, responding to emails, scheduling meetings, etc. These chores are necessary but by considering them 'mundane' we devalue them, failing to see that they provide endless opportunities for us to be grateful and positive. Isn't it good that we actually have a house to clean, work to do and food to eat? By recognising the inherent value in neutral things and activities we elevate the mundanity of everyday life into the profound.

MEDITATION – THE 15-SECOND POSITIVE PLUNGE

Do this anytime you feel happy – simple!

This is a very simple mindfulness technique that I created and that was inspired by the self-directed, positive neuroplasticity training I did with Rick Hanson, who writes, 'Positive emotions have standard-issue memory systems, and these require that something is held in awareness for many seconds in a row to transfer from short-term memory buffers to long-term storage.' The idea is to become aware of when you feel good and identify where you feel this in your body. Pay attention to moments when you feel present, loved, calm, confident, grateful, hopeful and happy. Positive emotions are far more elusive than negative ones; if we don't consciously feel them physically we may not even be aware of how happy we are.

The beauty of the 15-second positive plunge technique is that the more you practise it the more it becomes second nature. The habit of soaking in the positive transfers from the conscious mind to the subconscious.

You will enjoy this one, for sure!

+ + +

Five to One to Flourish

IN THE 1970s, John Gottman, a psychology professor and a leader in research-based approaches to relationships, teamed up with psychologist Robert Levenson to try to understand how some couples managed to be consistently happy. They were also having little luck with the ladies themselves, rather amusingly! If they could crack the code as to what makes couples happy it might be a great step forward for mankind and for themselves on a personal level.

In their now-famous study, Gottman and Levinson asked couples to come to a fake B & B environment where their interactions were scrutinised by hidden cameras and their urine tested for the stress hormone cortisol. In the beginning, by their own admission, they didn't seem to be learning much or helping anyone, much to the frustration of the people funding the research! Eventually, after almost 20 years, they discovered patterns that allowed them to predict with more than 90 per cent accuracy whether or not a couple would divorce.[33] Their predictions are based on the level of positive to negative interactions between the couples recorded when they were being monitored.

There is a magic ratio of five to one: we need five positive interactions to offset the strength of the one negative in order for a relationship to flourish.

Seems like quite a lot, doesn't it? Anything above five to one indicates a flourishing relationship and 0.8 positive to one negative indicates an unstable relationship that will most likely end in a breakup. If the results of this research are extended outwards to include our other relationships the ratio increases. For example, in the case of staff to customers it is 20 to one, with parents to adult kids it is 100 to one and with mothers-in-law it is around 1000 to one!

How many positive to negative emotions do you experience internally every day? When you pay attention to positive emotions you may discover that you have many more than you realise. It is also possible that you could be interpreting many positive moments as neutral. By following the exercises in this book you are raising your internal barometer of positive emotions to offset negative ones.

 IMAGINEERING

Imagine you are walking in an enchanting wood and see two pathways in front of you. One path spirals downwards – you have been on this path many times before. It is familiar and easy to navigate yet it is full of grey clouds and offers no new opportunities.

Imagine a second path that spirals upwards. It is bathed in lovely warm sunlight, lined with wildflowers, butterflies and birds. It is full of energy and possibilities and although this path is uphill, less familiar and may require effort, it looks inviting. On which path do you desire to walk?

Negativity has a downward spiral; one negative thought quickly leads to another and before long we can find ourselves lost in a pit of despair. Most of us know what this feels like in the form of either rumination or catastrophising.

> **Positive people are aware that positivity also has a spiral and this leads upwards.**

Positive thoughts lead to more positive thoughts, which increases your ratio of positive emotions. This process starts with awareness and presence, which is the subject of the next chapter. Observing yourself and your world is the strength of all strengths: positivity is presence and together we will create it.

THREE KEY TAKEAWAYS FROM THIS CHAPTER

1 You can programme your subconscious mind as you sleep.
2 The brain has a negativity bias that causes us to react to an 'old' system.
3 We need a ratio of five to one positive to negative emotions to flourish.

 MINDFUL SHOWERING

Imagine the water cleansing both your mind and body. Feel the water on your skin and continue to bring your mind back to the sensation each time your mind goes into planning mode.

ACKNOWLEDGE PROGRESS

Now mark how you are feeling on the positivity sundial below.

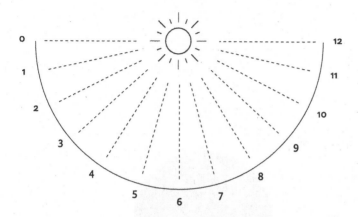

Remember to keep listening to your seven-minute morning and your sleep time hypnotherapies. Tick the days so far that you have listened in the grid at the back of the book. Be proud of the times you have listened and don't give yourself a hard time if you have missed one or two days; that is okay – keep going!

MEDITATIONS

+ Morning ritual

+ Sleep time hypnotherapy

+ The courage to sit with negative emotions

+ The 15-second positive plunge

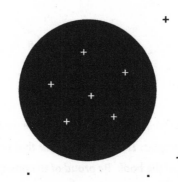

HOW TO CREATE PEACEFUL PRESENCE

'Everything flows and nothing abides,
everything gives way and nothing stays fixed.'
HERACLITUS

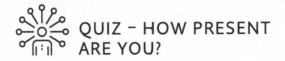

QUIZ – HOW PRESENT ARE YOU?

Please answer 'Yes' or 'No'. Answer honestly and without too much reflection. Go with the first response that springs to mind. In the past month have you:

1 Found yourself ruminating on the past?

2 Found yourself worrying about the future?

3 Found yourself over-analysing what someone meant by a comment they made?

4 Found it hard to focus your attention on the task at hand?

5 Found your to-do list invading your thoughts when in the shower or doing household tasks?

6 Found that you have not been listening to a loved one, a child or a family member?

7 Felt the pressure of not having enough time to complete all your tasks?

8 Felt impatient when something small didn't go your way, e.g. sitting in traffic, losing something, making a small mistake, etc.

9 Had intrusive thoughts about what people will think of you if you do or say something?

10 Felt your mind wander from the task you are doing to the next task and even the one after that so that you are not focused on the task at hand?

Make a note of how many 'No' answers you got and give yourself a point for each one. The higher the number of 'No' answers, the more mindful and present you are. Once again, wherever you are, this is where you need to be NOW.

Score =   /10

You will take this quiz again in the conclusion and I will, of course, remind you.

+ + +

Making Now a Habit

'Whatever the present moment contains, accept it as if you had chosen it.'

ECKHART TOLLE

POSITIVE PEOPLE ARE, first and foremost, present. Presence is positivity; when you are conscious you are aware and when you are aware you can choose to love life. If you are completely new to the practice of mindfulness or even if you have been practising meditation for years, this chapter will help you. Being present and aware is the beginning, the end and the continuation of your journey to emotional empowerment. In order for you to self-generate the six positive emotional habits of love, calmness, confidence, gratitude, hope and happiness, it is essential to first and foremost cultivate awareness – this is the bedrock that supports everything. Without presence you cannot and will not move past this point. It is the virtue of all virtues, the power of all powers and when you realise it every moment becomes one that lifts your soul.

The greatest addiction of our time is thinking. Our minds have never raced so fast: they are desperately trying to keep up with a world that is speeding faster than we can process. As a result, our attention spans are now officially less than a goldfish – a study carried out by Microsoft on 2000 participants illustrates that goldfish have an average attention span of nine seconds while humans now have eight![34] It remains unknown exactly how many thoughts a person has per day, but it is roughly 12,000 to 60,000, with as many as 98 per cent of them the same ones as the day before and 80 per cent of them broadly negative. This means that we are thinking the same negative thoughts almost all the time! To say that this needs our attention is an understatement.

Fortunately, as most thoughts are repetitive, we can quickly see a pattern and take action. It tends to be the case that negative thoughts are the ones that are repeated, thanks to the negativity bias.

Thinking is a habit like any other, with a trigger, routine and reward. Due to the speed and volume of your thoughts, it is hard to see this three-part structure at play, so slowing down your thoughts will help you to identify and understand them.

You may recognise that your **negative** and persistent thinking habit loops all follow the three-part structure:

1 **The trigger** – resisting what 'is'; something or someone you want to change, fix, or control.

2 **The routine** – thinking of **how** to do something, how bad or hard something is.

3 **The reward** – the illusion that you will 'solve' and/or 'control' whatever the issue is even though this is often completely outside your control.

The mind is constantly striving to close the loop, to solve the problem; and here's the rub – the problem is not actually the perceived problem but the fact that once one issue seems to be resolved another one presents itself. We can see both of these habit structures in the process of rumination and catastrophising discussed in the last chapter. Here is an example of this unfortunate loop:

Anna is a 25-year-old trainee solicitor, stuck in a negative thinking habit loop:

1 **Trigger thought:** I should be able to cope better at work and I need to get noticed by the partners.

2 **Routine thought:** This is so hard, I'm exhausted, there is nothing I can do, everyone else is working long hours and seems fine. I just have to work harder.

3 **Reward:** I will be successful if I work harder.

In this scenario it is likely that Anna will be 'successful' in the way we are conditioned to believe (money and recognition) but it is also likely that she will work herself into the ground and ultimately burn out from exhaustion and pressure by the age of 40. The negative thinking habit loop keeps spiralling when it is left unattended to and it keeps us stuck at the level of the problem. Solutions cannot emerge from the fog of too many thoughts.

It is vital to understand that in the first instance it is not the thinking habit loops themselves that need to change but your relationship to them. In Anna's case, transforming the pressure of 'should' to a realisation that she is doing her best will allow her to set clear and healthy work boundaries that allow her to be successful and also to build a career.

> **By softening the pressure to become compassionate, negative thinking habits ease and with time lessen.**

Moving your mind from fear to love and self-compassion clears the ground in preparation for building the foundations we need for the six core positive emotional habits. The word 'mindfulness' touted by so many is perhaps an oxymoron as it suggests that your mind is *full*; in fact, this is not the case when you are being mindful – your mind is *less full*. It is not completely empty and neither should it be, as trying to achieve this actually puts pressure on the mind. Instead we are trying to move from a state of persistent thought to one of open awareness.

One day recently while on holiday I was meditating as I do most days. On this occasion a fly decided to make my body its home. My initial reaction was irritation, as you can imagine. I caught myself and decided that rather than resist the fly by brushing it off, I would embrace the irritation and use the feeling of the fly on my skin as the focus of my meditation. I found that the more I accepted it the less irritating and more interesting it became. The little legs tickled me and I could feel the energy of life as it danced across my body. When it landed on my nose that was the end of the challenge! Life is full of such minor 'irritations', from forgetting passwords to people skipping queues; mindfulness teaches us to be curious rather than critical about these irritations, to be open rather than closed.

In many Asian countries the word for mind and heart is the same. The practice of mindfulness is deepened when heartfulness is incorporated into the practice. I shall expand on the heart's intelligence in the next chapter, the Love Habit.

+ + +

What Has the Buddha
Got to Do with It?

THE STORY OF THE BUDDHA, if you don't already know it, begins with a prince named Siddhartha Gautama, who lived roughly 2600 years ago on the border of Nepal and India. He lived a life of opulence and luxury but never felt contentment. At the age of 29, he was overcome with the fear of getting old, dying and losing the people he loved. He realised that the certainty he was seeking could only be found within himself and not externally. This is an important thing to realise at any age. Subsequently, he left his home, his family and all his worldly possessions to seek enlightenment and for six years he travelled and studied with the great meditation teachers of his time yet still did not attain the inner peace he was seeking.

He therefore decided to sit and meditate continuously until he felt the shift in his mind. After six days and six nights with a full moon high in the sky, it is said, Siddhartha awoke as Buddha (he who is awake). He became 'the now' and embodied the present moment. He spent the rest of his life as a spiritual teacher. At the time of his death, when he was nearly 80 years of age, he said, 'I can die happily. I have not kept a single teaching hidden in a closed hand. Everything that is useful for you, I have already given. Be your own guiding light.'

The Buddha's four noble truths are often misrepresented as a focus on the negative, that life is really about suffering. In reality, their wisdom creates the opportunity for us to love ourselves and the world free from attachment.

Below is a brief synopsis of his teachings but I do recommend further reading on this. In *The Heart of the Buddha's Teaching*, Thich Nhat Hanh, the Vietnamese spiritual leader, provides us with a deeper exploration.

The four noble truths:

1 The truth of suffering (*dukkha*) often translates to the concept that all life is suffering. However, the word 'suffering' in this case actually means 'incapable of satisfying.' We have to recognise and accept the presence of this 'suffering' and touch it.

2 The truth about the cause of suffering (*samudaya*) requires us to look deeply at the nature of the suffering to see how it came to be. We need to recognise both the spiritual and material foods we have ingested that are causing us to suffer.

3 The truth of the end of suffering (*nirodha*) is that the cessation of suffering can be found by not doing the things that make us suffer. Healing becomes possible.

4 The truth of the path that frees us from suffering (*magga*) is the path that leads to us stopping the things that cause us to suffer. This path is called the 'Noble Eightfold Path' and it incorporates the cultivation of right view, right thinking, right speech, right action, right livelihood, right diligence, right mindfulness and right concentration.

In reality, you don't need to spend six days in India sitting under a tree. However, incorporating the mindfulness practices in this book as part of your self-care routine will certainly help you on your ladder to happiness. This is the first and most crucial step.

> **The practice of mindfulness is
> the practice of life.**

The breath is the most immediate tool you have at your disposal and, as you will read in the Calmness Habit chapter, it is your strongest ally in softening the mind. In this chapter you will learn two fundamental techniques, the seven deep belly breaths and the ARK method to deal with negative thoughts. Both techniques can be used anywhere, anytime and will become automatic for you gradually.

+ + +

Tune Out to Tune In

IF THE MIND is a radio that never turns off, what station are you tuned into? Is it a negative, self-critical one that always predicts the worst possible outcomes and won't let you rest until your to-do list is complete? Does it say you are not good enough? If so, why do you keep listening? I sincerely hope that you are listening to a kinder, wiser station, but is it still always turned on? Your mind needs space, it needs silence. There is power in stillness.

It is through silence that our creativity emerges.

Have you ever experienced a moment when a solution to a problem emerges from nowhere? When you are mindful you turn off that radio, you breathe deeply, you take in your surroundings, you listen to others with an open heart, you hear all the sounds of life and you see everything in colour. In order for you to truly tune in to life you need first to tune out. If you honestly want to help make the world a better place you need to dig deep into the stillness within.

There are times in our lives when we very naturally become present. When we travel to new and far-flung destinations we automatically and easily become mindful; our senses are alive with what we see, hear and smell. Similarly, when we fall in love or meet a new person, it is easy to be present and when we are present we feel alive. Also in the middle of life-changing moments such as the birth of a child or the death of a loved one, we are completely and entirely present. Positive people, however, do not become present in these heightened moments alone; they are fully alive to each moment no matter what it offers – they realise that in order to attain this awareness they need time to grow within.

Bringing awareness to everyday tasks helps to stop the conscious mind from wandering too far either into rumination about the past or catastrophising about the future.

Eckhart Tolle is one of the greatest spiritual teachers of our time. His classic book *The Power of Now* has changed the lives of millions. When it was first published in Canada in 1997 by a small publishing house aptly named Namaste, only 3000 copies were printed.[35] The book was later picked up by a New York publishing house and was subsequently recommended by Oprah Winfrey. The rest, as they say, is history. Enlightenment for Tolle came literally overnight when he was 29, the same age as the Buddha! Maybe there is something in that? Tolle had been suffering from terrible depression but experienced an inner transformation that changed his relationship to himself and to life. His ego, or 'pain body' as he also calls it, had died. When we change our relationship to the present moment we change our relationship to ourselves.

I first read *The Power of Now* in the early noughties having heard how transformational it was and I desperately wanted a piece of this 'living in the moment' action! Although I tried really hard to understand it, I have to confess that it went right over my head. I simply could not understand the key concept, which is 'we are not our thoughts'. I thought about it way too much and as a result, my young mind was confused. The idea was not invented by Tolle and is in the teachings of all the great spiritual leaders such as the Buddha, Christ, the Dalai Lama and Marcus Aurelius. I understand it now and this has transformed my life but unlike Tolle and the Buddha, it has not happened overnight: it is something I work on every single day.

Forget drugs, smoking, gambling and other addictions, thinking too much is the hardest habit to break. It is also the root of all other addictions which provide a much-needed escape from the consistent noise of that radio of life that won't switch off. Master your mind and everything else will fall into place. There is no right or wrong way to create the Now Habit, but the things that will help you above all are patience, love and a desire to help yourself.

 IMAGINEERING

Imagine a beautiful summer's day. You are lying back gazing up at the blue sky. A white, fluffy cloud appears, you watch it and then let it pass and another one comes. Again, you watch it and gently let it pass. You are observing both of these thoughts. You can choose which thoughts to follow; some will be positive, others negative. As you observe the clouds, allow a gap to come between each cloud, each thought: in this space there is peace. You are not your thoughts; you are the presence that observes the thoughts.

It is this presence and the space between your thoughts that is the essence of peace and freedom from the thinking mind.

This concept, although simple in theory, can take time to put into practice, especially if your mind is caught up in a storm of negative thoughts. If you take anything from this chapter, take this: don't believe your dark thoughts; you are not your thoughts. I remember experiencing violent thoughts when my son was first born. I did not have postnatal depression but these strong thoughts would come like a bolt out of nowhere. It is common for new mothers to experience such thoughts as the hormones released in giving birth need time to settle. Thankfully, I understood that my thoughts were not facts but rumours in my mind which I could let go easily. However, if a new mum experiencing such thoughts were to identify with them they could quickly spiral out of control and cause great distress to both mum and baby.

While we should not identify with or depend on our thoughts, those that are positive should be nurtured and allowed to grow because positive thoughts create positive emotional states and the aim is then to progress from state to trait. Exercises such as the 15-second positive plunge (see page 93) can help you to achieve this.

With the Now Habit you choose your thoughts and create your emotional landscape. Take regular mindful moments that create a refuge from thinking. The following simple technique will help you with this.

MEDITATION – SEVEN DEEP BELLY BREATHS (2.5 MINUTES)

There are two types of breathing:

1   Thoracic (chest) breathing is shallow and short. People who suffer from stress and anxiety and racing thoughts or who are always rushing breathe like this. This is the type of breathing most people do without being aware of it.

2   Diaphragmatic (abdominal) breathing is deep and slow. Babies and young children do this and we also breathe like this when we sleep. This type of breathing will calm your mind and body and we will practise it in exercises in the book.

'Seven deep belly breaths' is a mindful technique that should be practised at least three times during the day. It is short enough to do anywhere and long enough to calm your sympathetic nervous system, also known as the stress response. The audio can be found on The Positive Habit website.

Use the seven deep belly breaths in the following situations/when you are feeling the following emotions:

+ You feel overwhelmed, stressed and/or anxious.

+ You are faced with a life challenge such as an unexpected illness or being made redundant.

+ You already feel calm – this reinforces and deepens the Calmness Habit.

+ Before any important meeting, either professional or personal.

+ If you feel yourself rushing.

+ When your mind is racing.

+ When you are waiting in traffic.

+ When you are waiting in a queue.

+ When you are caring for children.

+ If you are with someone you find difficult to be around, for example a challenging member of your family or someone at work.

+ When you are in nature or in a beautiful place. This will help you to see the world with fresh eyes – colours, sounds and aromas all bounce with life.

+ When you are with people. Using this technique will help you to see the beauty in everyone and to feel in harmony with them.

+ ANYTIME you feel the need – the more often the better.

Listen to the audio clip now and prepare to change the way you breathe. You know you are doing it right when your shoulders no longer move when you breathe. It is helpful to place your hand on your belly so that you can feel it rise and fall.

+ + +

The Benefits of Presence

BEING PRESENT in the moment allows you to pause and move from reactive to responsive mode. When you react to a situation using your survival (mammalian) brain you will not be giving yourself, the people you love or the situation the credit they deserve.

When you are present, your head, heart and body inhabit the same space at the same time.

It may sound easy, but when was the last time you maintained that presence for more than a few moments? Very often the mind has wandered to the future or the past, the heart is being ignored and the body is not being cared for.

Observe your mind and notice if it is not present. Is it:

+ In the future, planning a moment that has yet to come?

+ In the past, ruminating on something that has happened?

There are so many benefits of cultivating the Now Habit. The practical benefits are that you:

+ Take better care of yourself physically.

+ Reduce the stress hormone cortisol and as a result live longer and stay healthier.

+ Switch off from work more easily.

+ Have a better memory, sense of direction and ability to focus and make decisions.

- Can manage pain better.

- Get to sleep faster both when you first go to sleep and also if you awaken during the night.

The psychological benefits are that you:

- Move from reacting to responding.

- Experience mental freedom from thought.

- Don't take anything personally.

- Detach from identification with your ego.

- Remove all judgement of yourself and others.

- Strengthen your relationships.

- Feel love and compassion for every creature including yourself.

- Contribute to the collective consciousness of those who are awakening to presence.

- Feel a great sense of inner peace.

The Now Habit is the lighthouse that illuminates all six positive emotional habits that you will cultivate with this book.

+ + +

The Comfort of Being Fully Present

FEELING SAFE IS fundamental to your wellbeing and being present can help to bring you this safety. Taking the time to quieten the mind takes courage, it takes effort and a genuine desire to be at peace with yourself. You are showing this courage now by listening to your morning and night time audios and by following the exercises in this book which are carefully crafted to break the habit loop of fear. You are building a sense of trust and safety in your own gentle presence in this very moment, now.

Jon Kabat-Zinn is an instrumental figure in the mindfulness movement; in the 1980s, his ground-breaking mindfulness-based stress reduction (MBSR) courses were introduced into hospitals and they are now run all over the world. There is a wealth of research that indicates those who follow these eight-week programmes experience a reduction in chronic pain and anxiety levels. Kabat-Zinn is the author of *Full Catastrophe Living*, a giant of a book that is an antidote for anxiety and stress.

Living a life with responsibilities takes courage because they expose us to many challenges. Your ability to live and love fully derives from rising to these challenges. For example, the fear of becoming a parent is understandable yet it should not stop you from participating in one of the most valuable of life's experiences, having a child.

Ironically, many of us find resources we didn't know we had when we face true catastrophe. For example, when we lose a person we love we may, after grieving, find a new lease of life and a change of perspective allowing us to do things we may never have considered before. In loss, we see the full fragility of life and this can make us more determined to live life to the full.

Do you want to wait for a tragedy to wake you up?

Of course, you will have suffered already and whatever you have gone through has helped make you who you are today. The question is, have you learned from this suffering or have you sheltered behind it? Being in the now means that it is never too late to learn from what is going on within yourself.

It is often everyday stresses and strains that collectively cause a lot of our suffering; the car won't start, a deadline looms, your email inbox is full, the kids won't eat their vegetables. However, most of this suffering is unnecessary; problems are only problems if you view them as such. Remember the fly that irritated me as I meditated? Life is not a journey without bumps and if it were it would be dull and mundane with no room for progress. Using your trigger list is a major contribution to creating peace in your mind. Practising the Now Habit allows minor irritations to take on little or no meaning and they cease to have a major impact on your emotional state. They are forced to take their place in the full 'catastrophe' of living.

Kabat-Zinn stresses that having an open mind is essential to the effective practice of mindfulness. Your attitude to the process and the more open you are to it, the easier it is to cultivate. The Now Habit is a skill that you develop through what Kabat-Zinn calls the seven foundations of mindfulness practice.[36]

1 **Non-judging** – not judging yourself in your practice of mindfulness. Being with whatever arises in the mind is true self-compassion.

2 **Patience** – give yourself time and each time the mind wanders, gently, kindly bring it back to the moment.

3 **Beginner's mind** – always be open to learning. Each time

you practise meditation, bring wonder and curiosity to the process, like a child.

4 **Trust** – self-trust is golden. Cultivate the precious ability to rely on your own mind and let go of the harsh inner critic.

5 **Non-striving** – letting go of the need to 'achieve'. With mindfulness there is no goal, no end result – this is true freedom.

6 **Acceptance** – you have to accept yourself as you are before you can really change.

7 **Letting go** – practising non-attachment to all things, thoughts and feelings, both positive and negative.

I will be touching on all of these areas throughout the book as they are important and offer us the essence of compassion. Now let's start with the concept of acceptance.

Acceptance is the beginning, not the end.

Much of our inability to live in the present is a habit and it is caused by the habit of resistance to what *is*. Observe yourself – are you living in resistance to each moment as it unfolds? Common examples of this include complaining when:

+ Something breaks, whether it is a car, a computer or a jug!

+ Waiting in a queue at the bank, in a traffic jam or for a friend who is late.

+ Plans are changed, flights delayed or meetings postponed.

+ Things are lost, for example, keys, phones, glasses, passport ...

+ You have minor physical ailments.

All of these examples contain one or both of the following:

1 A change or something that is not planned.

2 A situation outside your control or a person who is not behaving the way you would like them to.

While many of the wonderful people who come to see me in my clinical practice *are* aware that they are stressed, anxious and finding it hard to cope, when I ask them to accept it, they find this much more difficult. This is entirely understandable – acceptance feels like giving up! Yet, imagine you are walking down a street in the wrong direction and someone kindly taps you on the shoulder to let you know you are going the wrong way. If you refuse to accept their help you will continue to be lost.

Acceptance of the darker and more complicated parts of our psyches takes courage. Our survival instinct tells us to get as far away as we possibly can from the pain we feel, and yet, until we accept the negative we are stuck.

Imagine someone in a dysfunctional relationship who cannot accept that they are being abused; they simply 'cannot believe it' each time 'it' happens and they convince themselves that it will never happen again. As long as the protective cycle of resistance to the reality continues, they will remain in that relationship.

The first step in affecting real change, as Kabat-Zinn points out, is to accept what *is* before we can take positive steps to change it. To truly experience how to implement acceptance into your thoughts, your relationships and your life, consider the following technique.

+ + +

The ARK Method – Transform Negative Thinking to Positive

MOST NEGATIVE THOUGHTS linger and multiply because we feel shame and guilt for feeling them. It's a vicious cycle. For example, one of my clients who suffered from a huge amount of anger would mentally beat himself up for being stupid, not good enough and then get more angry with himself for feeling like that. He felt totally powerless to control his thoughts. The harder he was on himself and the more shame he felt, the more intense the negative thoughts became.

The following technique is effective in catching negative thoughts early, before they become feelings and are harder to shift.

> **There is no shame in feeling negative; replace shame with kindness.**

The ARK method is about creating an ark of transformation that brings you from feeling negative to feeling positive. It is a bit like Noah's ark, which saved all the animals; using it will save yourself from the toxicity of unnecessary negative thoughts. There is no audio for this exercise, you simply read it.

ACCEPT

1 **Accept unconditionally** the first negative thought you have. Let's say for argument's sake it is, 'I'm not good enough' (the most common one that I hear regularly from clients). Catch this first thought (through awareness) and simply *accept* it.

2 Repeat several times, 'It is okay that I think like this.' This is the *hardest* step as the instinct is to fight it but all that does is bring more negative thoughts.

Doing this will lessen the impact of the negativity bias and associated shame that comes in the form of, 'I **should** or feel this way or that.' Banish 'shoulds'. There are a myriad of reasons that led to the creation of that thought and it is not your fault. Getting annoyed with yourself for thinking the thought turns that one thought into a full story.

RELEASE

1 It is now time to let the negative thought go. Shake your hands to physically release the toxicity of the thought from your body. This part is easier but only possible once it has been accepted.

2 Repeat the phrase, 'I let this thought go now.' You may have to follow these two steps in the beginning up to 100 times a day, but that is okay! It will get so much easier and just like the four-second positive pause (see page 62), over time it will become automatic.

KINDNESS

1 The next step involves showing kindness towards yourself and this is the lovely part! What words would help you right now? If you were talking to a child or a friend, what would you say? Probably something like, 'that's not true,' 'you are great', 'I am proud of you' or 'you are doing your best'. The voice in your mind is on your side, it loves you and has infinite patience.

Repeat these words consistently and you have created an ARK from negative thinking to positive, from resistance to acceptance and from self-loathing to self-love.

Your moment is now.

The Now Habit will bring awe and awareness to both the new and the familiar in your life. Consider for a moment people you know who are 'present'. Do you notice they also possess other positive qualities, such as calmness and confidence? When we encounter presence in a person, we feel it as they create a powerful impression that is almost tangible. They see things that nobody else notices and have an energy that draws people to them naturally. You can seize this moment to be that person and to exude a loving presence.

To do this, take the time to observe yourself properly. Socrates, a man who died (with a calm acceptance) for his beliefs, once said, 'The unexamined life is not worth living.' If you live without knowing or understanding who you really are, you live with a stranger, which can be very uncomfortable; until you get to know yourself, you can't fully trust yourself.

You have all the ingredients you need in the present moment to transform your life and to experience the six positive habits of love, calmness, confidence, gratitude, hope and, ultimately, happiness. Becoming present in your life is a form of re-awakening, a returning to the divine light within yourself. The gap between your thoughts (remember the clouds?) is where real peace exists; as your thoughts become slower this gap gets wider and you consequently become more positive. Presence itself is not a transformation but a returning to the source, a coming home to now.

Remove yourself from thought and become like a young child again, breathe deeply and marvel at the world.

Let me extend my admiration to you now that you have done the necessary work to take your first step on your ladder to happiness and positivity, which is love. Love is the most primary emotional habit that you will self-generate and which will significantly impact on you reaching your full positive potential. Your undivided attention and ability to be present for yourself and the people in your life creates the purest and most profound love.

THREE KEY TAKEAWAYS FROM THIS CHAPTER

1 You are not your negative thoughts. There is a space that exists between you and your thoughts; this is presence, this is peace. Do *not* believe your negative thoughts.

2 Being mindful is simply being aware and is something you can incorporate into your daily life.

3 Acceptance, as opposed to resistance to thoughts, situations or people, will help you to recreate your powerful presence.

 MINDFUL SHOWERING

Imagine the water cleansing both your mind and body. Feel the water on your skin and continue to bring your mind back to the sensation each time it goes into planning mode.

ACKNOWLEDGE PROGRESS

Now mark how you are feeling on the positivity sundial below.

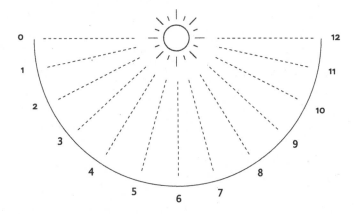

Remember to keep listening to your seven-minute morning and your sleep time hypnotherapies. Tick the days so far that you have listened in the grid at the back of the book. Be proud of the times you have listened and don't give yourself a hard time if you have missed one or two days; that is okay – keep going!

MEDITATIONS

+ Morning ritual

+ Sleep time hypnotherapy

+ The seven deep belly breaths

PART TWO

THE LOVE HABIT

HOW TO LOVE YOURSELF AND OTHERS

*'Every heart sings a song incomplete
until another heart whispers back.'*

PLATO

+

INTERRELATED

Closeness   *Connection*   *Bonding*   *Affection*   *Tenderness*   *Devotion*

AFFIRMATIONAL TOOTH BRUSHING

Write the following three affirmations in your journal and say them to yourself as you brush your teeth each morning and night. Make sure to cultivate the feelings in your heart that the words create. Closing your eyes will help with this.

1   I love myself just the way I am.

2   It is safe for me to connect with others.

3   I trust the divine light in my heart to guide me with love.

If you cannot remember the exact words, it doesn't matter; simply repeat the phrase 'I am loved' silently to yourself, over and over, as you brush.

Please note that at the end of the chapter I will ask you to write down three examples to support the affirmations outlined above. For example, in the case of the first affirmation, you might write, 'I did not obsess over my weight this week,' or for the second, you might write, 'I had an honest conversation with a friend.'

PADDY'S STORY, BUSINESS OWNER, 64

'I would say that I love everybody in the world and can see something lovable in everyone. The weakness with me personally was self-love which I didn't apply to myself maybe because, as a child, I was taught that loving yourself was selfish. I was conditioned to believe that love was only towards other people, not towards yourself. Seeing self-obsessed people really put me off the idea of self-love in the extreme.

'This lack of self-love is a huge issue for many men and to be perfectly honest led me into a very abusive marriage that I ended up staying in for thirty years. Like many men who have been in abusive relationships, I didn't get out of it until my children left home. What I realise now is that my lack of self-love probably kept me in that situation longer and looking back at that now is a huge thing for me. There are so few resources for men suffering domestic abuse and they end up feeling ashamed and trying to hide it. It is, therefore, no surprise to me how high the suicide rate is in Ireland for men. A lot goes on behind closed doors.

'Real love, to me, always meant putting others' needs ahead of my own; I had a sick child and had to work and look after him as my wife was generally in no fit state mentally or physically to care for him or our other three children. I didn't question it – I didn't have time to. My son had a heart condition from the age of six that eventually, a few years ago, took his life before his thirtieth birthday.

'I don't regret putting my children first even though I was in a bad place because of my relationship with my wife. A year after the death of my son I suffered a heart attack. I was a smoker and this is why I first met Fiona – to help me give up smoking. When I was in the hospital a young nurse approached my bed and said, "care". I often think she was like an angel but at the time I looked at her blankly. "You need to care for yourself now, it's time," she whispered. Although she knew nothing about my background her message resonated with me and so sometime after that I contacted Fiona. I haven't smoked since and that was almost five years ago. I still come to see Fiona once a month as my way of continuing to care for and love myself. I am now healthy, strong and I have carved out a new life for myself, I travel and see the world.

'I'm calm and in control. I might sometimes get anxious for around ten seconds and then I stop myself. It is a choice I make. It is self-love, I have a chance at last. It's my time now.'

THE POSITIVE HABIT
EMOTIONS QUIZ #2

Take the quiz now and allocate a point for each Yes answer that you give. Go with the first answer that comes to mind and do not spend too much time thinking about the question.

1 Do you feel present most of the time?

2 Do you make time to care for your mind each day?

3 Do you love yourself?

4 Do you believe you are a compassionate person?

5 Are you able not to take anything other people do or say personally?

6 If you feel stress or anxiety, do you use your breath to calm your mind?

7 Do you protect your mind from negative information, people and places, for example having regular digital breaks/avoiding people who drain your energy?

8 Do you feel confident to speak your mind and feel equal to others?

9 Are you kind to yourself if you make a mistake?

10 Do you feel grateful each day?

11 Do you let go of grudges from the past?

12 Do you visualise a bright future?

13 Do you feel you are living your life's purpose?

14 Do you take care of your physical needs, such as getting eight hours' sleep a night, exercising and eating a balanced diet?

15 Do you feel that you are good enough as a person?

16 Do you trust that no matter what happens you will be able to cope?

Score from quiz #1 on page 8 =   Score from quiz #2 =
What do you notice? Can you see progress? Which answers have changed?
Which ones need more work? Keep learning – you are doing great!

+ + +

What Does Love Mean to You?

ANCIENT GREEKS HAD six different words for love, each indicating a different form of love:

1 **Eros** – sexual passion and desire

2 **Philia** – deep friendship (generally far more valued than Eros)

3 **Ludos** – playful love

4 **Agape** – love for everyone, family and strangers alike

5 **Pragma** – long-standing love

6 **Philautia** – love of the self.

The Greeks were quick to identify two types of self-love; narcissism (clearly not to be encouraged) and self-compassion, one to be nurtured.

NOTEBOOK
LOVE TRIGGERS

Take a moment to brainstorm and write down in your notebook what love means to you, when you most feel it and how. This list is important as it will help you to create a positive habit loop of love in your life.

To help get you started, I'm sharing here some examples from my clients:

+ Spending time with my family

+ Watching my children sleep

+ Feeling safe and cosy

+ Laughing with friends

+ Being listened to

+ Feeling equal to others

+ My mum rubbing my tummy when I was a child

+ Making love with my partner

+ Being comfortable on my own

+ Helping people

+ Being part of a group

+ Hugging my loved ones

+ Caring for my family when they are not well

+ Being cared for

+ Saying 'I love you'

Look at your list and allow it to resonate with you. In the same way that we created a trigger list for stress and negative emotional habits (page 61), we now start to assemble a positive emotional trigger list for love. We are turning creation of habits a full 180 degrees to the positive.

Start to scan each day for positive triggers that open opportunities for you to create the Love Habit in your life. Remember, habits are motivated by reward and operate by repetition.

THE HABIT LOOP OF LOVE

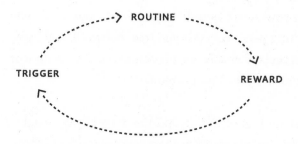

In this example, the following triggers may be appropriate:

1 **Positive trigger** – being listened to.

2 **Positive routine** – finding someone I can trust. Speaking from my heart.

3 **Positive reward** – feeling loved.

+ + +

Love – The
First Emotional Habit

NOW THAT YOU are cultivating presence you are conscious and awake to creating the king and queen of all positive emotions – love. Positive people are acutely aware of how fundamental love is to their happiness. They understand that love is life and it is to be found everywhere when you open your eyes. In this chapter, I want to challenge your perception of love, explain why you need to operate from your heart as well as your head, and show why not taking anything personally sets you free. Above all, I will give you the practical tools to enable you to increase your daily dose of oxytocin, also known as the love hormone.

Love is the most supreme emotion and the most highly sought-after; people will do literally anything because of it and for it. There is no greater pain than to feel a lack of love. When we are born we crave love as much as we crave food and if we remain unloved in infancy we can spend our lives suffering, both consciously and unconsciously.

In the film *Castaway*, Tom Hanks plays a man shipwrecked on a desert island who finds the most difficult thing to endure is his isolation from other people and so he creates a companion called 'Wilson' who is not a real person but a volleyball. Despite this Hanks loves Wilson and confides in him daily. Wilson paradoxically helps to keep him sane. In one dramatic and heartbreaking scene, Hanks loses Wilson from his raft and we, the audience, feel the tragedy of the lost friend just as if it were a real person. The human need for love is so strong we fear Hanks will die bereft.

Without love our hearts harden to the point that we become like the living dead.

There has been extensive research on the detrimental effects on orphans who are brought up in an environment devoid of love and human touch. When the Romanian Communist leader Nicolae Ceauşescu was overthrown in 1989, 170,000 children were discovered living in brutally inhumane conditions in Romania's many orphanages. During Ceauşescu's reign from 1965 to 1989 both contraception and abortion were illegal and, as a result, orphanages were inundated with unwanted babies. Conditions were so bad that many babies received no affection or love and often spent hours staring at the ceiling. In addition, many of them were left naked and strapped to their beds where they were also subjected to emotional, physical and sexual abuse.

A study conducted by Professor Edmund Sonuga-Barke and Professor Sir Michael Rutter from King's College London on 165 Romanian children between the ages of 0 and 42 months who were adopted in the UK illustrates the impact of early trauma on the mental health of the adoptee.[37] The study examined the children by talking to their adoptive parents and teachers and by using MRI scans of their brains at 4, 6, 11 and 15 years of age. The findings were compared with those of 52 non-neglected children adopted within the UK. Unsurprisingly, they found that the Romanian children demonstrated significantly increased maladaptive behaviours and emotional difficulties, with 40 per cent of them presenting for mental health care. Crucially, the amount of time an infant is deprived of love and care has a direct link with their development; children adopted at less than six months old generally displayed normal behaviours and made healthier attachments. Professor Edmund Sonuga-Barke commented, *'Getting children out of those neglected situations as soon as possible and into a loving family was crucial.'*[38]

A genuine or perceived lack of love and connection at the formative stage and indeed in any period of our lives can lead to depression and anxiety.

So, on that cheerful note, let us examine how you can bring more love into your life.

+ + +

The Age of Romance?

IN HIS BOOK *The Art of Happiness,* the Dalai Lama suggests that in the West, we are conditioned to believe that romantic love is the secret to our happiness. If you haven't found 'the one', you are doomed to a life of loneliness and despair. The development of the concept of romantic love springs from Romanticism, the artistic, literary, and intellectual movement that originated in Europe in the early 19th century and which has had a major influence on how we view love in the West. When you add to this fairytale happy endings remembered from childhood and Hollywood projections of perfection, serious ructions can occur between long-term partners. Couples can feel the romance has gone out of their relationship and many end up turning their backs on potentially fulfilling relationships.

In the East, people tend to live and love in a wider community and that opens the possibility for love to flow in all relationships. This is more in line with the Greek word *agape*, meaning the love of all. Whatever your relationship status, when you are open to this wider concept of love then it can be found everywhere and within every encounter.

+ + +

The Heart of Love

'A good head and a good heart is a formidable combination.'

NELSON MANDELA

ARISTOTLE VIEWED the heart as the most important organ in the body; in ancient Egypt, during the mummification process the brain was thrown away and the heart kept. Ivor Browne, former chief psychiatrist of the Eastern Health Board (Ireland) and a pioneer in mental health, has always sought to see the 'patient' as a person who needs love and he greets all he meets with a hug. He has practised *Sahaj Marg*, a system of Raja Yoga meditation, more commonly known as 'heartfulness' since the late 1970s (he is now 89). Personally, I, like many, have a lot to be grateful to Browne for; he introduced me to my heart's intelligence.[39] When we first met I was living from my shoulders up, busy talking about the brain, neuroplasticity and the hope it provides for people, and he said, like the wise old owl he is, 'Indeed, but what about the heart? Don't forget about your heart.'

We use the word 'heart' to express our emotions in so many different ways: from the bottom of your heart, to break someone's heart, to cross your heart, to eat your heart out, to be half-hearted about something, to have a change of heart, to have a heart of gold … the list goes on. It has become a cartoon-like symbol and is one of the most-used emojis in social media. On the one hand, this illustrates an implicit connection and understanding we have with our hearts, but on the other, it has the potential to cheapen the true intelligence of the heart.

By moving away from the purely mechanical view of the heart you can slow the busyness of the thinking mind towards the stillness of an open and uncluttered heart.

To ignore the intelligence of the heart is to cut out one of the most important routes to establishing a balanced, emotional intelligence as well as connecting to ourselves and others.

By listening to your morning and sleep time audios, you will feel a growing awareness of your own heart.

+ + +

Connect for Longevity

YOU MAY KNOW that 'happy' hormones boost our immune systems but did you know that the happier you are the longer you are likely to live? Harvard's renowned Grant and Glueck study is the longest-running study on happiness in the world. For more than 80 years it has tracked the physical and emotional wellbeing of two populations: 456 poor men growing up in Boston from 1939 to 2014 (the Grant Study), and 268 males who graduated from Harvard between the years 1939 and 1944 (the Glueck study).[40] Because of the length of the study, it has required multiple generations of researchers; since before World War II they have diligently analysed blood samples, conducted brain scans (once they became available), and pored over self-reported surveys, as well as having actual interactions with these men to compile the findings. The conclusion? According to Robert Waldinger, director of the *Harvard Study of Adult Development*, one thing surpasses all the rest in terms of importance: 'the secret to a long and happy life is our *connection* to other humans'.

Today if someone asks you to connect, it is usually in a digital format; send me an email, follow me on social media. Replacing face-to-face interaction with digital connection is not the same as we miss many of the important nuances of face-to-face connection and can actually miscommunicate as a result. How many times has the recipient of an email picked it up the wrong way and inferred something else? Technology, like most things, is very useful only as long as we know how, when and for what purposes to use it. It is, however, not a substitute for real-time face-to-face interaction. Positive people are present and use technology appropriately but are not slaves to it – they live their lives rather than spending them endlessly scrolling on a screen. They carefully allocate screen time and then carve out time to be away from it, having and building real relationships.

One of the most interesting discoveries in neuroscience in the last 15 years is that of mirror neurons. From infancy we reflect back to the world what we see in the expressions and behaviours of others. To put it plainly, a baby who smiles is smiled at often and a baby who frowns is likewise frowned at often. While it might seem pretty simple as a concept, we often tend to forget and ask questions like, 'Why is my child so anxious?' There are, of course, other factors at play but in the first place the answer may often be found by looking in the mirror.

Mirror neurons also fire when we feel empathy for others, which explains why we find it painful to see someone we love suffering. Our ability to have empathy for others is something many marketers and filmmakers are well aware of and they design their products and films to elicit an emotional response. The higher the level of emotion, the more likely we are to engage and to make a purchase.

+ + +

What if Your Empathy Goes Too Far?

'EMPATHS' ARE PEOPLE who feel intensely the emotions of others, which can cause them great suffering if they encounter toxic emotional environments. The empath often hopes, subconsciously, that experiencing another's pain will relieve it. Unfortunately, this does not work. Take the example of a therapist who becomes upset when their client is upset – now we have two people who need therapy! The empath is highly prone to a victim mentality. By absorbing the other person's emotional pain, rather than helping it they in fact compound it and it now becomes all about them. For example, an empath at a funeral may end up needing to be consoled by the grieving family. Perhaps you know someone like this – how does it feel to be in their company?

A compassionate therapist, on the other hand, has genuine concern but is emotionally resilient enough to help without losing their sense of self and this is necessary for all of our relationships. On my wedding day, my mother-in-law read the following from *The Prophet* (Kahlil Gibran) and this has guided me through my marriage on many occasions.

Love one another but make not a bond of love. Let it rather be a moving sea between the shores of your souls. Fill each other's cup but drink not from one cup.

The ideal relationship does exist!

 ## IMAGINEERING

Imagine waking up tomorrow morning and finding that you are in the best relationship of your entire life. You lie there for a few moments to reflect because you feel so in love, so full of joy and so connected. Your partner understands you so well and always knows the right thing to say. He/she supports you, soothes you and always sees the best in you. He/she accepts you entirely, loves you unconditionally, forgives your weaknesses and celebrates your strengths. He/she respects your boundaries and gives you all the time and space you need. If you feel emotional, anxious or sad he/she knows how to help you and gives you the courage to sit with painful emotions reminding you that they will soon pass.

He/she makes sure you take good care of yourself, reminds you to breathe deeply, cooks healthy meals, encourages you to exercise regularly and always makes sure you get a good night's sleep. When you are with him/her you feel safe, confident and that anything is possible.

Sounds good? Well, the good news is that it is possible and you don't have to find a new partner or go online to start dating; that person is, of course, you!

Who is the Most Important Person in Your Life?

WHEN I ASK my clients this question they usually say their children, partner, parent or friend. I rarely hear 'I am'. How would you answer this question?

By 'important' I really mean who you love and value most. Most people when answering instinctively do not refer the question to themselves as they may have been taught as children that this would be selfish. Think back to Paddy's story at the start of this chapter. Did well-intentioned adults tell you that in order to be a good person you must put others before yourself?

Self-love was not a concept I was familiar with growing up – it was considered vain, self-centred and possibly even selfish. The Greek myth of Narcissus, the handsome hunter who died from staring at his own reflection was something we all needed to be wary of.

If we were taught that to love ourselves is a negative thing, was the alternative – disliking ourselves – considered good? The message was not definitive but the formative mind sees many things in black and white.

Do you love yourself?

Perhaps the question makes you feel a little uneasy? Self-indulgent, even? Yet who are you with every moment of your life? Being in a dysfunctional relationship with yourself is actually selfish because it creates toxic energy both with the people you love and yourself. The tension and negative energy created when people argue is palpable and uncomfortable and the same is true when you have been fighting with yourself.

Self-love is not selfish.

The belief that self-love is selfish is still prevalent despite the popularity of taking selfies. In the era of social media it is easy to see why we equate loving yourself to how you look and what you achieve, but authentic self-love has nothing to do with vanity. There is a big difference between having an inflated ego and having a healthy and loving relationship with yourself. Having a big ego is in fact often reflective of high levels of insecurity and as narcissism increases, compassion decreases.

It can be useful to find out if you are feeding your ego. Are you:

1   **A constant giver?** Do you spend your time constantly putting everyone and everything else before yourself? The ego can feed off this identity; under all of the giving, resentment, frustration and exhaustion can build up. In this situation you simply don't have enough time or energy to take care of your own needs and you say yes to everything people ask of you both at work and on a personal level. The need for approval is what often drives this behaviour.

2   **A constant taker?** You may believe that you are selfish if you are always putting your own needs ahead of others. Do you always say no if you don't feel like doing something and look after yourself first? Do you indulge yourself both materially and emotionally? Do you identify closely with your

appearance and use this to compare yourself to others, either feeling superior or inferior? It may seem like these types of behaviour are a form of self-care but underneath lurks a very negative core belief that you are not a good person and are ultimately selfish.

Feeling superior or inferior to others is isolating. Feeling equal is love.

If the popular perception that self-love is selfish could be changed so that it came to be accepted as an essential requirement for good emotional intelligence, this would have a major impact. I therefore appeal to you to lead by example and demonstrate this to the younger generation. In order to do this you must first ask yourself: Do I feel worthy of love?

 IMAGINEERING

Imagine you are in a supermarket and at the checkout you see the cutest newborn baby girl sleeping peacefully in her pram, looking warm, cosy and well cared for. The baby opens her eyes for a brief moment and her tiny, twinkly eyes meet yours. Do you believe that she deserves to be loved, to live a happy life, to reach her full potential? Do you believe she has the capacity to love herself? Do you wish the best for her? Of course you do.

Babies naturally have presence, something that we all crave, and which was discussed in the previous chapter, How to Create Peaceful Presence. They live without ego and naturally love and accept themselves provided they are also being lovingly cared for. In the same way that they need milk and somewhere warm to sleep, they also need love and for them this comes naturally; the idea that love may be conditional on something or someone else has not yet been formulated in their minds and therefore there is no understanding of the concept of 'deserving'.

It is important to recognise that you were once a baby – pure, innocent and open to love, and that now there is still a part of you deep in your subconscious mind that recalls that feeling of self-love and total acceptance of yourself. It is this part that positive people have reawakened.

Mahatma Gandhi once said, 'Where there is love, there is life.' You were born to love yourself and others and to be loved.

+ + +

Approval-Seeking Belief

DO YOU APPROVE of yourself or are you constantly seeking approval from other people? As children we are vulnerable to how we believe others – in particular our parents – see us. The attitude of siblings towards us can also be significant in our development while the perception that parents may favour one sibling over another can cause psychological distress and jealousy. This 'green-eyed monster' eats away at the soul and can cause chronic self-doubt and feelings of inadequacy, along with a constant desire to be approved of.

An ex-client of mine, Sam, told me that as a child he always felt inferior to his elder brother; he felt he could never run as fast, be as clever or indeed be loved as much as his brother was. Consequently, as they grew up, Sam suffered from anxiety and very low self-esteem and began to compare himself negatively to everyone else: his colleagues were more intelligent, his friends more popular, his girlfriend more intelligent and so on.

Sam's brother was three years older, so when they were children, of course he could run faster and do more. Sam's father was an avid sports fan and regularly complimented the older brother for his speed and skill at soccer. Sam internalised what was merely a normal, developmental difference as 'not being good enough'. He had never taken the time to understand his childhood before as he had been too busy trying to compensate for his perceived lack of physical prowess. Understanding and then dispelling this belief was paramount to improving Sam's mental health. When he courageously had a conversation with his brother and parents he released years of pent-up stress and realised how much he was loved, that his father did not favour his brother but loved them both equally.

A lot of unnecessary pain can be avoided by seeking clarity from those we love.

Sam's confidence really started to improve and today Sam seeks only his own approval and more often than not, he gets it.

In the critical and formative early years, impressionable minds can easily confuse love and approval, equating what we do and achieve with how much love we *deserve*. For example, if I do my school homework well, I may well believe I will be loved more. This habit of approval-seeking behaviour when extended into adulthood is fundamentally detrimental to our self-esteem; craving external approval is exhausting and an entirely unreliable source of security.

Many people unconsciously replace the parent figure (authority) with their boss and they will do anything, including working themselves to the bone, to ensure they get that crucial nod of approval. The need for approval and fear of disappointing the boss/parent is often greater than finding the courage to say no.

Repeated experiences shape our belief systems and as much of the research on epigenetics (our genes are shaped by our experiences) suggests, we are conditioned creatures. In addition, many of us simply parrot the unconscious patterns of our parents and mimic their insecurities, which were never ours in the first place.

Negative emotional habits from the past must no longer define your present or your future.

+ + +

Attachment Theory

THE BRITISH CHILD PSYCHOLOGIST and psychiatrist John Bowlby's work on attachment theory is important in understanding our early conditioning. As infants we form either a secure or an insecure attachment to our primary caregiver, usually our mother.

Forming one of the three insecure attachment types may cause lifelong feelings that there was a of lack of love displayed by the primary caregiver to the child. In adulthood this is likely to lead to anxiety, depression and anger issues. By knowing what type of attachment you formed and taking appropriate steps to understand your early years, you will no longer be governed by old, unconscious patterns of behaviour.

Bowlby identified four key attachment types depending on the early bond that was formed or not.[41]

1 **Secure attachment:** This is displayed by babies who are happy and smile often. Such babies feel secure even when their mother is not present, are easily soothed by their mother and tend to favour her over anyone else. The mother is usually kind, patient and reliable. As an adult the person who has made a secure attachment tends to have healthy relationships and to be accepting and non-judgemental. Such people are usually self-sufficient, confident and allow their partner freedom to do as they wish; they do not suffer from jealousy or the need to control.

2 **Anxious-avoidant insecure attachment:** This is displayed by babies who are withdrawn and do not trust their mothers to meet their needs. They will be indifferent if the mother is present or not but will be anxious inside. In such situations the mother is often withdrawn and could be suffering from postnatal depression. As an adult, the person who has made this kind of attachment will find it hard to let people become close to them and will often be introverted, shy and prefer their own company. They have a deep fear of trusting others and believe if they do so they will only be hurt. Their hearts are closed.

3 **Anxious-resistant insecure (ambivalent) attachment:** This attachment is displayed by babies who can become easily angered and distressed. Their mother displays great affection interspaced with frustration and anger which is often projected onto the baby. This mixed message is very damaging and adults who have made this kind of attachment often display erratic behaviour. Their relationships are often filled with tension, stress and dramatic arguments. They are generally very clingy as children and adults.

4 **Disorganised/disoriented attachment:** This category is for those who do not fit into any of the other categories. As a baby, their behaviour can swing from anger to apathy. The mother is often anxious herself. As an adult, a person with this type of attachment may flare up quickly towards partners and/or withdraw into themselves and suppress their emotions for fear of how they will be judged. As a result he or she will be prone to depression.

NOTEBOOK ATTACHMENT

In applying attachment theory to yourself you may feel that you display a mix of the attachment types and this is quite often the case. Nevertheless, you are probably closer to one of these types. As you were reading the descriptions above which one did you most identify with?

Please take some time to answer the following questions in your notebook, leaving aside any blame or judgement. If you feel that those early years were hard and the situation was far from perfect, you have my sympathy, but this will only get you so far; you don't need sympathy, you need to own the experience – the good, the bad and the ugly parts. Learning about the first 18 months of your life takes courage and you have it.

Work with what you know now and if possible/if you feel comfortable you might ask your parents and/or siblings for some insights. Do this to learn about their point of view rather than how you may have seen things.

Take seven deep belly breaths and answer the following questions in relation to your first 18 months of life.

1   In photos were you smiling or did you seem with-
     drawn?

2   What was happening in your parents' lives at the time?
     What pressures did they have?

3   What was your mother's (or caregiver's) own mental
     health like at the time?

4   What stories have you heard about yourself? Were you
     described as a 'good' or 'difficult' baby?

5   Were you compared to your siblings in either a positive
     or negative way?

Answering these questions will help you to understand those early
months and years from the perspective of your parents. This can be
a very useful thing as you look at your life with a very different lens. If
you are a parent yourself now, you will know what a joy and challenge
parenthood is.

+ + +

Were You Labelled?

FAMILIES CAN BE notorious places for labelling their members;
Mary, a client of mine, had five sisters and each sister had a title
such as Anne – the pretty one, Helen – the kind one, Catherine
– the clever one. Mary, daughter number four, was known as the
difficult one who always cried and never slept. With that label, it is
easy to see how Mary may have had low self-esteem even though,
in essence, she was no more difficult or less pretty, kind or clever
than her sisters. She was responding to the environment into
which she was born and trying to form a secure attachment with

her mother who was overwhelmed and exhausted with looking after four young girls.

Even as fully independent adults many people struggle to come to terms with the actions of their parents. It is not about finding fault, it is about understanding first, and then compassion.

Parents generally do their best for their children with what resources they have available to them at the time; by this, I mean what state their own mental and physical health is in, the type of childhood they had themselves and the negative beliefs they may have unwittingly inherited.

The best gift we can give our children is to mind ourselves so we can put an end to a legacy of faults and pain that our families may have unconsciously passed down the line. Remember, you are not stuck and unable to change; being willing to understand yourself and practising the exercises in this book to self-direct your neuroplasticity will enable you to transform yourself from the maladaptive attachment type to the highly adaptive and secure attachment type.

Part of becoming an adult means being able to provide self-approval without relying on others for it. Self-approval is an infinite supply of love that helps you to connect with others and to contribute to the world as an emotionally intelligent adult.

The Habit of Self-Love

IF AT THIS STAGE of the book you feel that you already do love yourself, I am thrilled. However, all relationships need ongoing care and attention to keep them flourishing. If you still find the idea of self-love nauseating and indulgent then we have more work to do.

Your experiences have shaped who you are now, so your subconscious mind only has the capacity to operate from the world it is exposed to. An accumulation of small and apparently minor experiences that we interpret as negative can build feelings of insecurity and anxiety. Remember Sam who was jealous of his brother? No terrible trauma, just his way of interpreting his world.

It can be common to attach conditions to self-acceptance (never mind love), for example when a certain weight is reached, a new job acquired, an exam passed or an 'ideal' partner found. But unconditional self-love removes the need to compare or judge and replaces it instead with pure acceptance of you, just the way you are now.

Being content with yourself provides a springboard for success.

Compassion rather than pressure will fuel you to move forward. When you love someone deeply, you truly want the best for them, isn't that so? Can you do this for yourself? It sounds easy but it takes consistent practice to turn self-love into a habit.

How do you care for yourself?

It is a sad fact that many of us care better for our pet dogs than ourselves. Those without a dog will probably also take even less care of themselves; they don't have to take the dog for walks and so may miss out on some valuable fresh air and exercise. Tending to our own needs can often come last, if at all, on a very long to-do list that has everything and everyone else at the top of it.

Jordan Bernt Peterson, a Canadian clinical psychologist, is author of the recent bestseller, *12 Rules for Life*. In this remarkable book he poses the question, 'What could it be about people that makes them prefer their pets to themselves?'[42] In order to answer this perplexing question, Peterson brings us back to the story of Adam and Eve and postulates that their shame of discovering themselves as naked and imperfect is at the root of human dissatisfaction with the self. It is perhaps this awareness of our flaws that gives them their strength; dogs do not feel shame, ruminate or catastrophise and they are naturally present. It seems we have a lot to learn from dogs!

+ + +

Meeting Your Needs

ABRAHAM MASLOW, the American psychologist best known for creating his famous 'hierarchy of needs', clearly states that our fundamental needs must be met for us to attain self-actualisation, which is when we move from surviving to thriving and can then reach our full positive potential.[43]

Take a look at the pyramid below and assess your own situation in terms of the five levels. If, for example, you are not drinking enough water, getting enough sleep or eating a nutritious diet, these issues must be noted and dealt with. Neglecting your basic needs keeps you languishing at the bottom and heading towards burnout.

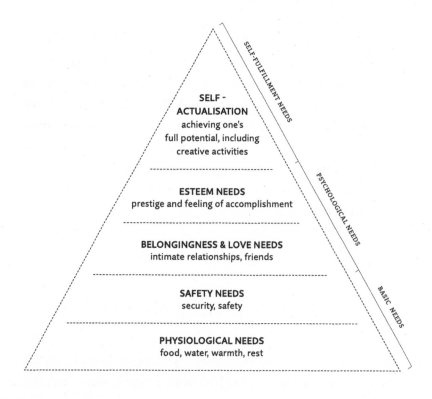

In order to reach full self-actualisation you need to take responsibility for meeting your needs, starting with the basic needs and moving upwards.

One cannot progress up the pyramid until the previous needs have been met, in much the same way that you cannot progress to the next rung on your ladder to happiness until you have made the effort to take the first step. With each step upwards you see the world from a more positive and open perspective; what was once considered impossible becomes achievable. Your potential for happiness is always grounded in the moment, in the now.

Let's now take a look at how you can start to meet those needs both practically and psychologically.

+ + +

Consciously Parenting Yourself

WHATEVER WAY YOU were parented, it is now in the past; you are an adult now and as such need to take responsibility for yourself and your mental and emotional health. This means becoming the type of parent you always wanted to yourself.

Adults who remain emotionally stunted and blighted by their pasts do not reach self-actualisation.

So how do you do this? It can help to think of your conscious mind as the adult who takes care of the child, the subconscious. How does the adult talk to the child? Is it with compassion or criticism?

This voice is often referred to as the 'inner critic' and can be very harsh and judgemental. In fact, social services would probably be called if we spoke to our children the way we speak to ourselves!

+ + +

Turn Your Inner Critic into Your Inner Companion

1 Consider your own inner voice. Is it critical or is it one of love?

2 Write down all the words your inner critic uses. Did your parents use any of these terms regularly about you, for example 'bad', 'unhelpful', 'lazy', 'dishonest', 'not good enough'?

BY CONSCIOUSLY choosing to monitor, regulate and transform your inner critic into your inner companion you are becoming a loving parent to your subconscious mind (the part that is vulnerable and indeed very much like a child) in order to change the patterns of the past and to ensure that whatever disapproval or criticism you felt is not carried into the future.

Brené Brown, famous for her work on vulnerability and shame and author of *Daring Greatly*, commented, 'If we want to fully experience love and belonging, we must first believe we are worthy of love and belonging'.[44] Children who feel they are bad often do not feel worthy and will question and doubt their parents' love. In order for us to 'grow up,' we must actively make our conscious mind the parent to the more vulnerable subconscious mind and make our love unconditional.

If you have suffered from an internal critical voice that beats you up mentally, especially when you are tired, irritable or overwhelmed, listening every day to your morning and sleep time audios is a direct way to train your brain for unconditional self-love, which is at the heart of the Positive Habit. It might take some time for your neural networks to fully habitualise this change, so it is important to keep going!

To help you understand this further, please see my TEDx, 'Your Subconscious Power, How to be Anxiety Free,' available on YouTube and at www.thepositivehabit.com.

+ + +

Embracing Unconditional Love

WHAT DO YOU understand by 'unconditional love'? To me it is total acceptance without precondition. Acceptance of ourselves and others as we/they are may sound simple in theory but, as we've discussed, is an ongoing process of constant awareness and mindfulness.

In general, we are constantly trying to mould others into how we think they should be and we do the same with ourselves.

This unfortunate habit stems from those early messages where the distinction between love and approval was so blurred. For example, our younger selves may have thought, 'I'd better do what I'm told or I'll be in trouble,' which years later becomes, 'I'd better not say what I really think or I'll upset my boss/partner.'

In general, the pattern is that people are not kind or compassionate to themselves until they reach a state of perfection and achievement and unfortunately, that time never comes because, first, there is no such thing as perfection and second, as we age, the list gets bigger, more demanding and often less attainable. Once we have achieved something we are already looking for the next thing, always operating psychologically from a place of lack rather than abundance. Loving yourself just as you are in this moment creates the desire to care for yourself now and to live in the present moment.

Unconditional love does not mean that if someone is abusing you, you should put up with it. On the contrary, you need to get yourself away from that person. But what if the person abusing you is yourself? Many people try to get away from themselves and to escape the critical voice in their mind by comfort eating, drinking, obsessive internet use, shopping, gambling, using drugs and many other mind-numbing and addictive means. These methods are based on avoidance and cannot be ultimately successful and at heart we all know this. Turning towards yourself with love, kindness and compassion will actually provide the refuge you seek.

Where there is love, there is no need to escape.

The audio exercise on page 164 is particularly useful for this so I advise you to practise it often, especially if you are feeling anxious or down.

The Love Habit for Relationships

IF SELF-LOVE is the first step, the second involves moving to the external and sharing and spreading love around. Positive people have learned to love themselves unconditionally and as a result they form loving bonds and are sociable, popular and successful. As you cultivate the Love Habit you will move yourself from a world of petty conflicts to a universe where you connect openly and honestly with others.

Every interaction is an opportunity to connect and lengthen both your life and that of others.

It's a good analogy to think of people as 'radiators' who exude positive energy and as 'drains' who sap it. 'Radiators' consciously and actively seek out like-minded individuals while also maintaining and nurturing meaningful relationships.

NOTEBOOK
HEART OPEN/HEART CLOSED

Use your heart intelligence rather than your mind for this exercise; the mind tends to quickly shift to judging and using mechanisms of guilt. If you operate from the heart your answer will be authentic.

It takes valour to do this exercise honestly, so please take out your notebook and let's begin.

1   Think of every person in your life, your close family, your friends, colleagues and acquaintances. Basically, everyone you interact with regularly. Write their names on the left-hand side of your page.

2   Now divide the rest of the page into two columns, and label the first column 'Heart open' and the second 'Heart closed'. Those who 'open' your heart are 'radiators' who make you feel lighter and brighter and are likely to make you laugh and smile as well as feel safe and secure. Those who 'close' your heart are 'drains' who make you feel tired, irritable and quite possibly down. They sap your energy.

3   Look at each person's name in the left-hand column and visualise them for a moment. Taking a deep breath, put your hand on your heart and select by ticking the column that applies to them. Do this with each person without analysing or justifying your decision. Don't stop until you have finished the exercise.

Well done! This is not an easy exercise but it is worth it and important for your progress. Please don't feel guilty if some of the people you truly love have ended up in the 'heart closed' column; it doesn't mean that the relationship is doomed or that you need to cut this person out of your life. It may simply indicate that the relationship needs more of your love and honesty. Those entered in the 'heart open' column you should seek out as often as you can; positive energy is infectious and you deserve to be with people who encourage you to feel good about yourself.

Now, put one last name on the list, your own, and do the same thing. Take a deep breath, put your hand on your heart and answer honestly. Are you a 'radiator' or a 'drain'? How do you feel about yourself? How do you think people feel when you enter a room? Be as honest as you can; if you end up in the 'heart closed' list that is okay. It is good to know this now – with time you will find yourself moving very easily into the 'heart open' column.

+ + +

Don't Take Anything Personally, Ever!

'Whatever happens around you, don't take it personally ... Nothing other people do is because of you. It is because of themselves.'

Don Miguel Ruiz

'BRAIN TATTOO' these words; that is, fix them in your mind forever. This is perhaps the single most important thing you can do to love yourself and others. Unfortunately, we live in a world where taking things personally is endemic and as a result, on a personal level, relationships are tumultuous while on a societal and international level, conflict and mistrust proliferate.

Taking offence when someone insults you or being flattered when they compliment you means that you are taking things personally and have allowed your ego to take charge of your consciousness. In most cases, when someone behaves badly towards you they are not being personal but are venting their own frustrations, unhappiness or anger.

I was fortunate to learn this message early on; if I came home sad because another kid had been unkind to me my mum would encourage me to feel sorry for them, saying, 'they are not happy in themselves if they are unkind to you'. This can be hard for a 'mature' adult to grasp, let alone a sensitive ten-year-old but believe me, it has helped me to become resilient to the whims of others. Thank you, Mum.

The quote above comes from the international bestseller, *The Four Agreements* by Don Miguel Ruiz, which I highly recommend. The Four Agreements are:[45]

1 **Be impeccable with your word.** Always tell the truth; you have nothing to hide. This is great for building confidence because when you lie you erode your sense of self.

2 **Don't take anything personally.** Reasons for this are explained above.

3 **Don't make assumptions**. Never presume to understand without asking questions.

4 **Always do your best.** This applies to any situation; also let your best be good enough. This is great for those with high standards that always seem to get higher.

Look back at your list of people from the exercise above and consider how applying the principle of not taking anything personally to those who ended up in the 'heart closed' category would change things.

When you use your heart intelligence, especially with your relationships, you will start to operate from an entirely different level. You move from making mental judgements to using the softness and compassion of the heart.

Everyone, yourself included, desires and deserves to be loved.

IMAGINEERING

Imagine the most vibrant pink rose you have ever seen; the aroma of the rose meets your nostrils and you breathe in the sweet, flowery scent. You reach out and touch the petals, which are like thin velvet in your fingers. Imagine now that the rose is covered with so many brambles that you can't touch it quite so easily; it takes more effort, you need to move carefully and be patient but you know the reward is worth the effort.

Now think of someone who has a beautiful heart that they hide behind barbed comments and irritability. Seeing the best in yourself opens your heart to see the best in everyone else even if they don't make it easy for you. They are probably not consciously trying to be prickly and difficult – it is a defensive, unconscious action. Always remember to look at their behaviour, don't react and practise the agreement not to take anything personally.

Is your heart surrounded by brambles? Do you unintentionally make it hard for people to see your goodness? If you are struggling with any relationship in your life right now, it is helpful to look at it objectively and ask yourself where your responsibility lies in any disagreement/conflict. Try to see it from their perspective; how do they perceive your behaviour? Relationships are built on trust and require honesty. Sometimes the relationship is more important than asserting your point of view to the extent that you hold it against them if they don't see things 'your way'.

With 7.6 billion people in the world, expecting them all to see things 'your way' is fairly unlikely.

In all conflicts there are two sides to the story and it is important that both are listened to objectively. If someone has lied to you or hurt you, ask yourself why they feel they need to do this? Putting your ego gently to one side and really listening to the other party is a valiant act of love that will serve you well.

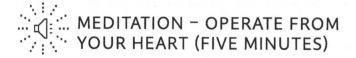

MEDITATION – OPERATE FROM YOUR HEART (FIVE MINUTES)

This is an empowering exercise that will help you to see the best in yourself and others, allowing you to develop the courage to ease frustration, to connect with love and to see the bigger picture in petty conflicts or stressful situations.

+ + +

Feeling at One with Everyone

IMAGINE WE LIVED in a world where fear was replaced with love. Much of the horror and tragedy that exists arises because people are operating from the 'them and us' mode of thinking. Differences in religion, race or politics all give rise to fear and fear creates anger and intolerance. Many see people who are different as being dangerous as they threaten their concept of order in a chaotic world.

There is, however, plenty of space for us all to be different. Until we see being different as a positive thing rather than a threat we will remain in the dark ages, operating solely from the reptilian brain (see page 82). So how can you create more love and tolerance in your daily habits?

Dr Barbara Fredrickson, referred to in the last chapter, believes that this can achieved by creating 'micro-moments' of love as often as we can. In her book *Love 2.0*, Fredrickson explains that we can find love with everyone, from our children to strangers.[46] When we hold a gaze, smile and hug someone we are flooded with positive nourishment that aids our emotional growth and mental health. The longer and more frequent these loving moments are, the more oxytocin is released.

When I was a child, my granny and Auntie Lally (actually her sister) used to say that everyone in the world was my brother and sister. These two ladies lived from their hearts and were quite possibly the kindest people I have ever had the privilege to love and be loved by. Their message that we are all connected, all equal and, metaphorically, all related was an important message of universal love and it resonates deeply with me to this day.

THREE KEY TAKEAWAYS FROM THIS CHAPTER

1 Self-love is **not** selfish; it is essential for you to truly love others.

2 The heart contains 10,000 neurons similar to those in the brain and this is known as the 'little brain'. Operating from an open heart allows you to be guided by love, not by the fear of the overthinking mind.

3 Don't take anything personally. Nothing people say or do is because of you. Do this and all your relationships will flourish.

THE LOVE HABIT –
DAILY MINDFULNESS

1 Greet everyone you meet with a smile and, if you feel comfortable, a hug. Hold the embrace for 15 seconds to increase the release of oxytocin.

2 Listen often to the *'operating from the heart'* audio to help you improve all the relationships in your life, especially if you are struggling with any of them.

3 Look into the mirror regularly and say 'I love you' while maintaining eye contact with yourself. Practise non-judgement and always look beyond the purely physical.

4 Create micro-moments of love every day; take time to stop and chat with people, especially people who may be lonely, such as an elderly or homeless person. Social interaction is nourishment for the soul.

5 Use the positive plunge technique for the moments you feel love or loved.

AFFIRMATIONAL
TOOTH BRUSHING

Repeat your love habit affirmations every day while you brush your teeth. Remember to feel the emotion they create in your heart as you repeat them.

MINDFUL SHOWERING

Take time as you shower and dry yourself to be loving and patient with yourself. Use this habit as a time to connect with yourself without judgement.

ACKNOWLEDGE PROGRESS

Evidence to support your affirmations. For example, in the case of the first affirmation, you might write, 'I did not obsess over my weight this week,' or for the second, you might write, 'I had an honest conversation with a friend.'

+ I love myself just the way I am.

+ It is safe for me to connect with others.

+ I trust the divine light in my heart to guide me with love.

Now mark how you are feeling on the positivity sundial below.

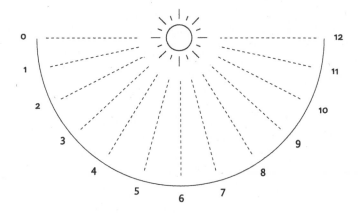

Remember to keep listening to your seven-minute morning and your sleep time hypnotherapies. Tick the days so far that you have listened at the back of this book. Be proud of the times you have listened and don't give yourself a hard time if you have missed one or two days; that is okay – keep going!

 MEDITATION

+ Morning ritual

+ Sleep time hypnotherapy

+ Operate from the heart

THE CALMNESS HABIT

HOW TO SOOTHE ANXIETY

'He who is of a calm and happy nature will hardly feel the pressure of age.'

PLATO

+

INTERRELATED

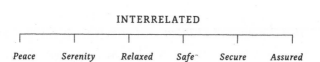

Peace Serenity Relaxed Safe Secure Assured

AFFIRMATIONAL TOOTH BRUSHING

Write these affirmations in your journal. If you cannot remember the exact words it doesn't matter, simply repeat to yourself, over and over as you brush, 'I am calm'. Remember to feel the calmness as you repeat the words.

1 I breathe deeply to calm my mind.

2 I flow calmly in all situations that I find myself in.

3 My mind is as calm as a still lake.

Note *that at the end of the chapter, I will ask you to write down three examples to support the affirmations. For example, for number 2 above you might write, 'I was calm before and during my appraisal in work.'*

VICKI NOTARO'S STORY, 32, JOURNALIST

'I started suffering badly with panic attacks about two years ago. I'm not sure what the trigger was really; a lot of things came to a head I guess, and there was some personal trauma in my recent past that I hadn't dealt with. All of a sudden, and out of nowhere, I found myself feeling very frightened. I thought I was going nowhere, that I had no future, that I was an awful, worthless person who wouldn't amount to anything. All of this made me want to hide in my bed feeling entirely overwhelmed, with a racing heart. This led to me disappointing friends and family and missing work commitments, which only added to my sense of panic and fear. But to look at me on the surface, you would have seen someone quite successful both personally and professionally, so it just didn't add up.

'I had tried therapy and CBT, but neither were really clicking with me. Then someone told me about Fiona Brennan and her Positive Habit

method. The combination of audios and questionnaires and reading within that programme is designed to literally rewire the brain and build more positive pathways where the negative ones had surfaced. I was sceptical and cynical, but it really worked for me. Over a matter of weeks, I was able to pinpoint what it was that was making me feel bad, and to go about my business thinking more positively about them. Over time I found myself becoming calmer, more able and happier in myself. I rediscovered confidence that had been lost along the way, and before long I was giving my mood a seven out of ten, where it had been a two out of ten just weeks earlier.

'I've had hiccups since with anxiety and returned to the programme when I've been feeling down to give me a boost, and to remind myself of the power of positive thinking. It's non-judgemental and private, and that's what I like most about it. When I feel calm, I know I can handle whatever comes my way.'

 ## THE POSITIVE HABIT EMOTIONS QUIZ #3

Take the quiz now and allocate a point for each 'Yes' answer that you give. Go with the first answer that comes to mind and do not spend too much time thinking about the question.

1 Do you feel present most of the time?

2 Do you make time to care for your mind each day?

3 Do you love yourself?

4 Do you believe you are a compassionate person?

5 Are you able *not* to take *anything* other people do or say personally?

6 If you feel stress or anxiety, do you use your breath to calm your mind?

7 Do you protect your mind from negative information, people and places, for example having regular digital breaks/avoiding people who drain your energy?

8 Do you feel confident to speak your mind and feel equal to others?

9 Are you kind to yourself if you make a mistake?

10 Do you feel grateful each day?

11 Do you let go of grudges from the past?

12 Do you visualise a bright future?

13 Do you feel you are living your life's purpose?

14 Do you take care of your physical needs, such as getting eight hours' sleep a night, exercising and eating a balanced diet?

15 Do you feel that you are good enough as a person?

16 Do you trust that no matter what happens you will be able to cope?

Score from quiz #1 on page 8 =
Score from quiz #2 on page 130 =
Score from quiz #3 =

Make a note of any progress. If you see a shift forward, please acknowledge this fully, own it! What areas continue to need your attention? Keep learning about yourself.

+ + +

What Does Calmness Mean to You?

THE ORIGINS of the word 'calm,' come from the ancient Greek word *kauma*, which means 'heat', specifically that of the midday sun when everyone winds down due to the intense heat; there really is no choice but to retreat inside to escape this heat and to have the all-important siesta.

In Greek mythology, Pasithea was one of the graces of relaxation, meditation and altered states of consciousness and she was married to Hypnos, the god of sleep. This could explain the roots of why hypnotherapy is so calming.

NOTEBOOK
CALMNESS TRIGGERS

Take a moment to brainstorm ideas of what calmness means to you and how you can cultivate it.

Here are some examples from my clients to help you get started:

+ Waking up before the rest of my family early in the morning when the house is lovely and quiet

+ Being with other people but not feeling that I need to say anything – a 'comfortable' silence

+ Meditation/deep breathing

+ Being in nature

- Doing mindful yoga

- Gazing at the flames of a real fire

- Watching someone I love sleeping

- Getting home after a long trip or even a long day

- A lie-in on a Sunday morning

- Soaking in a long, hot bath

- A good chat with someone I feel safe with

- The silence in a library or a bookshop

Look at your list and allow it to resonate. Use the 15-second positive plunge technique to absorb the calm moments in your life when they arise. By doing so you are training your brain to seek out opportunities to be at peace.

+ + +

The Habit Loop of Calmness

AS WITH ANY HABIT, the brain is focused on and motivated by the reward, which in this case is to feel calm and relaxed. By following this chapter you are learning to show it how to do so effectively and consistently. Use the habit loop diagram opposite to identify some of your own.

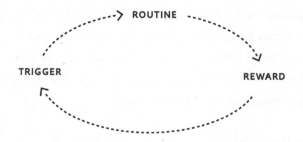

For example:

1 **Positive trigger** – A lie-in on a Sunday morning.

2 **Positive routine** – Keeping Sunday mornings sacred with no plans or pressure to 'do' anything.

3 **Positive reward** – Feeling calm and relaxed.

+ + +

Calmness – The Second Emotional Habit

'Calmness of mind is one of the beautiful jewels of wisdom. It is the result of long and patient effort in self-control.'

JAMES ALLEN

CALMNESS IS A SUPERPOWER: of that there is no doubt. Now that you are becoming more present and understand the essence of self-love and connection with others, you are ripe to create inner feelings of security and safety, which is the essence of calmness. Positive people exude calmness in any given situation. Whether it is a family holiday, a presentation at work or a genuine crisis, they remain unruffled. It's now time for you to develop the habit of calmness, which will become your best friend and your greatest ally. In this chapter, I will illustrate how being calm could save your life, how to cultivate calmness on a physical level and also the important role compassion plays in creating calmness and soothing anxiety.

Feeling calm is the ultimate expression of empowerment.

Authentic calmness differs from pretending to be calm, which is what many people do when underneath there is a turmoil of emotion. Faking any positive emotion always does more harm than good as it is dishonest both to yourself and to others. Many people strive to create calmness in their external environment, for example by keeping everything tidy and/or attempting to control the people they love. This need for control is common and often stems from a need to feel safe and secure. Unfortunately, this type of control has the opposite effect and creates untold stress and tension both in ourselves and in our relationships.

The place where you have *real* control is in your mind and nobody else can mess it up unless you allow them to. A calm mind is the highest expression of self-control, no matter how much laundry needs to be done or how many tasks remain unticked on your to-do list. Calmness is one core positive emotional habit that will serve you well both physically and mentally; serotonin (the neurotransmitter linked to good mood and a greater sense of wellbeing) and oxytocin (commonly known as the love hormone) are released as a protective balm to help you to feel secure. Calmness also acts as a springboard for the third habit of positive people, confidence, which will be discussed in the next chapter.

Is Calmness an Emotion?

ALTHOUGH NOT IMMEDIATELY identifiable as an emotion, calmness is a psychological state that softens and soothes negative emotions like anxiety and stress but also softens anger and frustration. It is the state that encourages the other five emotional habits. Being calm deepens your ability to love and to connect with people, as they feel safer in your company. In addition, your focus is sharper, so you feel more confident; and you notice more of the goodness in your life, so you feel grateful. Calmness opens up space for you to feel hope in a crisis and ultimately it is a key component of happiness. Many of my clients report feeling more and more calm as they progress on their journey. It is an integral rung on the ladder to your happiness, as it is hard to feel joy while you are stressed.

Perhaps you have been asked during an interview how you cope with pressure. Can you keep your head while everyone else is losing theirs? These are good questions and most of us will answer that we can deal with the situation – after all, we want the job! Is it really true, though? Imagine being able to answer that question totally honestly with a deep inner knowledge that you *are* good at making decisions under pressure and that you *are* one of those people who has a calming effect on others.

Calmness Could Save Your Life

THE 'MIRACLE ON THE HUDSON' is the miraculous true story of an American pilot, Captain 'Sully' Sullenberger who in 2009 faced a potentially fatal crash but was able to land his stricken aircraft on the Hudson River in New York.[47] Captain Sully made a split-second decision that saved all 155 passengers on board, but how did he do this under such immense pressure? In panic the amygdala is fired up and we react emotionally rather than responding rationally. Because of his ability to stay calm, Captain Sully was capable of finding a solution, which would not have happened if he had been panic-stricken. Eyewitnesses claimed that Captain Sully was so calm that he went back after the crash landing to check that all his passengers were safe. You may not be an airline pilot, but feeling calm on a motorway when someone cuts in in front of you will help your reaction times to be at their optimum.

Kyra Kopestonsky[48] was out hiking on her own in Colorado when she had a potentially fatal encounter with a mountain lion. But she saved her own life by remaining calm: on seeing the lion, Kopestonsky calmly retreated, did not scream or run, held her composure and started to sing opera to the full capacity of her lungs! The lion backed away and she survived. The important point here is that by remaining calm she was able to think creatively and so survived.

+ + +

How Calm are You?

PERHAPS YOU ALREADY consider yourself to be calm. Do you feel calm, yet other people say you seem stressed? Or do you often feel stressed but give the impression of being calm? This is particularly prevalent in the workplace where people often hide their stress levels as best as they can. It is helpful to separate how you really feel from how you portray yourself. If you are giving the illusion of calmness do you feel as if you are wearing a mask and hoping that nobody will see through it?

Really feeling calm is only possible when it is authentic.

Consider the following two 'types' of people:

THE LAID-BACK ONE

Is being 'laid-back' a form of calmness? Not necessarily. People who are described as being 'laid-back' or 'easy-going' are generally viewed as calm, yet there is often a negative association with this description; in being calm they become indifferent and never seem to care what is happening, where they go or what they do – they exude apathy. They may lack drive or at least appear to, so this is not the kind of calmness I suggest you cultivate. When calmness becomes outward indifference, there are often self-worth issues. The roots of this could lie in being shy or timid as a child and thus going along with anything that pleases others (remember attachment theory in the Love Habit, page 147?). Such people may appear calm but can be busy fighting a cascade of concern and panic inside their heads. Is this you?

THE DRAMATIC ONE

People who are described as 'worriers' or 'wound up' can be very vocal at expressing their inner turmoil or worry. They may crave calmness but genuinely don't have the skills to create it. Have you ever been described as a 'drama queen', 'hot-headed' or the 'difficult' one in the family? Your parents may have made unhelpful comments either directly or indirectly such as, 'Why can't you be more like your brother or sister?' or 'You are just like your mother/father ... so moody'.

It is important that you identify wherever you are in the continuum between the two extremes of being totally laid-back or constantly stressed and anxious. Many people live in the middle ground but this means they are probably still carrying an unnecessary amount of stress and anxiety that no longer serves them and that keeps them from reaching the top of Maslow's pyramid of self-actualisation (see page 154).

 CALMNESS QUIZ

Please take a moment to answer the following questions, which will further help you to identify how calm you are. Allocate one point for each 'Yes' answer.

In the last month, have you:

1 Worried a lot about something bad happening that in the end turned out just fine?

2 Had trouble sleeping because your mind was too busy with racing thoughts and/or your heart was pounding?

3 Worried about being late/not having enough time?

4 Had problems with your digestion?

5 Experienced shallow breathing because of anxious thoughts before an exam, presentation or important meeting at work/awkward social meeting?

6 Lost your train of thought in a conversation and found it hard to focus on what the other person is saying?

7 Avoided social occasions by making up an excuse or white lie or simply not turned up because you couldn't face people?

8 Felt overly concerned if someone was late that something bad had happened to them?

9 Felt overwhelmed by having too much to do?

10 Felt intense anxiety or panic?

Score: /10

A score of three or more 'Yes' answers indicates that your calmness levels need love and attention. So let me now introduce you to a technique that instantly induces calmness.

 ## THE BUZZING BEE BREATH TECHNIQUE (1.5 MINUTES)

This exercise is speedy and effective for times when the mind is really racing and you just want it to stop. It is one of the many yogic 'pranayama' (breathwork) styles of breathing designed to soothe anxiety, and it brings immediate relief. Use it for any of the situations described in the questions above. Because of its use of a buzzing sound, most people prefer to practise this alone.

+ + +

Follow Your Breath, not Your Thoughts

THE SEVEN deep belly breath technique that we learned on page 111 guides you through how to breathe and it is something that you need to practise. While most of my clients try to practise breathing deeply every day, in the heat of a stressful moment they may forget to use this technique. This is not their fault or even intentional – the 'old' brain patterns of panic and anxiety have automatically kicked in and hijacked their ability to use the deep breathing technique. On a scale of threats, breathing deeply is irrelevant to the fear they are experiencing. It is important to establish the habit of deep breathing so that when you are being triggered you will automatically start to soothe yourself. In other words, waiting until you feel stressed or anxious to start deep breathing is too late. The habit of breathing deeply creates a constant state of calmness that stops you from triggering into reactive patterns of panic and anxiety.

Many of us need to re-learn how to breathe properly.

Trying to create calmness by using the mind to control the mind is simply not effective; the mind is full of thoughts that jump from one catastrophic thought to the next and this only adds to the physical sensations that come with fear. In order to have a calm mind, we need to use the body and breathing deeply and consciously is the quickest and most effective method to generate calmness and by so doing to create feelings of self-control which counteract racing thoughts.

It may seem counterintuitive to 'practise' breathing, but deep belly breathing leads to a focused awareness, which is the essence of calmness. Look at a baby or a young child breathing, and you will notice that it is their belly and not their chest that moves with the breath. This is the type of breathing you need to return to.

If you suffer from chronic anxiety that leads to panic attacks it is essential to know that when you are breathing deeply and consciously you cannot have a panic attack the same time. Remember this!

This simple but powerful information has transformed many people's lives.

+ + +

The Huge Gap Between Feeling Anxious and Chronic Anxiety

HAVING ANSWERED the questions in the quiz above and also by keeping a regular score on the Positive Habit quiz, you will be more aware of the areas you need to work on and in particular your stress and anxiety levels. The higher the number of 'Yes' answers you gave in the quiz above, the more likely you are to be suffering from chronic anxiety and therefore the more you need to bring the habit of calmness into your daily life. It is important at this stage to clarify the difference between occasional feelings of anxiety, which we all have, and chronic anxiety. A healthy level of nerves before an exam or presentation is very different from living in a state of constant fear and worry.

Chronic anxiety has many physical manifestations and if you suffer from it, your body will most definitely let you know.

Please tick each of the following ailments that you have suffered from in the last month:

- ◯ Tightness in the chest – a knot-like feeling in the chest "

- ◯ Pounding heart

- ◯ Shallow breathing – getting out of breath very quickly even if you are fit

- ◯ Dry mouth

- ◯ Sweating hands

- ◯ Blushing, particularly in social situations

- ◯ Constricted throat

- ◯ Headaches

- ◯ Dizziness

- ◯ Shaking or trembling

- ◯ Difficulty in speaking clearly

- ◯ Constant muscle tension – often in the shoulders and back

- ◯ IBS symptoms – poor indigestion, bloated stomach, diarrhoea and/or constipation

- ◯ The worst of all – insomnia!

Observe these physical symptoms in the coming days and notice if they are aggravated by stress/anxiety or fraught thoughts andor situations.

Living with even one of the above symptoms every day is a toxic cocktail and can be exhausting. Such symptoms can be completely overwhelming and seriously hinder your ability to cope with everyday stresses and challenges.

If your anxiety has been there for years untreated you may not even notice these symptoms and think that it is normal to feel this way. Henry David Thoreau, author of the classic book *Walden* written in 1854, commented, 'The mass of men lead lives of quiet desperation.' Thoreau lived and breathed the spirit of a calm and mindful life; in *Walden* he recounts how he retreated to live in a simple log cabin for two years simply to be with nature. While this may not be practical, appropriate or even desirable for most of us, cultivating inner stillness is paramount for positive mental health.

As you complete the self-exploratory exercises and listen to the morning and sleep time rituals, you will begin to notice the gradual lessening and eventual absence of any chronic physical discomfort and at the same time begin to experience the freedom of living with a healthy body and a calm mind. The reward of feeling healthy and strong starts to drive your behaviour and to create a positive habit. In order to reinforce this habit loop you need to pay close attention to the physical benefits that positivity brings by regularly asking yourself the following questions:

+ What does the absence of pain and discomfort feel like?

+ What does normal, healthy digestion feel like?

+ What does it feel like to have more energy?

+ What does it feel like to sleep deeply and peacefully and to wake up refreshed?

You are now training your body and mind to see, feel and live the rewards of the six positive emotional habits.

If you have become used to living with chronic anxiety, now is the time to change the habit of stress to the habit of calmness. Remember, I am with you each calm step of the way guiding and helping.

+ + +

Imagine Calmness

AS YOU LEARNED on page 74, the imagination is the gateway to the subconscious mind. When you imagine something, it is real as far as the subconscious mind is concerned. While the imagination can be used to accelerate anxiety, it can also be used to create calmness if you so choose. Read the following two scenarios, and being honest, decide which outcome (A or B) you would usually identify with.

1 You give a presentation at work at an important meeting and feel it went reasonably well. Your boss asks to speak to you later that day. Do you:

a. Believe that you must have made a mistake, that you will be in trouble and that it could be serious? Did you forget something important in the presentation?

b. Imagine they want to have an informal chat about the meeting, possibly even to congratulate you on your presentation?

2 You go to the doctor about a small mole you have noticed has changed shape. The doctor informs you that it is probably nothing but that to be sure you should have a biopsy. You have to wait for three weeks. During that time do you:

a. Convince yourself you have cancer and will probably die soon and ruminate on how you are going to tell the people you love?

b. Feel a little worried but **imagine** it will be fine and for the most part put it out of your mind?

The answers (a and b) in these two examples are polar opposites and I appreciate that some people will be somewhere in the middle. Nevertheless, which side of the scale are you closer to? Also, note that the word 'imagine' in option B is highlighted to illustrate that imagination can be used to feel calm. Choosing option B in both examples will help you to stay calm and come up with ideas and solutions.

+ + +

The Stress Habit

IF THERE WAS tension in your home as a child (even in the most 'idyllic' of childhoods there often is in some shape or form) or if you lived in a constant state of fear about the moods of one of your family members, it is possible that you have unintentionally brought with you the habit of feeling stress. Left unattended to, this can turn into anxiety. Of course, it is also possible that you developed the stress habit later in life; at college or when you had your own family and had to face responsibility for the first time. When we feel overwhelmed we tend to stress and think of the worst-case scenario.

So where is the reward for stress or anxiety?

Many people feel that without stress and pressure they would not be motivated to achieve anything. They believe that pressure fuels progress. And it does, for a while. The problem is that eventually this approach leads to burnout: the body stops functioning properly, especially if the stress habit has been there since childhood. The anticipated reward of success never arrives because if you are not living in the now and are anticipating the future you will always be looking for the next thing and this constant pressure is damaging to the body and the mind. It is an unfortunate unconscious cycle that many of us suffer. So, what can you do?

Find the positive in stress.

Eustress is positive stress; *Eu* is the prefix in Greek for 'good', so, in essence, it means good or beneficial stress. Kelly McGonigal, a health psychologist at Stanford, gave a famous TED Talk called 'How to Make Stress Your Friend,' the thrust of which is that how we view stress is paramount to the effect it has on us.[49] The less negatively we view it, the less toxic it is for us. Perception is paramount.

The more you view stress as a feeling of excitement and healthy nerves as opposed to negative energy, the less stressed you will feel.

Eustress is very useful for an important meeting, presentation or on your wedding day. Our bodies can create high levels of adrenaline and this helps us to perform at our peak. However, far too often what may have started off as eustress tips into toxic stress, excitement turns into nerves and adrenaline becomes the stress hormone cortisol. When your body is flooded with stress hormones, you are far from performing at your peak. You will struggle to think clearly, to focus, to communicate and it will take all of your energy just to stay in the room. Eustress is not well known as a term but it needs to become so; recognising the positive aspects of stress allows us to differentiate it from the negative. So spread the word!

+ + +

Compassion Precedes Calmness

MANY PEOPLE are particularly harsh on themselves precisely in the moments they need more kindness, understanding and compassion. If you hear the internal voice in your head saying things like, 'come on, snap out of it' or 'I can't believe you are so stupid' or especially, 'You should be able to handle this, what is wrong with you?', it's time to recognise these thoughts for what they are – self-critical, judgemental and unhelpful. Focusing on the kindness step from the ARK (Accept, Release and Kindness) technique, please try the following exercise.

 IMAGINEERING

1 *Imagine that you are addressing a person you love who
is feeling anxious or stressed about an area of their life,
be it a friend, a child, your partner or a parent. How
would you speak to them? Would you dream of saying
any of the critical phrases above to them when they are
obviously feeling vulnerable?*

2 *What words would you use to help them? Perhaps you
would say, 'it's normal to feel nervous' or 'you're going
to do great.' You may remind them to breathe deeply
and that you believe in their ability, that you love them
no matter what.*

*Imagine the difference they feel with this level of understanding and com-
passion. Now imagine applying this to yourself. Instead of being critical, be
kind and compassionate and reap the rewards. This habit becomes easier
over time and the practical way to employ it is by first using the breath to
calm the body – the mind will then follow suit.*

+ + +

A Calm Body is a Calm Brain

IF YOU ARE not fighting a sabre-toothed tiger or dealing with a
really traumatic event there is no reason why you can't feel calm
and relaxed most of the time. The Hope Habit looks more at how
to cope during difficult periods. But for the moment, let's focus
on what happens to your brain when you are calm. Why is it so
good for you? Can it really lengthen your life? And, if you are so
calm, how will you achieve what you want to achieve? Many of us

unconsciously hold the notion that calmness is complacency or even boring. It most definitely is not. A calm state of mind allows you to achieve success and abundance.

Dr Gayatri Devi, a neurologist and author of *A Calm Brain*, explains how you can tap into 'the neurology and physiology of our body's innate calm mechanisms to achieve greater health, happiness and success.'[50] Just as we need our stress system for survival reasons, we also have a calming and rest response system called the parasympathetic nervous system, also known as 'rest and digest' and 'feed and breed'.

The parasympathetic nervous system is responsible for bodily functions when we are at rest: it stimulates digestion, activates various metabolic processes and helps us to relax. Unfortunately, for many of us, this system is switched off while the ironically named 'sympathetic' (stress system) system is turned on by default. The sympathetic system is, of course, vital to our survival as it increases our mental and physical energy, increases our heart rate, opens up our airways and inhibits digestion (hence many people who are stressed/anxious will have bad digestion). We need time to digest our food properly, but do we give it to ourselves? Often, we rush from eating to the next activity. It is all yin with no yang; there is no balance. By the same measure, we understand that what goes up must come down and if we are always up we will eventually have to come down. Emotionally intelligent and positive people realise that resting is a skill that must be cultivated in order to flourish.

Living only from the sympathetic stress system is not sustainable.

Using your innate ability to tap into the parasympathetic system, you can access the neurotransmitters that you need to create any feeling that you desire. In much the same way that young children are instinctively able to switch off in a healthy way after having a tantrum (they become quiet, retreat within themselves and often fall peacefully asleep), accessing the parasympathetic system through the breath and the repetition of your audio and affirmations can help you to switch off when you need to.

+ + +

The Wonder of the Vagus Nerve

IF YOU CAN recall the layout of the brain (see page 82), you will remember that the 'old brain' is the part that is mainly unconscious and is programmed to bring on the stress response fast. It is also where the vagus nerve is located, right at the base of the skull – that little hollow part.

The vagus nerve acts as a brake to buffer you from unnecessary stress and is activated when you focus on feeling calm. Think of it as the lever to the parasympathetic system, the messenger between body and brain. You can self-soothe when you need to by choosing activities that activate the vagus, such as a simple walk with your dog or a hug with someone you love. According to Dr Gayatri Devi, 'you can choose your emotional state just as you can choose to move your arm or your leg. And you can choose calm over panic when confronting a stressful situation.' If someone you love is in despair, the best gift you can give them is to listen and at the same time, reach out physically – put your hand on theirs or on their shoulder and keep it there while they talk. By doing this you are stimulating the healing effects of their vagus nerve.

+ + +

The Physical Rewards of Inhabiting a Calm Body

SOME OF THE MANY benefits of a calm body are:

+ **YOUR SLEEP IMPROVES.**
This is logical. When you feel calm your conscious mind easily switches off and lets the subconscious take over. This is one of the prime advantages of listening to your sleep time hypnotherapy audio: you are teaching your conscious mind to trust your subconscious mind; when you fall asleep, instead of tossing and turning and worrying about the next day, listening to the powerful positive suggestions naturally aids a peaceful night's sleep and, at the same time, helps you to change negative thought patterns into positive ones.

+ **YOUR CHANCE OF DISEASE IS LESSENED.**
The stress hormone cortisol leads to high levels of inflammation in the body. Researchers have found that chronic stress changes the gene activity of immune cells before they enter the bloodstream so that they are ready to fight infection or trauma – even when there is no infection or trauma to fight and it is this that leads to inflammation.[51] If you have any illness which causes inflammation such as arthritis, heart disease or early signs of aging, keeping calm will decrease the symptoms and give your body a chance to fight the illness.

- **YOU WILL LOSE WEIGHT AND/OR MAINTAIN A HEALTHY WEIGHT.**
  You make healthier food choices when you feel calm. When we are stressed we often grab 'convenience' food which is often carbohydrate-heavy and contains high levels of sugar, salt and fat. Psychologists term this behaviour 'cognitive overload', which occurs when we feel too overwhelmed to make healthy choices and settle for the easiest and quickest option. If you are busy but have a calm mind you are more likely to make sure you have access to healthy foods.

- **YOU WILL EXPERIENCE FEWER MUSCLE SPASMS.**
  When you are stressed your body uses up a lot of magnesium to try to relax the muscles. It stands to reason that if you are chronically stressed you will have less magnesium in your system and suffer from back and shoulder pain and stiffness.

- **YOUR DIGESTION WILL IMPROVE.**
  As you know, the parasympathetic system activates healthy digestion and this only happens properly when you are feeling calm. For some people with even mild anxiety, having an upset stomach is a regular feature and this often involves difficulties with bowel movements, cramps and feeling bloated. This can be exhausting and is an extra drain on the body's resources. A drop in magnesium levels in the body caused by stress can also lead to constipation.

 IMAGINEERING

Imagine waking up late for work because you were out the evening before and forgot to set your alarm. You have an important meeting at work but

failed to keep your promise to yourself to get an early night. Imagine that from the moment you wake you accept the situation entirely, you don't panic or give yourself a hard time, you simply say to yourself 'this could happen to anyone'. You clearly need to rush, but at the same time you breathe deeply, aware that there is external pressure. You therefore rush calmly and in a highly focused manner, which enables you to leave just five minutes later than usual. Because you continue to breathe deeply and remain calm, everything flows: your meeting goes really well, and you confidently make many valuable contributions. Afterwards, you take a pause and smile to yourself. 'Well done,' you think, and you feel empowered that you can handle whatever comes your way.

Being calm does not mean operating at such a slow pace that nothing gets done. It means having a focused awareness that enables you to move at speed to achieve what you need to without panic and stress. It also reminds the body and the subconscious mind that all is essentially well.

+ + +

Calmness, the Doorway to Inner Peace

PEACE IS SOMETHING we all crave and yet we often look in all the wrong places to find it. The only type of lasting peace is inner peace; being in harmony with yourself. Offering yourself unconditional love will help you to feel serenity within. The more often you feel calm the more those peaceful moments will open out to you. People often feel this level of peace when in nature, witnessing a stunning sunset, gazing at the stars or after lovemaking. These moments are truly wonderful, but what if there is no visible sunset or you don't have a partner?

Positive people cultivate inner peace and confidence by being present and fully alert to each moment of their lives, by operating from the heart, and by being calm.

The third emotional habit of positive people is the Confidence Habit. Once you feel safe, loved and calm inside it is time to conquer the world with confidence and take that next step.

THREE KEY TAKEAWAYS FROM THIS CHAPTER:

1 Calmness could save your life in an emergency – your brain can focus and come up with solutions much more quickly.

2 Follow your breath, not your thoughts; the way to calm the mind is through the body, not the mind.

3 The physical rewards of being calm are multiple and will help you to feel strong and healthy.

 ## DAILY PRACTICE – THE CALMNESS HABIT

1 If you are waiting in a queue or stuck in traffic, take the opportunity to take seven deep belly breaths. Do these often and before any event that could cause you to feel stressed or anxious such as a meeting, a presentation, a social event.

2 Visualise your mind as a calm lake or sea, still and peaceful and with depth.

3 If you need to feel instantly calm, use the buzzing bee technique. This is good if you feel overwhelmed and your mind is racing.

4   If you make a mistake, say to yourself, 'it's okay, it could
    happen to anyone'.

5   Show yourself compassion as you would with some-
    one you love.

6   Spend as much time as you can in nature – being out in
    nature is life-affirming and calming.

AFFIRMATIONAL TOOTH BRUSHING

Repeat your calmness habit affirmations every day while you brush your teeth.

MINDFUL SHOWERING

Take time as you shower and dry yourself to be loving and patient with yourself. Use this habit as a time to connect towards yourself without judgement.

ACKNOWLEDGE PROGRESS

Evidence to support your three affirmations. Provide an example from your life when you have experienced these.

1   I breathe deeply to calm my mind.

2   I flow calmly in all situations that I find myself in.

3   My mind is as calm as a still lake.

Now mark how you are feeling on the positivity sundial below.

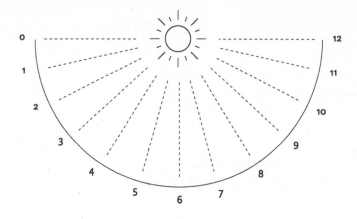

Remember to keep listening to your seven-minute morning and your sleep time hypnotherapies. Tick the days so far that you have listened on your grid on page 344, and remember we are aiming for 66 days. Be proud of the times you have listened and don't give yourself a hard time if you have missed one or two days; that is okay – keep going!

 ## MEDITATIONS

+ Morning ritual

+ Sleep time hypnotherapy

+ Buzzing bee technique

THE CONFIDENCE HABIT

HOW TO SHINE BRIGHT

'Let him who would move the world,
first move himself.'

SOCRATES

+

INTERRELATED

Self-belief *Agency* *Determined* *Certain* *Courageous* *Motivated*

AFFIRMATIONAL TOOTH BRUSHING

Write these affirmations in your journal. If you cannot remember the exact words, it doesn't matter, simply repeat to yourself, over and over as you brush, 'I am confident'. Remember to feel the emotion of the affirmation.

1   I am equal to everyone I meet.

2   I can achieve anything I put my mind to.

3   I have faith in the best of me.

Please note that at the end of the chapter, I will ask you to write down three examples to support the affirmations. For example, for number 3 above, 'I asked someone out on a date with the belief that I am worthy and equal'.

MICHAEL'S STORY, 42, MATURE STUDENT

'Confidence is something I had as a young child but it began to evaporate on my first day of school. That is one of my earliest memories. With the passing of the years my confidence ebbed away and I was left with very little. Having little or no confidence impacted every aspect of my life and without realising I developed a way of living where I could not grow or be the best version of myself.

'Returning to an environment that caused great psychological difficulties and anxiety in early life can trigger very potent memories wrapped up in feelings of distress, as I know to my cost. A short synopsis: I had a difficult childhood, especially at school. Reading, writing and comprehension were somewhat elusive skills for me to master. Teachers and peers labelled me as 'stupid' and 'lazy' and beatings were used as incentives to learn. Years of such indoctrination imposed by those around me manifested in long-term

anxiety and left me with the core belief that I was stupid. Fast-forward to my early thirties when I was first diagnosed as dyslexic, which resulted in my epiphany, and I returned to the classroom. This, however, awoke the old negative core beliefs coupled with automatic negative thoughts.

'Core beliefs are powerful. So powerful in fact that whenever I sit in a classroom or in group scenarios my anxiety is triggered. I first came to see Fiona because I had to give a presentation at university and I needed help.

'Having to give a presentation made me feel nauseous with anxiety. I could not sleep or think clearly and the thought of the presentation invaded my life. I believed I would fail and let the others in my group down. I was convinced my voice would shake and I would expose myself as a fool and run out of the room halfway through the presentation.

'These negative thoughts and beliefs stem from my days in school, standing in front of a class and struggling to read out loud. Not knowing why everyone else didn't seem to have a problem reading and I just couldn't get it right.

'I became very aware that my lack of confidence was really holding me back and making my life difficult. After my first meeting with Fiona I walked home and knew something had changed within; I just felt really good about myself and knew I had started on a journey. Fiona's words made a deep impact on my psyche and I knew there was a LOT of work to do because my confidence was non-existent or fleeting at best. So I got with the programme and made a habit of listening to the hypnotherapies every night and sometimes during the day. I instantly began to sleep better and to slowly feel more positive about myself and the world around me.

'I now view myself through a different lens and as a result I'm kinder to myself. My internal dialogue is now compassionate in much the same way *that I speak to my family and friends, with compassion. I'm also more confident deep down, in my soul. I no longer accept the old negative beliefs about myself. They may raise their heads from time to time but they are quite small and erode quickly. I've learned to be confident, to close the lid on self-criticism and negative beliefs through cultivating the positive habit. Confidence is a habit. Fiona gave it back to me and I make a habit of listening to the audios at least twice a week now.'*

THE POSITIVE HABIT EMOTIONS QUIZ # 4

Please allocate a point for each 'Yes' answer that you give.

1 Do you feel present most of the time?

2 Do you make time to care for your mind each day?

3 Do you love yourself?

4 Do you believe you are a compassionate person?

5 Are you able not to take anything other people do or say personally?

6 If you feel stress or anxiety, do you use your breath to calm your mind?

7 Do you protect your mind from negative information, people and places, for example having regular digital breaks/avoiding people who drain your energy?

8 Do you feel confident to speak your mind and feel equal to others?

9 Are you kind to yourself if you make a mistake?

10 Do you feel grateful each day?

11 Do you let go of grudges from the past?

12 Do you visualise a bright future?

13 Do you feel you are living your life purpose?

14 Do you take care of your physical needs, such as getting eight hours' sleep, exercising and eating a balanced diet?

15 Do you feel that you are good enough as a person?

16 Do you trust that no matter what happens you will be able to cope?

Score from quiz #1 on page 8 =
Score from quiz #2 on page 130 =
Score from quiz #3 on page 173 =
Score from quiz #4 =

+ + +

What Does Confidence Mean to You?

THE WORD 'CONFIDENCE' in Latin is *confidentia*, meaning to have full trust or reliance. Aristotle believed that confidence is cultivated through the absence of fear and a feeling of safety, which is why we have been working on the importance of self-love and calmness as the first steps to building trust and faith in yourself.

NOTEBOOK
CONFIDENCE TRIGGERS

Take a moment to brainstorm ideas on what confidence means to you and how you can cultivate it:

Here are some more examples from my clients to help you get started:

+ Feeling unstoppable

+ Walking into a room with my head held high

+ Making eye contact without being nervous

+ Feeling grounded

+ Believing that I am capable

+ Feeling equal to others

+ Being at ease with myself

+ Giving an amazing presentation

+ Speaking my mind at work and with my family

+ Being honest

+ Feeling independent and free

+ Having faith in myself

Look at your list and allow it to resonate. This list will now form the basis of positive triggers which will provide you with the reward of feeling confident.

+ + +

Confidence habit loop

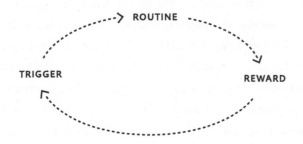

ROUTINE

TRIGGER

REWARD

1 **Positive trigger** – Believing that I am capable.

2 **Positive routine** – Contributing at a meeting.

3 **Positive reward** – Feeling confident.

+ + +

Confidence – the Third Emotional Habit

'You must find the place inside of you where nothing is impossible.'

DEEPAK CHOPRA

NOW THAT YOU are present, full of self-love and feeling safe, secure and calm, you are in a perfect position to climb the third rung of your ladder, confidence. This chapter looks at imposter syndrome, how to cultivate a growth mindset and how to make confidence an emotional habit you can rely on.

A confident person can achieve just about anything they choose and when one individual belief system takes on a collective momentum it can create either heaven or hell on Earth. Sam Harris, neuroscientist and author of *The End of Faith*, is the host of the controversial and popular podcast, *'Waking Up – A Guide to Spirituality Without Religion'*[52]. After the 9/11 tragedy, Harris made a determined effort to try to understand the causes of such extreme human behaviour. On the power of religious belief, he comments: 'This is the true horror of religion: It allows perfectly decent and sane people to believe by the billions what only lunatics could believe on their own.'

Contrasting examples from history illustrate how the self-confidence of individuals impacted the world; Hitler, Stalin and Pol Pot had huge self-confidence yet used it in destructive ways. Nelson Mandela, Martin Luther King and, more recently, Nobel laureate Malala Yousafzai used their self-confidence to try to improve the lives of others and to ameliorate specific conditions. Malala Yousafzai stood up against the terrible injustices wrought by the Taliban in Afghanistan, in particular their treatment of women and women's right to access education. Her self-belief and courage is inspiring: 'one child, one teacher, one book, one pen can change the world.'

When self-confidence becomes arrogance, it is driven by fear and elevated by the ego. This ultimately causes suffering. Self-confidence that is built on love propels humankind forward.

Cultivating authentic self-confidence based on love and compassion is essential for human development. Individuals and leaders who tap into the collective desire for peace and love rather than fear make the world a better place for all.

As you build a positive sense of yourself, what one thing could you do to make your life and that of others better? Each one of us has a special purpose to fulfil, your life is a miracle and if you dig deep enough your true meaning will emerge.

Turn self-consciousness into self-confidence and anything becomes possible.

In order for us to move beyond and above the self and change the world we need first to understand and love the self. Being fully in the present (the Now Habit), the Love Habit and the Calmness Habit provide you with the foundations for a positive self-image that is based on a real understanding of yourself. Feeling present, loved and safe boosts your confidence and self-esteem to heights you may never have dreamed of.

THE COLOUR OF CONFIDENCE (5 MINUTES)

Listen to this short exercise to help you to reconnect to the confidence you already have within yourself. It is designed to help you positively trigger the habit of confidence in times that you may need it most.

+ + +

Trust in Yourself

HAS ANYONE EVER told you in moments of self-doubt to 'just believe in yourself'? Perhaps a well-intentioned parent, teacher or friend? If so, you will know it is easier said than done. Self-doubt is part of being human, especially when you are out of your comfort zone, for example in a new job. The level and frequency that you doubt yourself matters and if it is chronic, it needs attention.

Feelings of low self-worth are in my experience one of the biggest contributing factors to stress, anxiety and low moods. I've listed below some of the most common negative beliefs I have heard in relation to self-esteem; please identify and tick those you have thought about yourself in the last three months.

○ *I'm not good enough.*

○ *I hate myself.*

○ *I'm stupid.*

○ *I'm no good at …*

○ *I'm not as intelligent/kind/funny/good-looking/fit as my partner/parent/ friend/colleague.*

○ *I'm going to be found out at work for not being as capable as I pretend to be.*

○ *I'm a fraud.*

○ *I'm selfish.*

○ *I'm not as good as …*

○ *I'm fat.*

- ○ *I'm lazy.*
- ○ *I'm good for nothing.*
- ○ *I'm useless.*
- ○ *I have no confidence.*
- ○ *I don't know what to say to people.*
- ○ *People are always judging me.*
- ○ *I'll never be confident.*
- ○ *I'll always be like this.*

NOTEBOOK
LIMITING BELIEFS

Look back at Michael's story on page 204 and consider the long-term, detrimental impact there would have been on him if he continued to believe his teachers; he would not be where he is today, a highly educated and confident person who is making a difference in the world.

Take a moment now to examine any negative beliefs that may be holding you back. All of us experience self-doubt at certain stages in our lives, especially when we embrace new challenges. Recall a time or times where your confidence was knocked, for example if someone said something humiliating or hurtful to you or if you couldn't remember a line in a play or if someone declined to go on a date with you.

The list above of negative self-beliefs that severely undermine confidence can debilitate even strong, capable and highly intelligent people. I saw this recently in an ex-client of mine, Paula, who had just been promoted to the role of vice president in a large corporation but suffered from a severe lack of self-confidence. Paula is an open and honest person who has always been ambitious and comes from a family who struggled on many levels. When she first came to see me, she had not been sleeping properly for three years and was living on a knife-edge, resorting to sleeping tablets that only aggravated her situation. As a result of her recent promotion she doubted her ability to do her job and wanted to walk away, even though she loved what she did and had worked very hard to get to where she was. Over the years as her responsibilities increased, her self-confidence had diminished and the effort of pretending to be super-confident was crippling her.

Paula was the eldest of a large family and her father was mainly absent due to alcohol issues. When she was 12 her mother, whom she was very close to, became very ill and Paula spent many sleepless nights caring for her while during the day she had to help with her younger siblings. Clearly, she was too young to manage the situation and so doubted her ability to look after her mother properly and manage her siblings. In addition, Paula felt ashamed of her home life, her sick mother, her drunk father, their lack of money. She didn't tell her friends or teachers about her difficult situation and worked hard at hiding it. She learned that in order to survive she must show no weakness, be an A student and always put others before herself. Paula also felt guilty for hiding her sick mother away from the world. When Paula's mother died, her insomnia started.

Paula had buried a lot of the traumatic memories from her past, she was strong and did not believe in 'navel gazing' or being self-indulgent. It was a big step for her to seek help – for many people this is often the hardest step. However, slowly and gently making connections to her childhood helped her to understand why her inner confidence had reached an all-time low. Through the hypnotherapy sessions we worked on healing her younger self, understanding her father's addiction, and clearing away the guilt and grief she felt for her mother. Her self-doubt had been triggered when she again found herself in a situation with a lot of responsibility and she constantly worried about the welfare of the many staff she was responsible for.

With time, her confidence and self-belief improved, she was able to delegate more at work and took time for herself every second morning to go swimming, an activity she loved but had given up due to the pressures of work. Eventually she started to trust herself to fall asleep. As a result of these positive changes in her life, she did not leave her job and continues to be an excellent leader who places an emphasis on the wellbeing of her staff.

If this story illustrates anything, it is that limiting beliefs can be overcome, but it is important first and foremost to identify them and then move to start to replace them with positive, life-affirming beliefs.

+ + +

Imposter Syndrome

I HAVE HAD many successful clients explain that they are just waiting for the day when their boss and/or colleagues walk into the office and say, 'The game's up, we know the truth, you are not good enough for this role.' This is imposter syndrome – the subject believes they are not really good enough and suffers chronic self-doubt and fear of being 'found out'. The more successful they become, the less confident they are. Fear of success and fear of failure are different sides of the same coin; either way, subconsciously the sufferer believes they must maintain pressure on themselves to remain successful. If they become complacent or 'believe in themselves' they will lose everything. While generally viewed as a condition affecting more women than men, it is actually an issue connected less to gender and more to high achievers.

While it is healthy and natural to question ourselves as we grow, it is unhealthy to question ourselves to the level where we stunt our progress and are stifled with anxiety.

Perfectionism is a major contributing factor to feelings of insecurity. The drive to *always* maintain impossibly high standards leaves many people exhausted, disillusioned and self-doubting their abilities.

In her now-famous commencement speech for new students, Hollywood actress and Harvard graduate Natalie Portman commented about her own experience starting university, 'I felt like there had been some mistake, that I wasn't smart enough to be in this company, and that every time I opened my mouth I would have to prove that I wasn't just a dumb actress.' Portman encouraged the students to be comfortable with being a novice; whether learning to drive or finding a new job in a café, we all experience the 'new person' feeling. Being patient with your progress, avoiding perfectionism and focusing less on results and more on effort will help you to feel more comfortable. All of the work you have done in following this book on building presence, love and calmness into your life will help you if you do feel you have imposter syndrome. Truthfully, we probably all feel it at some stage on some level. Like many unwanted feelings, it is not the feelings themselves that are the problem but your relationship to them that matters. Patience and kindness will always win out.

Growth Mindset for Confidence

More than 30 years ago American educational psychologist Dr Carol Dweck coined the terms 'growth mindset' and 'fixed mindset'.[53] Dweck was fascinated by children's attitudes to failure and carried out research on thousands of children, discovering that life experiences are less important than mindset in terms of measuring successful outcomes. In short, a child's belief system is crucial in their ability to bounce back from bad results at school or challenging situations at home.

Placing emphasis on effort rather than results can help overcome low self-esteem and imposter syndrome; believing that you can feel better about yourself and making a consistent effort to do so will result in you feeling more secure, which in turn leads to authentic confidence.

It is the belief and the effort that count, not the immediate result.

In Dweck's TED Talk she refers to a high school in Chicago that decided to remove the grade 'Fail' on a test and replace it with 'Not yet', indicating the possibility of growth and improvement so that a child who did not pass his or her test did not feel powerless but empowered to try again.[54] 'Fail' is so definitive and negative; if you don't pass first time this did not indicate that you will not pass next time. It is useful to remember that even Einstein made mistakes when he was testing the general law of relativity. Personally, I can proudly say that I succeeded in passing my driving test, after five attempts!

The aforementioned school inspired Dweck to conduct a study on ten-year-olds by giving them a task that was slightly too hard for them. Some of the children embraced the challenge while others were more suspicious, feeling that their intelligence was being judged. Scientists measured the brain waves of the pupils who displayed both 'fixed' and 'growth' mindset tendencies at the time when these pupils made a mistake. The brains of the children with 'fixed' mindsets saw little activity as the pupil 'failed' to engage with the task, while the brains of the pupils with 'growth' mindsets lit up with the challenge. Dweck, in her well-known TED Talk, poses the following questions: 'How are we raising our children? Are we raising kids who are obsessed with getting As? Are they carrying this need for constant validation with them into their future lives?'[55] These are highly pertinent questions that I think many of us can relate to.

A 'fixed' mindset in childhood leaves the door wide open for imposter syndrome to occur as an adult as the subject is always looking for acknowledgement and filled with self-doubt.

Why not apply a 'growth' mindset to your life and watch your confidence grow? These two simple ways of changing how you communicate about and with yourself are highly effective.

1 **'Not yet'** – Replace 'I can't do this,' with 'I can do this, just not yet.' Use this when you attempt to learn anything new or if you make a mistake.

2 **'Used to'** – Replace fixed ideas about yourself such as 'I've always been a worrier' with 'I used to be a worrier,' or 'I'm no good at' with 'I used to believe I was no good at.'

Developing a 'growth' mindset is a key component in building emotional intelligence. If you are a parent or work with children, try to apply these two principles to all that they do and focus always on their effort rather than their results.

+ + +

Inner Confidence

INNER CONFIDENCE is your sense of self-worth. If you are confident on the inside you feel equal to others whatever their social or financial status may be. Positive people feel at ease with themselves regardless of who they are with.

> **Authentic inner confidence rises above hierarchical and status-driven structures.**

Many of my clients cry during their first consultation and almost always apologise as if they have done something 'wrong'. They often tell me that they are not usually 'so weak', 'so silly' or 'so stupid'! Ironically, I am glad when I see their tears, not because I wish them to suffer, but because I know that my job of helping them will be easier; those clients who are removed from their emotions can take longer to reach.

We all feel vulnerable and exposed when we cry and this opens up a part of us that we desperately try to keep hidden. Remember Paula? Only when she had the courage to release and understand her emotions was she able to truly move on and to sleep peacefully.

 IMAGINEERING

Imagine you inherit an old but beautiful home that hasn't been lived in for years. You turn on the tap in the kitchen and a disgusting, foul-smelling green liquid pours out, so you quickly turn it off, leave the house and announce that you want to sell it immediately as there is far too much work to be done and you don't have the time or money to spend on it.

Perhaps if you had waited for the tap to run for a few moments, the water would have run clear and with it the potential of the beautiful home would have opened up to you.

Managing your emotions is no different; at first they can seem too much like hard work and it may appear easier to run from them than to let them flow freely. It takes courage, time and a great deal of self-knowledge for us to build an authentic feeling of self-worth. Feeling genuine confidence comes from when we feel calm inside, strong and at peace.

You are not pretending to be confident if you really are comfortable with your own vulnerability.

A positive person, when confronted publicly by a question they don't know the answer to, has the courage to admit this rather than feign knowledge or avoid the issue. Similarly, if someone is rude to them they choose to not take it personally and instead show compassion. Positive people display advanced emotional intelligence by admitting their foibles and apologising when they are in the wrong. As a result they exude a quiet confidence that you too are now creating by following the steps in this book.

+ + +

Outer Confidence

TAKE A MOMENT to consider the following questions:

1 How good are you at maintaining eye contact?

2 If you bump into someone you weren't expecting to see, does it shake you a little or do you feel happy to stop and chat?

3 How do you carry yourself – do you stand straight and walk tall?

4 Are you confident to speak your mind at a meeting?

5 Do you feel nervous at large social events?

6 If someone asks you to speak in public, what is your immediate reaction?

Some people may be inwardly confident but not appear outwardly confident. They lack the practical skills to communicate effectively at work, to give credible presentations or to fully relax at social events; they do not show their greatness to the world.

Amy Cuddy, a social psychologist famous for her work on power posing, demonstrates that when you change your body language you change your level of confidence. By consciously adopting high-status postures and holding these for two minutes you actually change the neural messages to your brain.

As with using the breath to cultivate calmness, body language can be used to create confidence as a habit; in both cases the body leads the mind in creating positive emotional habits rather than vice versa. Posture and stature are as important in humans as they are in animals, so if you want to feel confident and want other people to take you seriously, stand up straight. Cuddy's book *Presence: Bringing Your Boldest Self to Your Biggest Challenges*[56,] indicates that the key component is being present. It makes sense – how can you even remember to stand up tall if you are not living in the moment?

When you are present you are powerful.

Do you find that your confidence levels change depending on the type of event you are at (formal/informal)? Does the thought of giving a presentation at work fill you with dread? Does being asked to speak at a wedding really shake your confidence? Fear of public speaking is rooted in the old mammalian part of our brain; our ancient ancestors survived by living in packs and if for any reason you were seen as an outsider your life could be at risk. Nowadays, in the public speaking context, when we see a group of people staring at us a sense of threat is triggered and is accompanied by physical symptoms such as a beating heart, sweaty palms and a dry throat, which can only serve to make the situation worse.

Stepping out of your comfort zone in order to deliver presentations and speeches that resonate and help to transform people's lives is, however, well within your capability. I'm not suggesting we have to be incredible performers but the ability to say a few words confidently and from the heart is a gift that can propel you forward professionally. Overcoming fear of public speaking means that many brilliant ideas needn't languish unheard.

NOTEBOOK – LET'S BUILD YOUR CONFIDENCE

Write down every single thing you are proud of in your life. Remember to focus on your effort and not the result. Include everything that challenged you; every race you ran, every speech you gave, all the times in your life when you dared to be great. The outcome of the event is not what is important – if you did well, well done but the main point is that you took on a challenge and did your best. You jumped in the pool and got wet, you auditioned for the play, you sang in the choir.

Now, looking at this list, recall your state of mind when you made the decision to take on these challenges. You were probably apprehensive or even nervous but you did it anyway. Next, write down any feelings of confidence that arose from completing the event/action. Remember the feeling. Most people only measure their feelings of worth on what they achieve externally and yet the internal achievement of finding the courage and confidence to actually participate is what really needs to be acknowledged. In doing so, you are more likely to feel confident in the future and to take measured risks.

+ + +

The Benefits of Building Self-Esteem and Confidence

IN ORDER to make confidence a habit you need to see and feel the rewards. Confident people are more likely to experience positive mental health and feel the following:

1 A greater sense of self-worth

2 Greater enjoyment of life and activities

3 Freedom from self-doubt

4 Freedom from fear and all types of anxiety; less stress

5 More energy and motivation to act

6 More pleasure interacting with people at social gatherings.

Would you like to experience more of these in your life?

+ + +

The Potential of the Human Spirit

'Never underestimate the power of dreams and the influence of the human spirit. We are all the same in this notion. The potential for greatness lies within each of us.'

WILMA RUDOLPH

DESPITE MANY EARLY HEALTH issues, Wilma Rudolph became an Olympic Gold medal winner in both 1956 and 1960. She was born prematurely, weighing only 2kg, and at four years old contracted polio. At this point her doctor told her she would never walk again, but when her mother assured her that she would, she chose to believe her. Wilma was black and female in an era when social expectations dictated that she should become a maid. Despite all this she went on to become the fastest female runner in the world and a role model for both black and female athletes. In 1960 her welcome home party was the first racially integrated event in her home town in Tennessee.

Do you believe you deserve to be confident and to live your greatness?

Many people hold themselves back from truly reaching their full potential and from finding the greatness within themselves. They fear that if they believe they are great then they are getting 'too big for their boots' and becoming arrogant. Nobody likes a 'show off' or a 'know it all' or someone who exudes pretension. The word 'pretentious' comes from 'to pretend', to be something you are not. Having inner and outer confidence is the opposite – there is no need for pretence, it is authentic and genuine.

Being afraid of what other people will think if we are different, especially when we are children and teenagers, is common. Such beliefs often stem from well-intentioned parents warning about the perils of not conforming. This is the same mentality that views loving oneself as a bad thing. Perhaps you don't want to be an athlete or a movie star or any of the other clichés of fame and public greatness, but we all have the capacity to be an everyday hero, to take pride in what we do and to do it to the best of our abilities. Many reasons will be trotted out as to why we should not attempt to follow a purpose that is larger than we are, why it is safer to stay small. This is usually a reflection of the speaker's own limits, but you need to ask if this is good enough for you.

When you feel present, loved and calm you are more likely to push the boundaries; after all, how can you achieve greatness from the confines of your comfort zone? Positive people are constantly stretching themselves in new ways; they make it a habit to seek challenging experiences and as a result they are always growing, always learning.

Creating an abundant mindset which seeks to do the above will be the focus of the next rung of the ladder, the Gratitude Habit.

+ + +

Making Values a Habit

MANY OF US have values we can be proud of, but how many of us actually put them into practice every day or in the heat of the moment of a challenging situation?

Living a life where your values remain aspirational erodes your self-esteem.

For example, consider the mother who preaches honesty but lies to her kids, the teenager who was taught to value respect but screams at his parents, or the boss who values trust but is quick to doubt her staff. These are common examples that happen all the time, everywhere. When you behave in a way that opposes your values, you feel bad about yourself and when you feel bad about yourself your sense of self-worth diminishes significantly.

For values to be lived and breathed they need to become habitual. An empowering method to help achieve this comes in the form of a personal mission statement which will help you to identify (or realign yourself) with your three most important values and remind you to constantly practise what you believe in.

NOTEBOOK
PERSONAL VALUE-LED
MISSION STATEMENT

Take seven deep belly breaths, clear your mind and then commence.

1   Brainstorm and make a list of your values by asking what is important to you, what you believe in and what you value in yourself and others.

To help get you started, here is list of things that I value:

Honesty, kindness, trust, compassion, joy, connecting, helping, laughter, love, determination, peace, positivity, respect, courage, service to others, patience and loyalty.

1   Next, select what you consider to be the three most important and relevant values from your list.

2   Using those three values, write:

Today it is my intention, my desire and my promise to myself to cultivate habits of [insert values 1, 2 and 3]. If I deviate from these values, I will show compassion to myself, take responsibility for my actions and return to the practice of values [insert values 1, 2 and 3] each day.

3   Put your statement somewhere you can see it, for example on your desk, fridge or your phone's home screen and read it out loud every day to reinforce the values in your mind.

Beyond the Self

IF YOU DO NOT understand yourself, you are for ever stuck in your past habits. The ability to live outside of yourself and these habits, to see the bigger picture of your life and how you can contribute in a meaningful way to the world is what grows and maintains powerful confidence.

Viktor Frankl, the famous Jewish psychiatrist and Auschwitz survivor, wrote the book *Man's Search for Meaning* about the horrors of experiencing Auschwitz. Incredibly, Frankl did not blame the Nazi guards for their cruelty but instead saw them as prisoners too, prisoners of fear. Despite the hell he endured, he was able to find a meaning in his suffering and ultimately that meaning kept him alive; he promised himself that if he survived he would create a therapy that would lift people from the torture of their minds and help them to manage their response to life's hardships.

Frankl survived but the rest of his family, including his beloved wife, were murdered. True to his word, Frankl went on to develop 'logotherapy', which places meaning at the centre of positive mental health. *Logos* is the Greek for meaning and while it varies according to the individual, when found it transcends the self and its introspection.

Back to the Heart

Operating from the heart is the most profound way to feel confident; connecting to others with openness and without judging, and finding out how you can contribute to make the world a better place will all help to inspire self-confidence. The heartfulness-centred meditation referred to on page 164) and that I personally practise originated in India in 1975. Its mission statement is to 'awaken the divine consciousness and provide support on the path of human evolution'[57] by using the power of meditation to cleanse the heart each day.

To quote Indian Yoga Master Chariji,

> **'Do not love, do not seek to be love. Try to become love. Because when you become love, everybody will come to you like bees to a flower.'**

Extending this principle out in a practical way is very useful. Remember, self-confidence is the opposite of self-consciousness: if you possess genuine self-confidence you are able to focus on others; if you are self-conscious you will tend to focus on yourself. An example of this might be if you are giving a speech at a wedding. If you are self-confident you will focus on the couple's happiness, not yourself, and when you speak with an open heart the guests will feel it and believe in you because you believe in them. When you engage from the heart, they listen. Feeling their warm response leads us to the next step, the Gratitude Habit.

THREE KEY TAKEAWAYS FROM THIS CHAPTER:

1 Presence is powerful. Use the habit of being in the now to exude confidence.

2 It is healthy and natural to question ourselves when confronted by new challenges but it is unhealthy to question ourselves to the level where we stunt our progress and are stifled with anxiety.

3 Avoid imposter syndrome by dealing with your past and embrace a growth mindset to see all that you do as a learning opportunity.

 ## THE CONFIDENCE HABIT DAILY MINDFULNESS

+ Power posing – try to do this for two minutes every day and definitely before events such as interviews, presentations, exams and social events, whether you experience anxiety or not. Take two minutes before you enter the room – do it in the bathroom, car park, wherever. Always stand up straight, with your shoulders back and relaxed and your head held erect.

+ Remember the one word from the person you admire and the colour of confidence (see page 211). Bring the person, the word and the colour of the person to mind when you want a boost of confidence.

+ Develop a growth mindset when you are learning something new by simply adding the two little words 'not yet.'

+ Write out your mission statement and say it out loud, preferably in the morning. Keep it somewhere you can see easily. Read it, feel it, believe it and live it.

- Write your three most important values on your phone home screen, fridge door, sunshield of your car, front of your notebook or desktop.

- Surround yourself with confident people, big thinkers and those who take calculated risks and believe in themselves. Seek them out and spend as much time as you can with them.

- If you can, avoid people who give you all the reasons why you can't do something. Wish them well, but don't engage. If it is someone close to you, don't take it personally.

- Challenge yourself! Look back at your list of growth mindset achievements to remind you that you have felt this way before and pushed through successfully.

- Say 'yes' to events both at work and personally that you would previously have avoided. Feel the fear or nerves associated with this and then go to the event anyway!

AFFIRMATIONAL TOOTH BRUSHING

Repeat your confidence habit affirmations every morning and night while you brush your teeth. Feel them in your heart.

MINDFUL SHOWERING

Take time as you shower and dry yourself to be loving and patient with yourself. Use this habit as a time to connect towards yourself without judgement.

ACKNOWLEDGE
PROGRESS

Evidence to support your affirmations: Think of an example from your everyday life that illustrates the truth in your affirmations.

1   I have faith in the best of me, I am equal to everyone I meet.

2   I can achieve anything I put my mind to.

3   I am a confident and courageous person.

Now mark how you are feeling on the positivity sundial below.

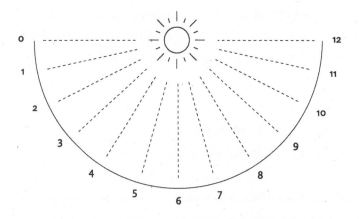

Remember to keep listening to your seven-minute morning and your sleep time hypnotherapies. Tick the days so far that you have listened on page 344. Be proud of the times you have listened and don't give yourself a hard time if you have missed one or two days; that is okay – keep going!

 **MEDITATIONS**

+ Morning ritual

+ Sleep time hypnotherapy

+ The colour of confidence

THE GRATITUDE HABIT

HOW TO APPRECIATE ABUNDANCE

'The fool's life is empty of gratitude and full of fears.'
EPICURUS

+

INTERRELATED

Contentment Acknowledgement Appreciation Thankfulness Grace

AFFIRMATIONAL TOOTH BRUSHING

Write these affirmations in your journal. If you cannot remember the exact words, it doesn't matter, simply repeat 'I am grateful', to yourself, over and over as you brush, feeling the emotion as you repeat it.

1 I wake each morning filled with gratitude for all the blessings in my life.

2 I am grateful for who I am.

3 My heart is filled with gratitude for everyone in my life.

Please note that at the end of the chapter, I will ask you to write down three examples to support the affirmations, for example I wake each day with gratitude for all the blessings I have, big and small.

BRIAN PENNIE'S STORY, 40, LECTURER IN THE NEUROSCIENCE OF MINDFULNESS

Although Brian is not a client of mine, I interviewed him for this book and as I listened to his story, I just knew I had to include it. It is rare to meet someone as present and grateful to be alive as Brian is. His story is one of love and courage. I hope his story helps you to see the greatness in gratitude. Personally, I'm eternally grateful to Brian for writing his story.

'On 8 October, 2013 I experienced my first day clean after 15 years of chronic heroin addiction.

'Prior to that day, I was an anxious, compulsive thinker, utterly derailed by the incessant chatter in my mind. This unrelenting inner voice was the source of many of my problems and drove me to the brink of death

through addiction. It is difficult to know exactly why I was such an anxious person, but I'm fairly convinced that it was rooted in childhood. Several traumatic milestones occurred during this time including a life-threatening operation, a long-term separation from my mother, an epic failure at emigration, and a dysfunctional family life which focused around alcoholism.

'It is very different for me today. During detox on a funny little farm on the outskirts of Dublin, I had a profound shift which empowered me to view life from a completely new perspective. I am not quite sure why or how, but the world just seemed to resonate with beauty. Colours were more colourful, sounds were more joyful, and food tasted like it never tasted before. And then there were the animals. I would sit on a fence in the October dew-soaked mornings, and Mollie, the resident cat, would crawl up my leg as I watched the sun come up from behind the trees. I was completely mesmerised by how colourful, fresh, and beautiful life had become. Despite the years I lost, I will be for ever grateful for the new perspective that my suffering has gifted me.

'Guided by a new-found love of mindfulness meditation, my increased sense of awareness led me to change nearly every aspect of my life. I overhauled my diet, began to exercise regularly, and became a student of life, devouring an obsessive amount of books on the nature of present moment awareness. I didn't realise it back then, but gratefulness was one of the key driving forces behind my new-found happiness. I was grateful for everything: reconnecting with old friends, new people who were entering my life, and of course my family who helped me to get back on my feet. I was also utterly grateful for the increased present moment awareness that was instilled inside of me. I was thriving, and my previously undiscovered spirit guided my every step.

'I should have been lost, but I wasn't. I had the world at my feet, and I

knew it. But it wasn't arrogance, I would have been happy listening to the birds for the rest of my life. I was just so grateful for all the opportunities that seemed available to me. I knew exactly what I wanted to do, however, and went to college to study the complexities of the human mind. I graduated with a degree in psychology in 2017 winning several awards, including a fully funded PhD scholarship in Trinity College's Institute of Neuroscience. Since then, I have become a self-development consultant, a lecturer in both Trinity College and University College Dublin, a published academic writer, blogger, speaker for mental health awareness, and one of the most energetic, positive and grateful people I know.

'With renewed intuition, I've also followed my gut and reached out to people further along the road. This boldness has paid off big time and I am now writing two books; one about mindfulness with Irish celebrity and mental health advocate Niall Breslin (aka Bressie), and the other about life advice that I have received from my interviews with some of Ireland's most successful individuals in the arts, sport, and business. I even consider world-renowned mindfulness expert Rick Hanson a friend. Life is truly wonderful.

'I don't take my new life for granted, however. I spend the first 35 to 45 minutes upon waking every morning pumping positive vibes through my body and soul, and this includes a big dose of gratefulness. My morning practice includes five minutes each of affirmations, visualisations and inner child work. I then spend ten minutes fully immersing myself in things I'm grateful for before my 15-minute meditation. I change what I'm grateful for each morning but it might include things like my breath, my bed, my family, the wind, or even one particular gust of wind. Getting specific works great. This gratefulness practice electrifies my body as much as any meditation. I feel like I'm powering my body for the day ahead with gratitude energy. And if I'm feeling a little low during the day, or get caught up in thinking, I use this tool as a way to come back again.

'You can't be fearful, angry or sad while you're being grateful, after all. The best thing is, the more I practise gratefulness, the easier it gets. It is, and will always be, one of the most important tools in my locker. And for that I will be forever grateful for gratefulness.'

THE POSITIVE HABIT EMOTIONS QUIZ #5

Please allocate a point for each 'Yes' answer that you give.

1 Do you feel present most of the time?

2 Do you make time to care for your mind each day?

3 Do you love yourself?

4 Do you believe you are a compassionate person?

5 Are you able not to take anything other people do or say personally?

6 If you feel stress or anxiety, do you use your breath to calm your mind?

7 Do you protect your mind from negative information, people and places, for example having regular digital breaks/avoiding people who drain your energy?

8 Do you feel confident to speak your mind and feel equal to others?

9 Are you kind to yourself if you make a mistake?

10 Do you feel grateful each day?

11 Do you let go of grudges from the past?

12 Do you visualise a bright future?

13 Do you feel you are living your life purpose?

14 Do you take care of your physical needs, such as getting eight hours' sleep, exercising and eating a balanced diet?

15 Do you feel that you are good enough as a person?

16 Do you trust that no matter what happens you will be able to cope?

Score from quiz #1 on page 8 =
Score from quiz #2 on page 130 =
Score from quiz #3 on page 173 =
Score from quiz #4 on page 207 =
Score from quiz #5 =

What do you notice? Lots of positive progress, I hope!

+ + +

What Does Gratitude Mean to You?

THE WORD GRATITUDE is derived from the Latin word *gratia*, which means grace, graciousness or gratefulness (depending on the context). Gratitude includes all of these meanings when we apply them to how we choose to live our lives. In Ancient Greece, the word for grace is *charis*; in mythology, when a person illustrated the spiritual practice of knowing their blessings, they became known as *charismata*, in modern-day English 'charismatic' which is often associated with grace.

From a positive psychology perspective, gratitude is much more than simply saying 'thank you' – it is a very powerful emotional state that transforms both individuals and societies. Harvard Medical School defines it as:

'A thankful appreciation for what an individual receives, whether tangible or intangible. With gratitude, people acknowledge the goodness in their lives ... As a result; gratitude also helps people connect to something larger than themselves as individuals – whether to other people, nature, or a higher power.'[58]

NOTEBOOK
GRATITUDE TRIGGER LIST

Write down everything you understand about gratitude, giving examples of when you feel most grateful.

Here are some examples from my clients to help you get started. Gratitude is ...

+ Being grateful for everything from opening my eyes and having the gift of another day

+ Showing respect

+ Seeing my daughter moving her toes after spinal surgery

+ Noticing and appreciating a moment when I tell myself I am truly blessed

+ An attitude

+ Being thankful for all that we mostly take for granted

+ The greatest prayer

+ Feeling alive

+ Truly essential for me to be happy

+ Showing grace and respect to other

+ My parents being healthy

+ My garden

+ My comfortable bed

+ + +

The habit loop of gratitude

ONCE AGAIN, let's get those positive emotional habit loops working in your mind, always focusing on the reward – in this case gratitude. Your list is a set of positive emotional triggers that you can use to notice all the moments you have already in your life to be grateful for.

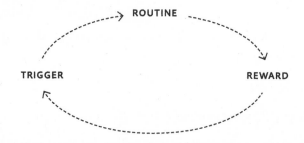

1 **Positive trigger** – showing grace and respect to others.

2 **Positive routine** – writing a thank you card to my friend after a lovely lunch.

3 **Positive reward** – feeling grateful.

Gratitude – the Fourth Emotional Habit

'Cultivate the habit of being grateful for every good thing that comes to you, and to give thanks continuously. And because all things have contributed to your advancement, you should include all things in your gratitude.'

RALPH WALDO EMERSON

AS WE HAVE MOVED mindfully through three of the positive emotional habits, you are now truly open to embrace the fourth emotional habit, gratitude. With each rung of the ladder you climb you are metaphorically getting higher and closer to an authentic level of happiness and contentment; each step naturally leads to the next, each positive emotion builds on the last, each step grounded in the Now Habit..

When you feel grateful every day you live in a state of contented bliss. The greatest gift you can give to yourself is gratitude and positive people instinctively know this.

While we may all know that being grateful is important and something we 'should' be, we don't always practise this. As children, most of us were required to say 'thank you' in certain situations and so we developed this automatic polite habit rather than the words having an authentic connection. If you ask a person what they are grateful for they will usually mention health, family and home. However, for gratitude's miraculous power to work you must feel it every day. It is therefore your duty to make it a habit. Positive people are grateful for both the good and the difficult in their lives as this presents them with the possibility of learning. Remaining grateful when life presents difficulties is the springboard to hope when we need it most.

It may seem obvious that having gratitude is important for positive mental wellbeing, but what you may not be aware of is how gratitude is one of the most effective tools for soothing anxiety, stress and low moods. In this chapter, we will examine why you cannot feel grateful and anxious at the same time, the social significance of gratitude and how to manifest what you want in the future by feeling grateful *now* for what will be. Again, the emphasis will be on *how* you can create it in your life.

Before we continue, let me extend my gratitude to you: my thankful heart expands and I am genuinely grateful that you are reading these words right now. This is also a gentle reminder to keep going with your audios!

+ + +

Optimistically Grateful

TWO LEADING PSYCHOLOGISTS studying gratitude, Dr Robert A. Emmons and Dr Michael E. McCullough, asked participants in a study to write a few sentences focusing on particular topics each week for ten weeks. One group wrote about things they were grateful for that had occurred during the week.[59] The second group wrote about daily irritations or things that had displeased them (a sure way to fire negative neural pathways) and the third group wrote about events that had affected them either positively or negatively.

After ten weeks, those who had written about gratitude were generally more optimistic and felt better about their lives. Surprisingly, they also exercised more and had fewer visits to medical practitioners than those who had focused on and written about sources of irritation. This study suggests that the act of being grateful helps us to become both mentally and physically healthier, both of which play a significant role in our happiness.

Another leading researcher in this field, positive psychologist Dr Martin E. P. Seligman (see also page 49) tested the impact of various positive psychology interventions on 411 people who were asked to write and personally deliver a letter of gratitude to someone who had never been properly thanked for his or her kindness.[60] Participants immediately exhibited a huge increase in happiness when this was measured. This impact was greater than from any other intervention, with benefits lasting up to a month.

If it is so obvious that gratitude makes us healthier and happier, why is this not reflected in the daily practices of families, schools and workplaces? The answer is probably that many of us simply forget to be grateful and the negativity bias is naturally stronger as it promotes survival.

Positive people make it a habit to consciously practise gratitude.

Jane Ransom, a clinical hypnotherapist, life coach and specialist on brain plasticity, has identified three key components that can be used to make gratitude a daily habit.[61]

1 **Emote:** It is not sufficient to be grateful; we must actually *feel* it. This is where we can apply self-directed, positive neuroplasticity. What does gratitude feel like physically for you?

2 **Extend:** True gratitude is not just for what we have but must be extended to people in our lives who help us each and every day. Gratitude works best as a social skill.

3 **Exercise:** Gratitude needs to be a daily exercise for it to become habitual.

The social aspect of gratitude will strengthen your relationships and help forge new friendships. When someone is truly grateful for something you have done for them in the past, you will be more likely to help them again. It is well known that people in the workplace are more prepared to tolerate lower pay and benefits if they are recognised and appreciated. If, on the other hand, hard work and efforts go unnoticed or ignored, this often leads to low morale and self-esteem.

Consider everyone in your life from your family to your friends, from your colleagues to the people who serve your coffee. Make a conscious choice to show them genuine gratitude for all that they do and notice the positive impact this has on all your relationships. Being specific about what you are grateful for is also recommended when thanking others as it shows them that you have paid attention to the details of their efforts. Very often we can be too quick to think of what people don't do rather than what they do. For example, a friend who forgets your birthday every year but is always there if you need them, or your partner who is reluctant to cook dinner but always cleans up afterwards.

Showing gratitude to others is the opposite of taking them for granted. Gratitude shows respect and respect is one of the highest and most practical forms of showing love to the self and others.

+ + +

Gratitude to Soothe Anxiety

GRATITUDE SOFTENS FEAR because it provides us with perspective; if you are struggling with something in your life and feel overwhelmed, being thankful for what you actually have erases imagined fears that fuel anxiety. Taking a step back and looking at everything the problem is *not* can help engender this. Often when we fixate on something that is challenging, either in our personal or professional lives, we lose the capacity to be grateful.

For example, take the case of Ella – she's 32 and really wants a baby but it's just not happening. She finds it really hard to be patient and obsesses over the perceived injustice that 'everyone else' can get pregnant even if they don't want a child! This is a hard situation; not being able to have children if you want them is heartbreaking. Everything the problem is *not* includes the fact that she is healthy and young, has a loving partner, still has time and has friends and family who support her. She can still hope to get pregnant naturally and seek medical help if she needs it.

To take another example, perhaps you have a difficult boss who always seems to take his or her bad mood out on you, but at the same time you have a bunch of amazing colleagues. If you focus only on the boss and his or her moods you may miss the opportunity to bond with your great colleagues.

Identify the positives in any situation, and the problems quickly fade into the greater scheme of your fortunate life.

Gratitude needs to be practised every day, not just at the times when you feel stressed or anxious. The following meditation visualisation is designed to really illustrate the point that holding gratitude and fear in your mind at the same time is near impossible.

TURN FEAR INTO GRATITUDE (5 MINUTES)

Please try this exercise now. It can be found on www.thepositivehabit.com.

+ + +

The Guilt Around Gratitude

IF FEELING GRATEFUL was a pathway and you came across a block, that block would be guilt. Many of us may feel guilty about 'not being grateful enough' for what we have when confronted by terrible injustices that affect others: homelessness, human trafficking, war. If you feel guilty, how can you be grateful? This gives us yet another reason to mentally beat ourselves up with thoughts such as:

+ 'I should be happy, I have a lovely family, a beautiful home, a good job, what on Earth is wrong with me?'

+ 'There are people in the world who have real problems; I'm so selfish.'

+ 'I'm so ashamed for not being thankful for what I have. I have no right to feel anxious or stressed when people in the world are starving or living in terror.'

Positive emotions such as gratitude cannot grow from shame.

Do any of the thoughts above sound familiar? Not being grateful enough or getting stressed, irritable or anxious brings up feelings of shame which, as you know, can be paralysing. If you feel shame for not feeling grateful, it is the shame that is causing the problem, not the lack of gratitude.

Therefore, it is important to deal with any shame or guilt you might feel about not feeling grateful enough. To do this we need to consider how the mind operates; the subconscious operates through emotion and imagination and does not concern itself with concepts of fairness. This is why when we tell children they 'should' be thankful for all they have, they often end up feeling worse about themselves and less grateful. The shame turns inwards.

NOTEBOOK
THE ROOTS OF GRATITUDE

Write answers to the following questions in your notebook.

1 Did you feel grateful as a child?

2 Did your parents remind you of how lucky you were compared to other children, or indeed compared to their own childhoods?

3 Do you feel that younger generations have it easier or more difficult?

4 Do you compare what you have to friends and family and do you feel envious of someone who has a bigger house/you feel is more attractive/has a 'happier family' and/or more money?

5 Do you compare your partner/children to those of other people? If you don't do this outwardly, do you do it in your own mind? For example, 'If only my X was more like Y'.

Some of these conditioned beliefs lead to the unfortunate habit of complaining, comparing and gossiping. We see this everywhere and it is, unfortunately, a common way for people to (both consciously and unconsciously) communicate and bond.

+ + +

Complaining Kills Gratitude

THE HABIT OF MOANING is something we can all fall into without even noticing it. The argument that it 'gets things off your chest' is, in my opinion, largely spurious. if your day has not gone smoothly and you insist on telling everyone every detail you are in fact prolonging rather than shedding the frustration and negative energy. This type of low-level, chronic negative thinking is rewiring and re-firing negative neural connections as you live through each small inconvenience not just once, but time and time again. Each micro-aggravation starts to accumulate and eventually dominates, affecting your thinking, outlook and behaviour as you stumble from one drama to another. Where is gratitude in this unfortunate dance with self-pity?

Your ability to accept that life has many hitches and that things often don't go according to plan keeps those minor irritations where they belong, as insignificant rather than significant events in the full scheme of your life. Your acceptance of them disempowers them so that they are no longer irritations, but simply part of life and of being human. Look for gratitude everywhere and you will find it pays dividends.

If you have a habit of gratuitous complaining, to break it I recommend initially that you journal your frustrations – unleash them on the page rather than burdening someone else who probably has their own issues to deal with. It is, however, imperative that *real* emotional pain and trauma be shared. If you have strong negative feelings and thoughts about yourself that you can't make sense of, *please* speak to someone you can trust – a friend, a family member or a therapist.

+ + +

The Miracle of You

'There are only two ways to live your life. One is as though nothing is a miracle. The other is as though everything is a miracle.'

ALBERT EINSTEIN

I STARTED THIS BOOK by saying that your life is a miracle and this was not just to flatter you as it is also true; the chance of you being born exactly as you are, is, according to science, about 1 to 400 trillion. Dr Ali Binazir, author and 'happiness engineer', calculated these odds by analysing statistically the chances of your parents getting together (considering how many people there are in the world) coupled with the chance that during conception the particular egg and particular sperm came together at an exact moment. Given that even before this happens the chances of all your ancestors mating to create your parents makes this a miracle.[62] Binazir said:

'A miracle is an event so unlikely as to be almost impossible. By that definition, I've just shown that you are a miracle. Now go forth and feel and act like the miracle that you are.'

Gratitude is generally focused on what we have and the people in our lives, which, are of course, important. However, expressing internal gratitude to yourself because of the preciousness of your life and not because of what you've achieved or what you have is supremely important. This follows from the same principle as outlined in the Love Habit chapter – love yourself first and then extend it out to others.

THANK YOU, MY HEART (4 MINUTES)

The heart's intelligence is infinite, but it does require daily fuel to keep pumping out positive emotions.

This short gratitude meditation is your way to thank your heart for simply being you. Listen to this often to feel the state of bliss that is a heart full of gratitude. This meditation can also help if you have recently been hard on yourself as it forces you to stop and acknowledge yourself with gratitude.

+ + +

Feel Grateful Every Morning

'When you arise in the morning, think of what a precious privilege it is to be alive, to breathe, to think, to enjoy, to love.'

<small>MARCUS AURELIUS</small>

LISTENING TO the morning ritual has been programming your mind so that you start each day in a grateful frame of mind and with a clear knowledge of which emotional habit you need to draw on most during the day, whether calmness, gratitude or one of the other habits. Remember how Brian Pennie spends time every morning carving gratitude into his neural network? Personally, I find it useful to not get out of my bed until I have genuinely created a deep feeling of grace and gratitude that I can bring with me during my day.

Shane, a client of mine, is a successful musician with a thriving career that he has built up over many years. When we first met, Shane, like many high achievers, put an immense amount of pressure on himself to be all things to everyone. At that time his three young children were all under five and he was the sole breadwinner. Shane felt he was stretched to capacity and his ability to create and focus on his work was being jeopardised by feelings of anxiety and low confidence. He was also constantly questioning his talent and his role as a father, which put further pressure on him.

His standards, both as a parent and in his career, were so high that he could never possibly meet them. When he was travelling for work he felt bad for not being with his kids and for leaving his wife to 'hold the fort'; when he was with his family he was distracted and worried about progressing his career.

To add to his frustration, he knew that he 'should' be grateful as he had created the life he had dreamed of when he was younger. If he tried to talk to family or friends they would be baffled, they would ask why he was worried – he 'had it all' and 'should' be happy.

At our first meeting Shane's confidence was at an all-time low and his anxiety had reached epic heights; his voice was beginning to shake when he was on stage and in the recording studio. He was terrified by this and would spend sleepless nights worrying about it happening again. He felt he could no longer hide these issues and he also began to suffer from 'brain fog' during important meetings.

The first thing we did together was to look at the thought processes that were fuelling his anxiety. We discovered persistent, negative thoughts such as:

+ 'I'm less smart than other people.'

+ 'If I mess up I won't have enough money to look after my family and maintain the lifestyle they enjoy.'

+ 'I'm the black sheep of the family, I'm not as talented as other artists and I don't see my kids as much as other fathers.'

+ 'I should be more grateful for my life, focus on the positives and just relax like most normal people.'

I taught Shane the ARK technique (see page 119) to deal with his negative thought patterns; the idea of accepting them had never occurred to him and he felt an immediate relief as he transformed pressure into kindness. Then we turned our attention to the guilt he felt about his success and how he felt he 'should' be happy with all that he had. As a child, Shane had always felt that he was the odd one out in his family; both his parents were senior academics and his two sisters were 'A' students, while he had never been good at school and simply wasn't interested in it. His parents had tried, but in the end could not understand why their son showed no enthusiasm for school work and was always 'messing around' on his guitar. We uncovered that the intense energy driving his success had been a way of showing his parents that creative pursuits were as worthy as academia. This was an unsustainable approach because each success led Shane to look for more approval.

During therapy, Shane found the courage to let go of this need to compete with and prove to his parents that what he was doing was important and worthy. He began to have compassion for his parents and their view of the world. Slowly, he was also able to begin to see how proud of him they were. Practising the 'thank you, my heart' mediation practice every morning (see page 252) was the principal technique that helped him to finally move on from his past conditioning. He finally became grateful for what was really important in his life – himself.

+ + +

How to Manifest Your Future Now

THOSE FAMILIAR with the bestselling books *The Law of Attraction* and *The Secret* will know that gratitude plays a large part in manifesting your desires into the world.

'You simply will not be the same person two months from now after consciously giving thanks each day for the abundance that exists in your life. And you will have set in motion an ancient spiritual law: the more you have and are grateful for, the more will be given you.'

SARAH BAN BREATHNACH

When you are aligned with the source energy of the universe you can manifest what you want through the power of your thoughts, emotions *and* the actions that you take.

The practical application of manifesting desires is often overlooked, or all too easily dispelled as naive, whimsical and a form of wishful thinking. But please keep an open mind as I explain how you can apply this transformative principle to better your life ...

One of the most famous psychological experiments on 'selective attention' was conducted in 1999 by two cognitive psychologists, Daniel Simons and Christopher Chabris at Harvard.[63] In the experiment they asked the study group to watch a video of six people playing basketball and to count the number of passes between the three players wearing white T-shirts. During this a person wearing a gorilla suit comes onto the screen, walks past and beats his chest. More than half of the people asked to participate in the study did not see the gorilla! I tried it myself and did not see the gorilla!

So why am I writing about gorillas and what has this got to do with manifesting your incredible future? Well, in essence, it is all about noticing things. You manifest what you pay attention to. Perspective is the key; the subconscious filters we apply to our world actually create our world. Remember Brian Pennie's dramatic perspective shift from craving heroin to cultivating presence? We only see what we focus on. Negative emotions are blinkers that keep us blind to other opportunities and possibilities. For example, if we are unhappy with a situation in our life such as a job or a relationship and all we do is focus on how hard it is, we cannot see the many possibilities that are also there. Just like the gorilla, they are invisible to us. This principle can also be the case in reverse; for example, when we decide we want to buy a new car, we see the desired model everywhere, or a pregnant woman will see other pregnant women everywhere.

You are subconsciously scanning the world for what you want to see.

Take this idea a step further and imagine starting to consciously use the power of your thoughts to perceive the world more positively. If you do this, you will naturally be attracted to positive opportunities and will grow and prosper.

Using gratitude as the emotional state for something that has not yet happened encourages you to seize moments to make your desires into realities. For example, if you want to change career, imagine yourself already in the new job that you want – by doing so, you will feel more confident so that when you go for the interview you will broadcast this confidence to the interview panel. It's likely they will pick up on your energy, giving you a greater chance of success in getting the job. What started out in your imagination is now your reality. Dr Joe Dispenza, a neuroscientist, advises that an elevated emotion combined with action will allow you to manifest your desires into reality.[64]

When you widen your lens of perception you enter a privileged and sacred space which will reveal opportunities that you would miss entirely if you had remain locked in the world of thoughts. The fog of thinking and analysing lifts. The steps are:

1 Become aware of what you wish to create.

2 Feel gratitude for what you desire as if it were already the case.

3 Act on the opportunities that are presented to you.

If followed, these three steps attract what you desire into your life.

When we convince the subconscious mind that we *already* have what it is we desire, it will start to feel and behave in a way that supports this new belief and it will organically search for opportunities that match the positive feelings that we have created.

You may well have been in the right place at the right time on many occasions, but if you remain unaware, opportunities are lost and you will continue to believe that you are not a lucky person. So, let's see *how* you can create your own ideal future.

Good luck is not a coincidence.

NOTEBOOK
BEING GRATEFUL
FOR THE FUTURE NOW!

Take a moment to answer these questions in your notebook. As always, clear your mind before you start and take seven deep belly breaths.

1   How often do you imagine your life one year or more from now? All the time, hourly, daily, weekly, monthly, rarely or never?

2   Describe in detail how you would like your life to be one year from now. Give as much detail as possible. Let your imagination run wild; don't hold back. Remember, in your imagination everything is possible.

3   Describe in detail how you would like your life to be five years from now. Again, the level of detail matters, so don't set boundaries. Dream of what you really want and remove yourself from the fear of what your conscious mind will tell you is realistic or not.

4   What principal positive emotion (from the six emotional habits identified in this book) do you feel when you imagine your ideal future in both one year and five years from now? Is it love, calmness, confidence, hope, gratitude or happiness?

When we construct mental models of the future with a high level of detail, the same areas of the brain are activated as when we remember the past. Memories of the future can therefore be created before they have even happened in the physical domain. When you radiate this energy it manifests into those future memories to make them a present reality.

It is important to note that this 'goal setting' is not about pressure or striving towards something. The 'goal' can be simply to be present in the moment, as there is no finer achievement than presence. Rather than using the word 'goals', let's instead call them 'intentions' and 'desires' as these are more positive and compassionate. So what are your intentions and desires for the present and the future?

Now answer the questions below – remember, the more detail the better. 'I want' becomes 'I am grateful for ...' as if this positive feeling is already the case.

1 How do you want to feel when you rise in the morning?

Example answer: *'I want to have energy and feel happy'* **becomes** *'I feel grateful that I wake up full of energy and happy.'*

2 How do you want to feel as you go through your day?

Example answer: *'I want to feel calm and confident at work'* **becomes** *'I feel grateful that I go through my day calm and confident at work.'*

Now write down three personal goals that you would like to achieve in the next year. For example:

1 Buy a new house

2 Run 10km

3 Start to learn Spanish

Write the goals as if they are already true. For example, 'I am so grateful for our new house, that I am healthy enough to run 10km and that I have started to learn Spanish.'

Next, write down three professional goals that you would like to achieve in the next five years. For example:

1   Start my own business

2   Employ 30 people

3   Contribute to saving the planet with my sustainable
    energy business

Again, write them down as if they are already the case: 'I am so grateful I started my own thriving business and that I now employ 30 staff. I'm really grateful I am contributing to saving the world with my sustainable energy business.'

How do you feel after doing this exercise? Does it make you feel more positive about your future?

+ + +

Positive Motivation

THE COMBINATION OF being very clear and specific about what you want, visualising it with a high level of emotion, then taking small incremental steps will make your wish a reality.

As outlined in the Introduction (see page 23), most people look to the outside world first to make changes, but the key to manifesting what you wish for in your life is to create it first internally and *then* to be proactive in your external environment to make it happen.

The *motivation* behind your desires is also very important. If the motivation is one of greed or revenge it is unlikely that any visualisation will work, as the energy source is toxic. That is not to say that cruel people do not achieve their goals, but these people tend to employ manipulation and bullying to build their desires.

Letting go of *attachment* to the outcome is the last and final step in the manifesting process. If something you have been working on doesn't manifest for whatever reason, trust that it was not meant to be for you. This requires a flexible trust in both yourself and the universe.

Think back on your life and acknowledge that in the past there were things you believed you really wanted and maybe wished for greatly that did not transpire. However, in hindsight you might be pleased that some of these things did not happen. This was the universe protecting you. Let yourself flow with life, relaxed and open while you also consciously create your world of joy.

The heart of gratitude lies in the present moment and is in the many small wonders of the world: the yellow butterfly, the smile of a child, the laughter of friends, the colour of leaves in autumn, the rain on a rooftop, a river gushing down from a mountain. If you want to feel grateful, the message is simple: stay in the moment and get out into nature with the people you love. You are now ready to climb higher again towards the next step, the Hope Habit. Consider for a moment: What is life devoid of hope?

THREE KEY TAKEAWAYS FROM THIS CHAPTER:

1 You cannot feel grateful and anxious at the same time.

2 Gratitude is a social skill. Extend gratitude to others as a way of relinquishing any guilt you might feel for not being grateful enough.

3   Manifest what you want into the future to feel grateful
    now for what will be.

THE GRATITUDE HABIT
DAILY MINDFULNESS

+   Be heartfelt in expressing thanks to *everyone* who helps you, from
    the person who holds a door open to a family member who supports
    you. If you go to a foreign country and learn only one phrase, let that
    be 'thank you'.

+   Quit complaining – if you hear yourself complaining about a person
    or situation use the four-second positive pause technique to stop
    yourself. Journal minor frustrations rather than vocalising them.

+   Journal every day what you are grateful for and be specific – list at
    least three things, more if possible.

+   Use the 'thank you, my heart' meditation often (see page 252).

+   Bring back 'saying grace' at the dinner table; if you can, select one
    meal a day where the majority of the family is together. If this is only
    on a Sunday then do it. In turn, each person says three things they
    are grateful for that day. This is a really good way for children to learn
    the habit of expressing gratitude.

+   Pay it forward – do a favour for someone and expect nothing in
    return, whether it is giving someone change for the ticket machine or
    buying someone a coffee.

+   If you drive, make it a habit to let out every second car that you see
    in traffic, even when you are in a rush. If you take public transport,
    let someone behind you go first and give your seat to someone who
    needs it. Be on the lookout for ways to help others daily.

+ **Gratitude letter:** Make space in your schedule to write a letter of gratitude to a person who you feel has really helped you in some way. It could be someone you feel has not been thanked properly, a family member, a friend, a doctor or a teacher. For example, one of my clients wrote to her primary school teacher 30 years later to thank her for inspiring her when she was young. Write from the heart and explain in detail why you are grateful to him/her. If possible, post it or give it to them in person rather than doing it digitally as this has a greater impact.

AFFIRMATIONAL TOOTH BRUSHING

Repeat your gratitude habit affirmations every day while you brush your teeth.

MINDFUL SHOWERING

Take time as you shower and dry yourself to be loving and patient with yourself. Use this habit as a time to connect towards yourself without judgement.

ACKNOWLEDGE PROGRESS

Write down three examples of when you have practised the Gratitude Habit and shown evidence of your affirmations. For example, 'I extend my gratitude to everyone in my life, from my family to strangers. On Monday I thanked my mum for all her help with the kids by taking her out to lunch.'

1 I wake each morning filled with gratitude for all the blessings in my life.

2 I am grateful for who I am.

3 My heart is filled with gratitude for everyone in my life.

Now mark how you are feeling on the positivity sundial below.

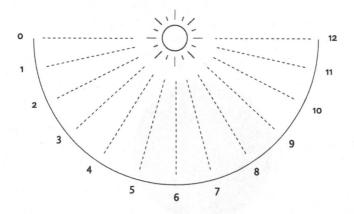

Remember to keep listening to your seven-minute morning and your sleep time hypnotherapies. On page 344, tick the days so far that you have listened. Remember, we are aiming for as close to 66 days as possible. Be proud of the times you have listened and don't give yourself a hard time if you have missed one or two days; that is okay – keep going!

 MEDITATIONS

+ Morning ritual

+ Sleep time hypnotherapy

+ Turn fear to gratitude

+ Thank you, my heart

THE HOPE HABIT

HOW TO BE FEARLESS

'Hope is a waking dream.'
ARISTOTLE

+

INTERRELATED

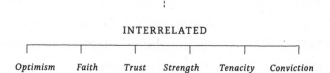

Optimism   Faith   Trust   Strength   Tenacity   Conviction

AFFIRMATIONAL
TOOTH BRUSHING

Write these affirmations in your journal. If you cannot remember the exact words, it doesn't matter, simply repeat to yourself, over and over as you brush, 'I am hopeful'.

1   Hope is in my heart, now and in the future.

2   I can cope with whatever the future may bring.

3   I turn walls into doors.

Note: *at the end of the chapter, I will ask you to write down three examples to support the affirmations. For example, in the case of number two you might write: 'I found out that I didn't get the job I applied for and I am now already looking for other opportunities; I am always hopeful.'*

KATE'S STORY, 44, HOMEMAKER

'I was always a "glass-half-full" kind of girl and full of fun. I was a mum with two wonderful kids that I had fought hard to have through five rounds of IVF, I had a lovely husband, great life, family and friends but somehow those things don't seem to matter when you suffer from anxiety which can be all-consuming. As a result, I found myself scared and losing my zest. These new emotions and feelings were alien to me, I simply did not know what was happening to me. The energy I was using to put on a front instead of making myself better was exhausting.

'I was heading for a crash but deep down knew there was hope buried there somewhere amongst my cluttered thoughts. I needed my mind and body to sync so when I stumbled on an article in a weekend paper about The Positive Habit online programme I cried, because the journalist seemed to be describing me. Here was the hope I was looking for.

'I registered for the programme and within a few days the veil started to lift – I really felt that the course was designed just for me. The hypnotherapies were like a lullaby at night and they would and still do send me off to the land of nod. After a few months, my mind had cleared and my days were bright again. Everything seemed so much more positive; I was laughing on the inside and out.

'I realised I had been suffering from a huge loss of confidence and a plethora of negative thoughts about feeling unworthy, coupled with a lot of guilt. The five IVF cycles had taken their toll on me; the stress and negativity stemmed from years of treatment and trying to conceive, and the many disappointments had led to my anxiety.

'On completion of the programme I felt a great sense of wellbeing, started to feel clearer and warm and fuzzy inside but I also started to feel physically sick and I thought, "what's going on?" Then, to my surprise I discovered I was seven weeks pregnant – for the first time in my life without IVF! I could not believe this little gift of positivity and hope had come into our lives. As this little miracle smiles up at me now with her toothless, wide grin she's living proof of how positive thinking can help. I can't believe it but in a funny way I'm glad I went through that angst as now I live more fully.

'I continue with Fiona's Sustaining Positivity programme and I use the tools and the techniques in my daily life, such as grasping the little, perfect parts of my day that root me in the present moment, like watching the kids play, looking at my garden, or hearing a song or a smell that evokes lovely memories.

'I am now a mum of three wonderful girls, I have a loving husband, great life, family and friends. The difference is I am now able to enjoy them all. Sometimes it is many small things that make big things happen. Hope for me is the strongest little word and thanks to The Positive Habit I hold on to hope now and for the future.'

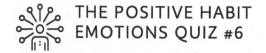

THE POSITIVE HABIT
EMOTIONS QUIZ #6

Please take the quiz now and allocate a point for each 'Yes' answer that you give. Go with the first answer that comes to mind and do not spend too much time thinking about the question.

1 Do you feel present most of the time?

2 Do you make time to care for your mind each day?

3 Do you love yourself?

4 Do you believe you are a compassionate person?

5 Are you able not to take anything other people do or say personally?

6 If you feel stress or anxiety, do you use your breath to calm your mind?

7 Do you protect your mind from negative information, people and places, for example having regular digital breaks/avoiding people who drain your energy?

8 Do you feel confident to speak your mind and feel equal to others?

9 Are you kind to yourself if you make a mistake?

10 Do you feel grateful each day?

11 Do you let go of grudges from the past?

12 Do you visualise a bright future?

13 Do you feel you are living your life purpose?

14 Do you take care of your physical needs, such as getting eight hours' sleep, exercising and eating a balanced diet?

15 Do you feel that you are good enough as a person?

16 Do you trust that no matter what happens you will be able to cope?

Score from quiz #1 on page 8 =
Score from quiz #2 on page 130 =
Score from quiz #3 on page 173 =
Score from quiz #4 on page 207 =
Score from quiz #5 on page 239 =
Score from quiz #6 =

Make a note of any progress If you see a shift forward, please acknowledge this fully and own it! What areas continue to need your attention? Keep learning about yourself.

+ + +

What Does Hope Mean to You?

THE WORD 'HOPE' in ancient Greek is *elpis*, meaning anticipating something positive in the future. Aristotle's view on hope was that we cannot cultivate hope without fear as they go hand in hand. He believed that having the courage to feel vulnerable and face fear are the key components of a hopeful person; after all, the certainty of the outcome we hope for cannot be guaranteed, so a hopeful person is also a brave one.

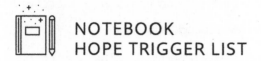

NOTEBOOK
HOPE TRIGGER LIST

Like all emotional states, hope is entirely personal. Take a moment to brainstorm and note down what hope means for you.

Here are some examples of what hope means to some of my clients:

+ That concrete slab to hold on to when everything else in my life shatters like glass

+ It's what gets me through my darkest days

+ A better life for my children than I have had

+ Realising that nothing is set in stone

+ It is all we have and it's what keeps the magic in life

+ Knowing I can cope

+ Being resilient

+ That everything will be okay

+ The only thing I have left

+ Something that produces miracles

+ The energy I need to continue

+ That everything is happening for a reason

THE HABIT LOOP OF HOPE

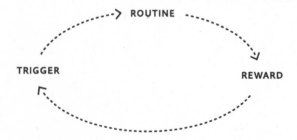

Use your positive trigger list to help you to create the habit of hope.

1 **Positive trigger** – knowing I can cope.

2 **Positive routine** – taking seven deep belly breaths.

3 **Positive reward** – feeling hopeful.

+ + +

Hope – the Fifth Emotional Habit

'Practice hope. As hopefulness becomes a habit, you can achieve a permanently happy spirit.'

NORMAN VINCENT PEALE

HOPE HAS AN INTANGIBLE, visceral quality to it. It inhabits a world that you cannot see or touch and incorporates a fantastical desire for something to improve. Hope is the human spirit at its best and is a consistent trait that positive people exhibit.

At this stage in the book you are emotionally resilient enough to fully embrace hope; the positive energy you have cultivated in feeling present, loved, calm, confident and grateful gives you every reason to be hopeful. Hope gives us the will to live when we have nothing else and without it, we wither and die both metaphorically and literally.

In this chapter we will examine how to hold on to hope in an uncertain world, how coupling hope with the neuroscience of mindfulness can help you, how the concept of compassion-based resilience works, and, as always, I will demonstrate how to create the Hope Habit in a very practical way.

While conducting research on hope I myself became really hopeful when I discovered Dr Shane Lopez, the world's leading authority on the science of hope. But during my research my new source of hope died, literally; Shane Lopez died suddenly in 2016 at the age of only 47, leaving behind a wife and son. My heart dropped when I read this, almost as if he were a personal friend. What happens to hope when the leading voice of hope is gone?

Lopez, like Viktor Frankl (see pages 62, 238) has left the world with a strong message about the true meaning of hope, which can be found even in the saddest of circumstances, like his own untimely death. Lopez defined hope as having three essential qualities: it is a choice, it can be learned and it is contagious. It is worth noting that these qualities also apply to the six core positive emotions.[65]

To remain hopeful in what appears to be a hopeless situation is what ultimately gives suffering meaning.

Barack Obama wrote the book *The Audacity of Hope – Thoughts on Reclaiming the American Dream* in 2006, just three months before he began and ultimately won the presidential campaign. Few had dared to hope that there would ever be a black president of the USA, especially when you consider the nation's history of slavery, civil war and the civil rights movement, with the assassination of Martin Luther King only 40 years before.

Hope makes the intangible real, the metaphysical physical.

Many positive people have used hope to rise above the self to create legacies that have changed the world. They refuse to be held back by the countless obstacles in their paths. Einstein is an example of this – he didn't learn to talk until he was four, failed the entrance exams to a technical school at 16, and worked as a salesman before he went on to become one of the greatest minds of all time. Another example is Oprah Winfrey, the most successful TV personality ever. She was born into poverty, sexually abused, which led to a pregnancy when she was just 14 years old, and gave birth prematurely to a baby who sadly died soon after. Her spirit has lifted the hearts of people all over the world. In an interview with David Letterman, she explained, 'I really did believe there was a power greater than myself.'

We can see in these and countless other examples that hope is paramount to overcoming tragedy, loss, illness or relationship breakups. Yet we misuse the word 'hope' for things that are well within our control and have nothing to do with tragedy. For example, 'I hope to go to the gym later.' Using the word 'hope' in this way implies that things are beyond your control, but the reality is usually the opposite. Life is uncertain enough; do not add any more ambiguity than you are already exposed to. Be decisive in both your speech and your actions.

Hope is too precious a commodity to take lightly: it needs to be nurtured and used correctly.

Bringing hope and optimism to the fore during difficult periods in your life will build your emotional resilience enough to navigate your way through these stormy waters. Many of us hold back on hope in much the same way we do with happiness, regarding it with suspicion. Don't let unwarranted fear keep you limited and stuck in negative habit loops. Dare to hope!

+ + +

Take the Fear Out of Hope

Being afraid to hope for a positive outcome is common and understandable, especially when the outcome is something you really want, for example having a bid accepted on a house you are trying to buy or getting the all-clear on a health condition. It can seem easier to prepare for the worst because that way you will not be disappointed if you do not get the desired result. Consider, though, that the time spent fearing for the worst is time that could equally be used to hope for the best and by doing this your body and mind will be at their optimum levels and be far more able to handle bad news *if* it comes.

To remove fear, base your hope not just on the desired outcome but on your ability to cope with the situation either way.

For example, if your bid for the house is not successful, acknowledge that you did your best and hope that a better house comes on the market. If you don't get the all-clear for the health condition, you will have more energy to deal with the illness. By being present, loving yourself, breathing calmly and, above all, having faith in yourself, you have every reason to hope. Ultimately there is no finer feeling than to know that you will be able to manage no matter what life throws at you. This is at the core of the six positive habits and is the view you enjoy from the top of the ladder.

How would you describe your outlook on life? Whether you describe yourself as an optimist, a pessimist or a realist, ultimately, we all want the best outcome in a difficult situation –

we just express it differently. For example, imagine the case of a sick mother who has three adult children. One is an optimist, one a pessimist and one a realist. The pessimist will predict the worst possible outcome, the optimist will focus on manifesting good news and the realist will keep an open mind and prepare himself/herself for either outcome. The difference is that the optimist has removed the fear and as a result has the resources to take action to support their hope regardless of the results.

Hope, when it is channelled through love and not fear, is life-changing.

+ + +

Hope for Now, Hope for the Future

Hope can be used as a positive force to create a better future for yourself and ultimately for the world even when there is no immediate tragedy, challenge or loss. You may just feel that your life is stagnant, that you are languishing. In this scenario hope can help you build your desired future now.

In the neuroscience of mindfulness there are two states. [66]

1 **The default mode network** (DMN) is a ruminative state where you are not focused on a particular task and are not fully present. For example, you may be chatting to your kids but at the same time worrying about a meeting at work tomorrow. In the default mode, the amygdala, which you may recall is the alarm bell of the mind (see page 82), is activated and this induces

stress and anxiety. This is why it is important to pay attention to what is unfolding in your life, moment-by-moment.

The default mode network was serendipitously discovered by Randy Buckner, Professor of Psychology and Neuroscience at Harvard University, when his team were analysing hundreds of MRI scans.[67] They discovered that when the brain is in baseline mode with nothing specific to do it will focus on the future and ruminate on the past. It is not present in the moment.

When the brain is at 'rest' we enter the daydreaming state which, contrary to popular belief, is not necessarily full of amazing fantasies but is usually quite mundane and often makes plans. For example, it may be thinking about whether there is time to have dinner before going out or if it is a good idea to go to the gym. This constant stream of micro-planning can put pressure on the mind and body. It should also be pointed out that the default mode can be more prone to the negativity bias.

2 **The task-positive network** (TPN) is an active state of being present in the here and now. When the TPN is activated, we relinquish rumination and worry; there is no past, no future, only the now. This will be further discussed in the Happiness Habit, as it is connected with 'flow', a state where we are highly engaged in what we are doing at that moment.

> **Consciously deciding to use hope as the lever to bring you from one state to another is powerful.**

Activating the TPN allows you to let go of petty mind wandering and embrace the full capacity of an awakened mind. Your planning mind is free to hope for what you wish to happen, and you then take actionable steps towards making this happen – see the previous chapter on how to manifest your desires (page 235).

The great thing about these two systems is that only one of them can be activated at any one time. As soon as you become aware of what's happening you shut down the DPM and the TPN goes into full positive flow. Now please write the answers to the following questions in your notebook.

NOTEBOOK
FUTURE PLANNING

1 How much of your time do you think you spend in the default mode network?

2 How often does your mind wander to the future, planning everyday things in the short term? All the time, hourly, daily or weekly?

3 How much of time do you spend in the task-positive network?

4 How often do you consciously visualise everything that you hope for? Look back to the work you did in the Gratitude Habit chapter and let yourself again focus on making all of those wonderful things your reality this time with the added ingredient of hope without fear.

5 What action can you take today to build the future you hope for? Each day do one small thing that gets you closer. Each small step is progress and it is vital you acknowledge it.

The Human Capacity for Hope

WHEN YOU OPENED this book and started to read it, you did so because of hope. Without hope there can be no action. When I meet a new client, I can often feel a heavy mix of hope and fear in his or her heart. As you read this book, listen to your morning and sleep time audios and complete the exercises, you are stepping into the unknown and it is hope and courage that propel you forward. The time you have dedicated to yourself illustrates the human capacity to make progress and to hope for better for yourself. I thank you for your hope.

A couple of years ago, I was invited to facilitate a series of charity workshops with a group of women who had been homeless and were now in sheltered accommodation. The charity helps women to rebuild their lives, not just by providing shelter but also by healing through the support of their community. Before my first workshop I was nervous; part of me doubted myself – how could I help these women who had lived through such great traumas? Many of them were from broken homes, had been separated from their children and suffered sexual and emotional abuse, a place very far from my privileged world and that of the majority of my private clients. Surviving on the streets, I imagine, takes a courage that is difficult to comprehend unless we too have suffered such conditions.

I did, however, *hope* that I could help the women and was determined to do so to the best of my ability.

The very first thing I did was to help the women feel safe by encouraging them to trust me and the work that I do. One of the women was very cynical and closed, and she laughed at and scorned my ideas. My heart ached for her but I did not stop trying to gently reach her as I knew that if I didn't I would lose the opportunity to help her and the rest of the women. I smiled at her and laughed at myself when she made fun of me and gradually she started to open up and the group had a chance to bond.

I could see that despite their traumatic experiences there was an energy of support and hope in their community. Hope was all I needed and over the weeks we embarked on a journey that saw many of the women move forward, step by step. The safer they felt, the more their hearts opened; women who would not even make eye contact with the rest of the group a few weeks previously were by the end happily going along with my hugging exercises! Ironically perhaps, the lady who had been the most sceptical in the beginning experienced one of the greatest perspective shifts and requested more hypnotherapy audios as they helped her sleep. Without their seeds of hope and my tenacity, I am certain little or no progress would have been made. Hope, as Dr Lopez pointed out, is contagious.

+ + +

Compassion-Based Resilience

THE TERM 'RESILIENCE' is one that is used a lot nowadays. Its Latin root, *resiliens*, means 'to rebound', and this is where the term 'to bounce back' originates. To be hopeful is one of the most important attributes of an emotionally resilient person.

Compassion-based resilience is a concept I have developed that focuses on compassion and kindness rather than judgement or pressure to keep you strong.

 IMAGINEERING

1 *Take seven deep belly breaths.*

2 *Think of something that is resilient, like a good pair of shoes, a beautiful antique, a reliable handbag – an item that was made to last and to stand the test of time and that you can depend on.*

3 *Now think of a person you know who matches this description, someone who, despite the challenges of life, always seems to bounce back smiling and positive. How do they do it? There are usually two key components.*

   + *Hopefulness is a habit they have cultivated.*

   + *They have learned to be kind to themselves when they are faced with pressure.*

 NOTEBOOK
CHALLENGES

Take a moment to consider and answer these questions in your journal:

1 When faced with a challenge, do you allow yourself to feel and work through the emotions that the difficulty has brought up for you?

2 Are you compassionate with yourself when you face a challenge?

3 Are you hard on others if they do not meet your expectations?

4 Are you hard on yourself if you do not meet your own expectations or those others have of you?

The Strength in Feeling Emotions

RESILIENCE IS OFTEN mistakenly seen as the ability to be emotionally strong. The concept of 'keeping a stiff upper lip' was commonly promoted in previous generations who were taught that to show emotions was a weakness and that it was necessary to be emotionally strong.

Repression of emotions ultimately leads to far greater pain than suffering the actual pain of the emotion at the time it is felt. For example, someone who does not give themselves the necessary time and space to grieve after a loss but instead pushes away or denies the pain each time it arises may eventually become sick; the trapped emotion in the body will cause damage both physically and mentally to them and to their families, possibly for generations.

Compassion-based resilience brings a more open and caring attitude to emotional pain, based on building the strength to sit with and face uncomfortable emotions.

Rejection is one of the most painful emotions, particularly when we are young. The anterior insula and the anterior cingulate cortex areas of the brain that are associated with physical pain also light up when we feel emotional pain like rejection. The thing is, the brain does not know the difference between physical pain and emotional pain. One of the many studies that highlights this phenomenon looked at the brains of 500 people who had recently suffered an unwanted breakup with a partner. When a picture of their loved one was shown, 'activation in these regions was highly diagnostic of physical pain, with positive predictive values up to 88%.[68]

You will have experienced rejection at some stage in your life – it happens to everyone. True resilience stems from the ability to depersonalise the exclusion and, most important, to remain a faithful friend to yourself. Cultivating this attitude will help to quickly heal your wounded soul.

Some examples of practising compassion-based resilience are:

+ Having the courage to be truly authentic, open and honest with yourself and those you care about by, for example, having an awkward conversation that you've been putting off.

+ Showing remorse if you have behaved unfairly and then showing yourself compassion for the reasons behind your behaviour.

+ Showing vulnerability to others by, for example, admitting when you don't know something or if you have made a mistake.

+ Naming unnecessary shame and being aware not to personally carry the weight of other people's issues.

+ Choosing to see the best in others even when they have behaved unkindly towards you. This goes back to not taking anything personally.

+ Remaining calm when emotions are high and taking steps after an event to release emotions in a healthy way by doing something like jogging, meditation, journaling or talking to the person concerned when the situation has cooled; this is emotional intelligence at its highest.

Hope in Loss

IF YOU HAVE recently suffered any type of loss you have my deepest sympathy. You are likely to be suffering a plethora of confusing and conflicting emotions from distress to sadness and your sleeping and eating patterns may be negatively affected. I sincerely hope and desire that following this book helps you to feel better, more empowered and more positive.

While we all deal with loss differently, it is important that you give yourself permission to cry.

Tears are a gift from the universe. Cry whenever you need to.

If you've been holding back tears you might find that they can spring up in uncomfortable places, like at work or on an evening out, and this may make you feel out of control, exposed and vulnerable. It is better to pre-empt these outbursts by crying in a place where you feel safe and with someone you love. However, if you do cry in public, so what? There is no shame in it and most of us have been there at some stage. Let the passing of time be your friend. Be very, very gentle with yourself, conserve your energy and rest when you can. Walk in nature, write your journal, spend time with people you trust and those who have a genuine desire to help you.

Do you recall Paddy's story from page 128? Paddy suffered the greatest loss imaginable, the death of a child. But, being a positive person, he no longer focuses upon what he has lost but the precious time he had with his son. Consequently, Paddy is not bitter about his tragedy, feeling instead that his son is with him every day, safe in his heart.

Hope and faith keep those we love eternally alive in our hearts.

I know from personal experience that one of the hardest things about suffering a bereavement is that life seems just to go on as if the dead person had never existed: buses come and go, people go to work, emails and phone calls are answered, the wheels of the world continue to turn while your heart is immobilised with pain. Like Paddy, I have come to understand that while life continues, it also changes because I change. The spirit of the loved one who has passed away lives on through me in the decisions I make and the work that I do.

+ + +

Turn Walls into Doors

NICK VUJICIC is an Australian/Serbian religious motivational speaker who was born with tetra-amelia, an extremely rare condition whereby the sufferer has no limbs and can thus operate physically only from his/her torso. In his TEDx talk 'Overcoming Hopelessness' Vujicic explains that after being bullied for years because of his 'dwarf' status he was without hope and at ten years old he tried to take his own life.

Fortunately, Nick's parents were very loving and supportive and always told him he was beautiful just the way he was. His parents actually taught him the power of choice, that he could focus on all that he had – a fully functional torso. Nick's epiphany came when he realised that he would actually be creating a burden for his parents rather than relieving them of one, if he killed himself.

The hope he felt as a result of this enabled him to continue and made him stronger and more resilient. His inspirational TEDx closes with him telling us, 'If I can dream big, so can you, there are no walls, find your peace, and you will make your walls, doors.'[69]

To actually turn a wall into a door, you need a hammer and a lot of strength and determination. Metaphorically speaking, it is much the same, minus the hammer. You are much stronger emotionally than you may give yourself credit for – often it is just a case of finding your strength.

NOTEBOOK
TURNING WALLS INTO DOORS

1   Take seven deep belly breaths.

2   Write down the three most difficult life events that happened in your childhood from the period 0 to 16 years old. Focus on establishing facts, not the emotions.

3   Write down the three most difficult times in your adulthood from the period 16 years old to now. Again, focus on facts, not emotions.

4   Acknowledge that we have all had difficult life events; don't compare yours with those that others may have experienced – what is minor to someone else may be major to you and vice versa.

Don't dwell on the past because it is the past – learn from it.

Now, review your two lists and using the wisdom of hindsight, find a positive lesson in each one. You will find when you look with insight at a situation that it has improved because of the difficult times.

Look at this example from a client of mine.

SARAH, 34

Childhood – 0 to 16 years old

1 Having to move primary school and house three times, because of my dad's job. Positive outcome – I make friends easily now and am not attached to being in one place.

2 Parents always arguing – I have learned with time not to shout at my husband if I am annoyed, I breathe deeply and cool down.

3 My grandfather, who I loved, died when I was 13 so I learned early on the meaning of death. Now I feel like he is still with me and guiding me from above.

Adulthood – 16 to 34 years old

1 Breaking up with a long-term boyfriend at 28 but now I can see that this gave me the opportunity to meet and fall in love with my husband.

2 Being made redundant during the recession but this enabled me to start a new career I love but would never have considered if I hadn't lost my job.

3 Having a miscarriage. Now, I remain hopeful I will get pregnant again soon and I know it is at least possible.

Out of what appears difficult, unexpected opportunities can appear, turning walls into doors.

When you feel lost or down, read the two lists you made and let them remind you of the importance of holding on to hope and that positive change and transformation are possible.

It is a law of physics that a vacuum must be filled with something. Similarly, when we lose something a space for the new to enter is created.

Hope lifts the soul. It is the energy from which everything unseen is created. The farmer who plants his field without knowing if it will rain, the teacher who sees the potential in a student who is unruly, the entrepreneur who creates an empire with no money are all built on hope.

Hope opens the door for you to take the final step upwards on the ladder of happiness. You may be surprised when you arrive that happiness is not a destination in isolation, but a journey that continues in each precious moment of your life.

THREE KEY TAKEAWAYS FROM THIS CHAPTER:

1 Never be afraid to hope. Let love guide you, not fear.

2 You can choose to move from the default network of rumination in your brain to the task-positivity network by coupling the Now Habit with hope.

3 Turn walls into doors; learning from past challenges will help you see that you have already overcome many difficulties.

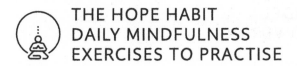

THE HOPE HABIT
DAILY MINDFULNESS
EXERCISES TO PRACTISE

+ Consciously direct your daydreams away from mundane planning and create an extraordinary future in great detail.

+ Find a piece of music that encapsulates hope for you. Listen to this any time you feel the smallest grain of hopelessness.

- When you are faced with bad news, big or small, give yourself time to process it, feel the emotions as they arise and use your breath to calm and soothe you. Let tears flow if they are there.

- Instil hope in others – if someone tells you of their future plans, no matter how far-fetched they may appear, encourage them. Do this especially with young people who are very suggestible and also vulnerable.

- Use the word 'hope' only when it is appropriate. Stop yourself from using it too lightly and change it to the affirmative. For example, change 'I hope we win the match,' to 'we will win the match.' The outcome is not what is important, it is the intention that counts.

- Look at the list from the 'turning walls into doors' exercise (page 287) when you face any challenges in your life.

AFFIRMATIONAL TOOTH BRUSHING

Repeat your hope habit affirmations every day while you brush your teeth, feeling the emotion as much as possible.

MINDFUL SHOWERING

Take time as you shower and dry yourself to be loving and patient with yourself. Use this habit as a time to connect towards yourself without judgement.

ACKNOWLEDGE
PROGRESS

Write down three examples of when you have practised the Hope Habit and shown evidence of your affirmations:

+ I can cope with whatever the future may bring.

+ Hope is in my heart, now and in the future.

+ I turn walls into doors.

Now mark how you are feeling on the positivity sundial below.

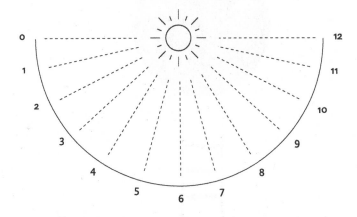

Remember to keep listening to your seven-minute morning and your sleep time hypnotherapies. On page 344, tick the days that you have listened so far. I hope you are really feeling the benefit of this continued practice. Be proud of the times you have listened and don't give your-self a hard time if you have missed one or two days; that is okay – keep going!

THE HAPPINESS HABIT

HOW TO CHOOSE HAPPINESS

'Happiness and freedom begin with a clear understanding of one principle. Some things are within your control and some things are not.'

EPICTETUS

+

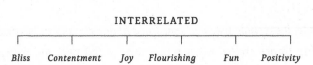

INTERRELATED

Bliss   Contentment   Joy   Flourishing   Fun   Positivity

AFFIRMATIONAL TOOTH BRUSHING

Repeat these silently to yourself when you brush your teeth. If you cannot remember the exact words, simply repeat, 'I am happy'.

1 I am responsible for my own happiness.

2 I spend time with people who make me happy and I do things that bring me joy.

3 I spread my happiness to everyone I meet.

Please note that at the end of the chapter, I will ask you to write down three examples to support the affirmations. For example, 'This week I rang Laura because she always makes me laugh and I spent time drawing as that brings me joy.'

KEITH'S STORY, 35, LAWYER

'My wife and I have just had our first child. My own childhood and teenage years were not the happiest, to say the least. The unsettling and traumatic experiences from my childhood and attitude of my parents wired me to believe I was worthless and deserving of nothing positive in my life. I always struggled to plug into life, to experience joy, to appreciate gratitude for all I have and was very numb to events both positive and negative. This feeling of numbness was like looking at life through a glass wall and I felt detached from life and the people I love. I felt I was worthless, incapable of anything and lacking hugely in terms of confidence which had an impact on my choices professionally and so I felt stuck.

'My wife, a psychologist, was concerned about me and in particular my inability to get excited when things were going well, for example, the

news that we were expecting our first baby. It's not that I wasn't happy, I just didn't feel as happy as I would have liked to be about something so wonderful.

'I was curious about how hypnotherapy would work and was open to trying any approach that would help. I had done CBT many years ago and found it great. Working with Fiona was transformational in that it helped me to live in the present moment and truly experience life. Her approach rewired my thought processes to appreciate myself, to be more caring to myself and to feel I was worthy of life. I now see that I have so much in life to be grateful for and I feel my lived experience is much happier. I catch negative thoughts and feelings before they run away on me.

'I won't lie, those negative beliefs from my childhood do arise from time to time but when they do I don't let them progress and take over. I now shut them down quickly with kindness. This ability to manage my thoughts has given me confidence and positive self-awareness and the fact that I manage them allows me to feel happy. I am more confident professionally and more present with my family and live for and enjoy experiences now that in the past I was completely numb to. To keep mentally fit I listen to Fiona's audio recordings and supplement them with exercise and apps like Headspace. I started to feel better from the first or second session. I have made it a habit to listen to the audios and they are brilliant at sustaining and cementing the positive suggestions from the sessions. They have not only helped me to sleep but I now have deeper and more restful sleep.

'I am very grateful to have worked through my issues with Fiona and I feel genuinely happy now. I am overjoyed when I can look into my son's eyes and know that the best gift I give to him is a happy father who is fully present. I intend to teach him all I have learned and hope that through my courage and kindness he will never have to feel those awful negative emotions that had become my daily diet.'

THE POSITIVE HABIT
EMOTIONS QUIZ #7

Please take the quiz now and allocate a point for each 'Yes' answer that you give. Go with the first answer that comes to mind and do not spend too much time thinking about the question.

1 Do you feel present most of the time?

2 Do you make time to care for your mind each day?

3 Do you love yourself?

4 Do you believe you are a compassionate person?

5 Are you able not to take anything other people do or say personally?

6 If you feel stress or anxiety, do you use your breath to calm your mind?

7 Do you protect your mind from negative information, people and places, for example having regular digital breaks/avoiding people who drain your energy?

8 Do you feel confident to speak your mind and feel equal to others?

9 Are you kind to yourself if you make a mistake?

10 Do you feel grateful each day?

11 Do you let go of grudges from the past?

12 Do you visualise a bright future?

13 Do you feel you are living your life purpose?

14 Do you take care of your physical needs, such as getting eight hours' sleep, exercising and eating a balanced diet?

15 Do you feel that you are good enough as a person?

16 Do you trust that no matter what happens you will be
able to cope?

Score from quiz #1 on page 8 =

Score from quiz #7 =

*Compare only the score from your first and last quiz. What difference
can you see? Acknowledge all progress.*

+ + +

What Does Happiness
Mean to You?

IN ARISTOTELIAN PHILOSOPHY, habit and happiness are eternally
intertwined. The word *eudaimonia* in ancient Greek translates
to 'happiness' or more specifically to 'flourishing' or 'thriving.'
In Aristotle's most celebrated body of work, *Nicomachean Ethics*,
he speculates on the nature of happiness and asks what people
need in order to live 'the good life'. The answer, he believes, lies
in employing the rational mind to lead you to do right actions to
reach your highest ideal through virtue, both intellectually and in
your character. Happiness is thus viewed as an active rather than
a passive state. Happiness isn't something that just happens to
you, you *make* it happen.

NOTEBOOK
HAPPINESS TRIGGER LIST

Take a moment to brainstorm and write down in your notebook what happiness means for you, when you most feel it and how. Happiness, of all the six positive emotional habits, is the most subjective; we all see happiness differently, so it is important for you to do this exercise.

Here are some examples from my clients to help you get started.

Happiness is:

+ Being carefree and relaxed in my day, no matter where I am or what I am doing

+ Being present to the moment

+ Feeling loved

+ Being in nature

+ Laughing with friends

+ Feeling full of positive, healthy energy

+ Being at home with my family

+ Having peace of mind on my own

+ Fishing and watching the dawn rise

+ Creating art

+ Reading my book

+ My child's smile

+ Being able to enjoy the small things in life

+ Helping other people

Eleanor Roosevelt once said,

> 'Someone once asked me what I regarded as the three most important requirements for happiness. My answer was, a feeling that you have been honest with yourself and those around you; a feeling that you have done the best you could both in your personal life and in your work; and the ability to love others.'

THE HABIT LOOP OF HAPPINESS

The list of things that make you happy now becomes your happy trigger list.

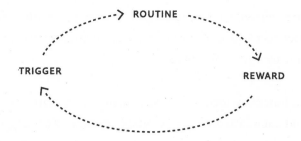

1 **Happy trigger** – being in nature
2 **Happy routine** – family walks every Sunday afternoon
3 **Happy reward** – feeling happy

Happiness – the Sixth Emotional Habit

'Happiness shouldn't be a goal, it should be a habit.'

RICHARD BRANSON

CONGRATULATIONS! I'm so happy you have reached the sixth and final emotional habit, happiness. You are now ready to take that ultimate step on the ladder towards the sun, the moon and the stars. Each rung supports you in this elevated position from where you now look at the world with a fresh perspective. Each emotional habit is, as you know, built on the strong foundation of being present in the moment and in your ability to ask yourself where you are now as opposed to where you would prefer to be. Being present sustains contentment rather than generating a state of striving.

The natural flow from love to calmness, confidence, gratitude and hope all lead cumulatively to emotional happiness. At times, one particular emotional habit may be needed more than another. For example, you may need to feel calm if you are stressed and this will again lead to your happiness. At other times you may need to cultivate hope if things are hard and again this ultimately leads to your emotional happiness. Regardless of the situation:

If you want to be happy your internal world must be richer than your external world.

Ultimately, we all have an innate desire to be happy and practising the six emotional habits will enable you to reach self-actualisation and pursue excellence in all that you do.

This chapter examines why pleasure does not lead to happiness, why happiness is a choice that takes great courage and, most important, it will show you *how* to foster happiness in your daily life, mindfully and lovingly.

The pursuit of happiness is a lifelong habit and one that needs a full heart and a peaceful mind. You may recall that happiness, presence and love are the natural default states of the unconditioned mind and therefore the quest is to return to this natural state rather than longing to create it. Happy people are not 'happy' all the time, which is not possible nor desirable.

'Trying' to be happy makes us desperately unhappy.

To be authentically happy you need to be able to feel the full range of emotions *including* negative ones such as anger, sadness and anxiety. Having the courage to turn towards emotional pain with love, especially when you feel disappointed or hurt by the actions of others, will build an inner resilience and calmness.

Eighty per cent of my clients identify that they want to be 'happier'. This is common – while many people are not unhappy, they also sense that they could be happier from the emotional imprints on their hearts and minds which remind them of times when they laughed more easily, felt joy each day and connected more closely with other people. The feeling that there must be 'more' to life, or feelings of numbness (like Keith earlier, page 294), indicate that we need to fully feel and connect with our emotions.

+ + +

The Feeling of Knowing
That We're Alive

POSITIVE PSYCHOLOGY is concerned primarily with helping people to rise above numbness and lack of joy to experience the state of 'flourishing'. Latest research in the science of happiness illustrates the power of having a positive mindset both for the prevention and treatment of disease.[70]

The two leading causes of the death in the United States are: first, lifestyle (poor diet, smoking and stress, lack of exercise); and second, the medication prescribed to deal with the poor lifestyle choices.[71] People generally make poor lifestyle choices because of lack of education, coupled with unhappiness. Sadly, in many cases, they don't have access to the appropriate mental health care that they desperately need. Prescribing medication for anxiety and depression is the default treatment and while it may offer a worthwhile short-term 'bridge' for some (placebo or otherwise), it does not deal with the root cause of the issue or empower people with the confidence or responsibility to help themselves to get better and to stay better.

Happiness is not something that we can prescribe – or is it?

Dr Mark Rowe, an Irish GP and author of *A Prescription for Happiness*, believes that it can be. Like Dr Deepak Chopra, Rowe questions the prevalent medical model and runs his practice holistically, having noticed that happier and more positive patients rarely got sick. In addition, they usually had healthier habits and recovered more quickly when they did get ill. Internationally, there is now a shift among the medical community and conferences on 'lifestyle medicine' have really taken off. Thankfully, there is a growing recognition of the importance of lifestyle for health and its interconnected nature; what you eat, how often you move your body, how many hours you sleep, what information you listen to, who you spend your time with and how you care for your heart and soul all contribute to your level of health and happiness.

NOTEBOOK
PLEASURE VERSUS HAPPINESS

1 Take a moment to list the things that bring you pleasure.

2 Now refer back to the list you wrote on what happiness means for you at the beginning of this chapter.

Can you see a difference in the type of activities in the two lists? You will notice perhaps that the pleasure-seeking activities are more external, transitory and superficial, for example, shopping for new clothes or drinking a glass of wine. The 'happy list' will be more about connection and internal peace, for example hugging your family or going for a walk in nature.

Epicurus, a major figure in ancient Greek philosophy and science, is famous for the idea that seeking pleasure is the worthiest of values. The word 'hedonism' comes from the ancient Greek word for pleasure, *hēdonē*. The people of Athens believed that Epicurus was a man of indulgence in all that he did, having orgies and gorging on food and drink so much that, it was rumoured, he had to make himself physically ill twice a day in order to cope with the amounts he consumed. However, such gossip among the Athenians was far from the truth and Epicurus's views on pleasure were far from what we view as hedonistic behaviour today. The pleasure he truly sought was in the simple life; he valued the company of his friends above all and he had a modest home where he established his 'pleasure garden' for friends and students to meet and discuss life. True pleasure, according to Epicurus, lies not in extravagance and luxury but in the pleasure of attaining inner tranquillity and in the meeting of minds between people.[72]

Many of us make the common mistake of confusing temporary pleasures with happiness. The emotional part of your brain is wired to seek pleasure and avoid pain. It is therefore not your fault that you seek out pleasure; it is an evolutionary process. The problem is that pleasures that form part of an unhealthy lifestyle can lead to heart disease or diabetes, two of the most common diseases.

Constantly seeking pleasure makes us fundamentally unhappy: pleasure quickly turns to displeasure.

If you live in a constant state of seeking your next pleasure, you are never content with what is now, the present moment, which is all we ever really have. It is a mistake to defer happiness to the future, to believe that you will be more fulfilled or happier at some future time. Genuine happiness means having a peaceful and rich inner life with no need to escape the self via transitory pleasures like eating, drinking, shopping, smoking and gambling, which give us a temporary, addictive dopamine hit. This does not mean you should become puritanical in your lifestyle choices; a glass of wine in the evening or an ice cream on a hot day are pleasures and enjoyable but they do not make you happier. But if you are suffering inner turmoil or are dealing with external conflict a glass of wine or an ice cream may distract you for a while; they cannot deliver the serenity you seek.

Creating positive habits that encourage you to turn towards yourself with love and compassion will certainly lead to your overall happiness. Listening to the hypnotherapy audios, journalling, going for a walk, meditating, spending quality time with friends and family and taking mindful moments are all habits used by positive people to create inner peace and happiness.

+ + +

The Courage to be Happy

'Do not cherish the unworthy desire that the changeable might become unchanging.'

THE BUDDHA

POSITIVE AND HAPPY people tend to share the trait of being courageous. The fear that everything we have could disappear holds many of us back from authentic happiness. Trying to control the uncertainties in your life will drive happiness away in much the same way as trying to control a partner will drive them away. Set them free and they will come to you. Let life flow and it will be abundant.

Have you ever felt nostalgic for the present moment?

In a conversation with mindfulness expert Rick Hanson he commented that there is 'no need for the fear, people are afraid that if they feel happy they will lower their guard, however, the opposite is true, it is possible to be happy and at the same time be vigilant'. He went on to explain, 'peak performers tend to be happy because they are in a position to sustain the high level of performance that cannot be sustained by those who are driven by fear'.[73] Ask yourself again, are you motivated by fear or love?

Remember, your choices matter.

**Making peace with impermanence is an
established route to courageous happiness.**

The knowledge that you will die should not be feared but accepted as the natural order of life. Would you want to live for ever and if so, what meaning would your life have? If we lived for ever what would we achieve? Complacency and lack of motivation are already common characteristics. Oscar Wilde's famous character Dorian Gray is a case in point. Narcissistically determined to stay young for ever, he found himself alone, unhappy and distraught. His life ultimately had no meaning.

In times of war, people often live as if each day is their last. They have a heightened sense of the present and are able to flow and live in the moment. Unfortunately, this is often coupled with forms of hedonism and gives rise to the confusion that such pleasure-seeking will make them happy.

+ + +

Your Happy Brain

MATTHIEU RICARD, a French monk, became known as the world's happiest man after he participated in one of the most conclusive neuroscientific studies on what the brain actually looks like. After wiring 256 sensors to Ricard's brain Richard Davidson and his team at the University of Wisconsin were stunned: 'the scans showed that when meditating on compassion, Ricard's brain produces a level of gamma waves (those linked to consciousness, attention, learning, and memory) never reported before in the neuroscience literature.' In addition, 'the scans also showed excessive activity in his brain's left prefrontal cortex compared to its right counterpart, allowing him an abnormally large capacity for happiness and a reduced propensity towards negativity.'[74]

As you listen to the hypnotherapy audios and practise the meditation/visualisation exercises you are actually creating the neurochemicals and firing the neural networks that will cause your brain to become happy.

+ + +

The Inner Laboratory of the Mind

LET'S HAVE A LOOK at the chemicals in the brain and nervous system that dictate moods.

Endorphins – these are produced in the central nervous system and help to soften physical pain.

+ The best way to create them is by doing aerobic exercise for at least 30 minutes. Walking fast, running, working out at the gym, basically anything that gets the heart racing will have you pumped full of endorphins, which is why we always feel better after exercise. Please note, though, that it is not possible to exercise away unwanted emotions. They will still be there no matter how far you run.

Serotonin – this is probably the queen of the 'happy' chemicals and the one most commonly used in medication for depression.

+ You can create this chemical for yourself every day by getting as much sunlight as possible. Using a UV lamp in winter can also help.

+ Positive thoughts create serotonin, so all the work you are doing with the affirmations and audios will make a significant difference.

+ Nutritional therapy also has a vital role to play: eat foods that are high in tryptophan, an amino acid that aids growth, a stable mood, and a good night's sleep. Foods rich in tryptophan include nuts, seeds, tofu, cheese, red meat, chicken, turkey, fish, oats, beans, lentils and eggs.

Dopamine – this is most commonly known as the 'reward' chemical which as you now know plays a huge role in habit formation. Dopamine is released when we feel we have hit a target or reached a goal, which can be a very positive thing, but the problem is that in the digital age our brains are constantly receiving dopamine hits in the form of emails, computer games and social media interaction. These are perceived by the brain as goal completions, but unfortunately, as with addictive drugs, we need more and more hits to get the level of reward (in this case dopamine) we require.

+ A far healthier way to produce dopamine that will, in fact, lead to genuine happiness as opposed to exhaustion is by helping others whether at work, with your family or by volunteering with a charity once a week, for example.

+ Once you have trained your subconscious to feel the reward in meditation and exercise it will seek them naturally for you.

+ Getting a non-negotiable eight hours' sleep a night will ensure that you produce enough dopamine.

+ Who said chocolate isn't good for you? Dark chocolate is a reward that you can use for motivation and at the same time it naturally releases antioxidants that produce dopamine.

Oxytocin – any woman who has given birth will know all about oxytocin. It is more commonly known as the love hormone. Women produce this in abundance during and after the birth of their baby. It is also a key ingredient of the drug ecstasy that creates feelings of loving everyone in users. It is not recommended that you go out and get pregnant or take ecstasy as ways to produce oxytocin and certainly not at the same time!

+ You can produce oxytocin every day by simply hugging someone you love or a pet for 15 seconds. We need to maintain the contact for at least that long to gain maximum benefits, similar to the positive plunge technique (see page 93). The more affection you give and receive in your life, the happier you will be.

 LOVING KINDNESS (5 MINUTES)

This meditation is similar to that practised by Matthieu Ricard (see above). In addition, Barbara Fredrickson, one of the world's leading positive psychologists (see page 43) has found that frequent use of loving kindness meditations creates the highest levels of positive emotions.

Practise now if you have the time and return to it as often as you can – the more frequently the better.

+ + +

Flow for Happiness

IF HAVING and maintaining close connections to other people is the number one route to happiness and longevity, doing what you love for a purpose which is beyond yourself is the most reliable route to sustaining happiness. When you become so immersed in an activity that you lose track of time you are in the state known as 'flow' in positive psychology. This is when you become powerfully present and time becomes timeless. Personally, this happens to me when I am working with clients, giving or participating in a workshop and above all, writing; hours pass like minutes and days like hours as I write these pages.

It was Mihaly Csikszentmihalyi, a Hungarian-American positive psychologist, who after years of research on the purpose of life, coined the term 'flow'. Echoing Aristotle and the Buddha, Csikszentmihalyi stated, 'Repression is not the way to virtue. When people restrain themselves out of fear, their lives are by necessity diminished. Only through freely chosen discipline can life be enjoyed and still kept within the bounds of reason.'[75]

Csikszentmihalyi describes the eight characteristics of flow as follows:

1 Complete concentration on a task

2 Clarity of goals and reward in mind and immediate feedback felt

3 Transformation of time (speeding up/slowing down of time)

4 The experience is intrinsically rewarding and has an end in itself

5 The activity seems effortlessness and is carried out with ease

6 There is a balance between the level of challenge and the skills utilised

7 Actions and awareness are merged, with the result that there is a loss of self-conscious rumination

8 There is a feeling of control over the task

Doing what you enjoy can help to make you happy, but how much of your day, your week, and your life do you spend in the flourishing state of flow?

Many of my clients are unhappy because they feel lost and have either forgotten to find or have never found true meaning in their lives, for example Sarah, who was suffering from anxiety and low moods that brought her very close to clinical depression. She has three children and had always worked outside the home so felt the pressure to earn a living and also to be a wonderful parent. Although she hated her job it paid well so she kept it up for years. When I first met her, she had actually left work on stress grounds, no longer able to keep up the pretence that her job meant something to her. Consequently, her confidence was very low and she felt ashamed that she was off work because of stress.

Over the course of our sessions she felt intense, internal pressure to return to work even though she was not psychologically ready to do so and financially her family were able to manage for the time being. In addition, her partner was understanding and wanted her to recover and feel well, so the pressure she felt was totally self-generated. I advised her to be patient and that returning to a job she hated when it was not imperative was not the solution. What she truly loved to do would emerge not from pressure but from self-compassion. According to Sarah, nothing brought her joy apart from her children so it felt at times that we were at a standstill. However, her desire to get better was very strong and she diligently applied herself to the exercises that I gave her.

One day, Sarah found by chance an old newspaper clipping of herself as a child winning a national art competition. The image of the smiling, happy ten-year old reminded her of something she had totally forgotten – she *loved* to draw. Slowly she started to sketch again – portraits, places, anything, and, as she drew, her confidence grew. After a while, she started to take classes and opened up to a new world that had been left dormant for 25 years. She had entered the state of flow and this restored her confidence. She subsequently used her creativity to start her own interior design business and this now allows her the autonomy and creativity her soul had craved.

NOTEBOOK
FIND YOUR PURPOSE

Perhaps you know what you love to do and if that is the case then I sincerely hope that you are doing it. Perhaps, though, you are doing something you don't enjoy and feel trapped or perhaps you have no idea what your purpose is? Looking back at Csikszentmihalyi's eight principles of flow, ask yourself what activities you do regularly that come close to producing this state.

Write down all your hobbies and the things you love to do. If you get blocked a good place to start is to identify what your favourite activities were as a child. Many people loved art or singing or playing sport but no longer follow these pursuits as they feel that they do not have the time or that they are no longer a priority. If you want to be happy, believe me, they are a priority.

Here is a sample list of what can create the flow state:

+ Playing the piano

+ Dancing

+ Baking

+ Writing

+ Painting

+ Mathematics

+ Public speaking

+ Being in the company of positive people

+ Walking in nature

+ Helping others by volunteering

If there is nothing in your life that produces this state, then it is time to do something about it and find something. It doesn't have to be in your work, although it is great if you can earn a living from doing what you love, and this may even come with time. When you start to practise whatever the activity is you will become happier and feel more confident in taking measured, responsible risks that will, with time, provide you with opportunities you may never have even considered. Just like Sarah above.

Laugh, Play, Fun

+ + +

'With the fearful strain that is on me, if I did not laugh, I should die.'

ABRAHAM LINCOLN

ALTHOUGH LINCOLN WAS speaking metaphorically, we now know that what he said is actually scientifically true – laughing regularly has multiple health benefits and can literally save your life if you are prone to cardiovascular disease.[76] We also know that stress kills and that laughter is one of the most effective antidotes to tension and works in an immediate way. When we laugh, the endothelium, the inner lining of our blood vessels, expands and increases blood flow. With stress the opposite is true; the blood vessels contract, which reduces blood flow.

Laughter also provides us with a global language that unites and bonds people. A heartfelt smile is often the beginning of laughter and we instantly feel warm and safe when someone smiles at us. Spoken language is often not needed. Laughter is one of the most 'human' of experiences and, as we all know, is highly contagious – can you recall getting a fit of the giggles in school and being unable to stop? In 1962 in a Tanzanian all-girls' boarding school there was an outbreak of laughter so infectious that it forced the temporary closure of the school![77] When laughter reaches this epidemic level it can actually be stress-induced rather than fun. Often when emotions are very strong, for example at a funeral, people laugh, which may seem inappropriate, but like tears this is the body's way of releasing tension.

NOTEBOOK
QUESTIONS

Take a moment to answer the following questions:

1   How often do you actively seek out fun in a week?

2   How often do you laugh on average in a day?

3   How much fun did you have when you were a younger
     adult/teenager?

4   How much fun did you have when you were a child?

5   How much fun did you have when you were a toddler
     (if you can remember)?

6   Who are the people in your life that you laugh most
     with? Seek them out.

It seems that the older we become the less fun we have and the less we laugh. Generally speaking, children naturally prioritise fun and adults don't.

Social conditioning expects adults to shut down our fundamental need for playfulness and fun and it is from this expectation that much unhappiness arises.

As soon as we take on responsibilities we feel it is time to 'grow up' and we become conditioned to the idea that responsibility is the enemy of fun. In his 1914 poem, 'Responsibilities', William Butler Yeats wrote, 'In dreams begin responsibilities'. Your responsibility is to your true self, to your younger self who always believed in you and who still has dreams and a desire to have fun. Responsibilities need not cancel fun; progress comes from learning and learning is always fun when you are stimulated by the subject matter.

In addition to learning, find time to play in your life for the sake of fun and fun alone. If you are invited to a party, go, even if it is not really your thing. Stay for a while and soak up the fun atmosphere. If you have an opportunity to spend time with children, take it and engage with them. Children love adults who play with them at their level and you will feel great afterwards even if physically tired; the mirror neurons in the children will spark your own desire to have fun and you will feel lighter and freer. At family parties I am often naturally drawn to seek out the kids as this energises me and lightens my mood.

+ + +

Why You Deserve to Enjoy Your Life

'The unexamined life is not worth living.'

SOCRATES

IF YOU LIVE without knowing and understanding yourself you live with a stranger and until you get to know them, you can't fully trust them and you can't be happy. By following the exercises in this book you have shown immense courage and made great efforts to get to know yourself better and as a result you now live in the presence of someone you love and that will in turn make you very happy.

Every day, positive people create countless opportunities to turn up the positive, fade out the neutral and diminish the negative and now you have the tools to do the same. The world needs your positive energy and if you decide to truly embrace your potential for happiness you will also create happiness habits in those you love.

It is in the multitude of 'micro-moments' that make up life true bliss is to be found: the impromptu walk with a friend, the laughter you share with friends, bringing light to someone's day with a smile and a kind word. Your heart already knows what makes you happy; all you need to do is create the time, the space and the commitment to hear its gentle whisper. You have now climbed to the top of the emotional ladder and it is my job to help you to stay there. In the conclusion I will show you *how* to sustain your positive shift and the pitfalls you need to be aware of to maintain balance.

THREE KEY TAKEAWAYS FROM THIS CHAPTER:

1   Idle and indulgent pleasures do not lead to happiness.

2   Happiness is a courageous choice you make each day.

3   Enter the state of flow by practising your true purpose every day.

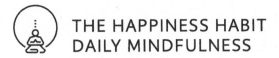

THE HAPPINESS HABIT
DAILY MINDFULNESS

+ Listen to your loving kindness meditation every day for seven days.

+ Do activities from your list that induce the state of flow.

+ Connect socially to at least one friend a day – a walk, a coffee or even a chat on the phone.

+ Smile at everyone you meet.

+ Spend time with children and play with them.

+ Actively seek experiences with only one goal – fun.

+ Take mindful moments throughout your day; when you feel happy, observe it, practise the 15-second positive plunge to get your neural network firing and serotonin rushing through your system.

AFFIRMATIONAL
TOOTH BRUSHING

Repeat your happiness habit affirmations every day while you brush your teeth. Feel the emotion of happiness as you do this.

MINDFUL
SHOWERING

Take time as you shower and dry yourself to be loving and patient with yourself. Use this habit as a time to connect towards yourself without judgement.

ACKNOWLEDGE
PROGRESS

Write down three examples of when you have practised the Happiness Habit and displayed evidence of your affirmations. For example:

1 I am responsible for my own happiness.

2 I spend time with people who make me happy and I do things that bring me joy.

3 I spread my happiness to everyone I meet.

Please now mark how you are feeling on the positivity sundial below.

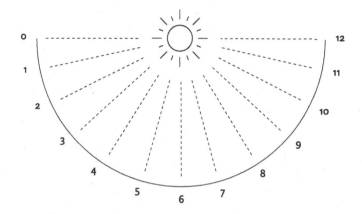

Remember to keep listening to your seven-minute morning and your sleep time hypnotherapies. Tick the days so far that you have listened on page 344. Be proud of the times you have listened and don't give yourself a hard time if you have missed one or two days; that is okay – keep going!

 ## MEDITATIONS

+ Morning ritual

+ Sleep time hypnotherapy

+ Loving kindness meditation

CONCLUSION

HOW TO SUSTAIN YOUR SIX POSITIVE HABITS

'Neither by nature, then, nor contrary to nature do the virtues arise in us; rather we are adapted by nature to receive them, and are made perfect by habit'

ARISTOTLE

QUIZ – HOW PRESENT ARE YOU?

Please answer 'Yes' or 'No'. Answer honestly and without too much reflection. Go with the first response that springs to mind. In the past month have you:

1. Found yourself ruminating on the past?

2. Found yourself worrying about the future?

3. Found yourself over-analysing what someone meant by a comment they made?

4. Found it hard to focus your attention on the task at hand?

5. Found your to-do list invading your thoughts when in the shower or doing household tasks?

6. Found that you have not been listening to a loved one, a child or a family member?

7. Felt the pressure of not having enough time to complete all your tasks?

8. Felt impatient when something small didn't go your way, e.g. sitting in traffic, losing something, making a small mistake, etc.

9. Had intrusive thoughts about what people will think of you if you do or say something?

10. Felt your mind wander from the task you are doing to the next task and even the one after that so that you are not focused on the task at hand?

Make a note on how many 'No' answers you get and give yourself a point for each one. The higher the number of 'No' answers, the more mindful and present you are.

Score from quiz on page 100 =

Score from quiz in Conclusion =

What differences can you see? Which areas have you improved on? Which ones need more work?

Presence is the strength of all strengths and it is the single most important way for you to maintain your positive shift. Always be present, always dwell in the Now Habit.

Mindfulness and being present is a skill that can be improved by habitual practice.

+ + +

Sustaining Your Positive Habit

You are now at the beginning of a long and uplifting love affair with life. Like all well-established habits, and once embedded into the subconscious, the Positive Habit can last a lifetime. The power of habit coupled with the skill of self-generating the six positive emotional states will help you to remain emotionally buoyant for as long you desire.

It is essential at this stage to evaluate your journey.

+ What are the key points you have learned about yourself?

+ Which meditations/visualisations really resonated with you?

+ Which areas still need some tender care and attention?

You are unique, and thus your self-care plan is unique to you. Nevertheless, I hope you can commit to the simple principle of listening to the audios each morning first thing and then last thing at night. If you do nothing else, take those precious 14 minutes each day to promote your own conscious ability to generate happiness.

Caring for your mind is an ongoing act of love and the neural pathways in your brain need constant attention. This may sound like an effort, but again, ask yourself, what is the alternative? To return to old emotional habits that were far more exhausting, and which didn't make you happy?

**Living unconsciously from fear is exhausting.
living consciously from love is empowering.**

Remember that presence is always within you and that you just need to connect with it. You are not, nor have you ever been, broken; by following the exercises in this book you are returning to your unconditioned default setting of happiness and reconnecting with your presence.

You have nurtured your heart and soul with what it needs most – love. You have taken the time and found the courage to be with yourself and consequently you shall live in peace.

You now see the world from an elevated perspective. The world has not changed, but your perception of it has moved from fear to love. Where you once saw negativity, you now see positivity; what

> 'I have learned that champions aren't just born; champions can be made when they embrace and commit to life-changing, positive habits.'
>
> LEWIS HOWES

once annoyed you no longer bothers you; what once offended you is no longer personal. Your heart may have been closed but now it is open and you see the world as a beautiful place. You see the goodness in other people because there is goodness there. Again, this is not naive or unrealistic, it is the cultivation of a mindset that empowers you to deal with life's difficulties as they arise.

It is my job now to ensure that you maintain your six positive emotional habits by caring for your shift in perspective with all the love and tenderness that you would give to a child who relies on you to guide them through the maze of life. Your commitment to yourself is crucial to your continued success. Listen to your needs and meet them, be guided by your desires and not your fears. Be with yourself.

+ + +

Trust

MANY YEARS AGO, when I was with a friend on holiday in New York and we were trying to find an elusive restaurant we had heard about, a guy, probably in his thirties, approached us with the biggest smile and asked in this wonderful New York accent, 'Can I help you guys, are you lost?' After we explained our predicament he said, 'forget that place, I know a great spot just down the block' and led the way. On arrival, our new buddy asked if he could join us and, a little surprised but also flattered that this hip New Yorker wanted to hang out with us, we agreed. I'll never forget his kindness, his desire to tell us about his city, what we should see and what tourist traps to avoid, but after a few beers (too many), I became a little suspicious of him. Was it his trick to find naive young tourists, bring them to expensive bars and get them to buy him drink? If so, at this stage I was happy enough to pay for him as his company as our very own tour guide had been invaluable. However, my suspicion kept me a little guarded and as the evening progressed I held back a little. Suddenly, our new friend bounced up and said, 'I have to hit the road' and after he left I went up to pay the bill. My heart dropped in shame when the waiter informed me, 'Don't worry, your friend settled up.' There was never any issue with the bill. It was about trust – in this case, my lack of it.

This year I was on holiday in France and was having lunch with two girlfriends when I saw a street artist approaching tables offering to do sketches. Nobody was agreeing so when he approached our table and said in his very French accent, 'I like to make a drawing for you, I don't want money, it eez a gift from the heart, I love this passion,' I invited him to sit at our table, much to the horror of my friends! He then drew two beautiful sketches for us. When I asked Pierre, the artist, why he does this for nothing he explained, 'I want to connect with the others, to bring a happiness for people.'

These two stories illustrate not that the world has changed, but that my perspective has taken a 180-degree turn. In New York I was in my early twenties, didn't know myself very well, didn't really trust myself, and as a result, found it hard to trust others. If you listen to the media regularly, it is understandable you might feel the world is full of dangerous people and that you should trust nobody. A diet of negative news is not good for your mental health. The media business is to a large extent a peddler of 'misery porn' and takes a biased and destructive view of humanity. It feeds the inbuilt negativity bias that is part of the human survival system. In my view, a more balanced approach to news reportage which also displays the positives in humanity would be more appropriate and lead to an increase in trust between people.

Trust in yourself that you can sustain the six positive habits through both the good and the tough times.

+ + +

Believe in the Goodness of Humanity

PSYCHOPATHS ARE RARE and deeply unfortunate individuals who lack empathy for other people and there are many conflicting theories about why and how this occurs. Psychopaths are estimated to make up just 1 per cent of the world's population, which means that 99 per cent do not have this condition and are essentially good although they may also sometimes act out in an unconscious way,[78] for example the alcoholic who lashes out at their family.

One day recently, my ten-year old son Luca was telling me about a kid who had teased him with hurtful and personal remarks. Although he was upset he said, 'There are no bad people in the world, only unconscious ones, and people who think others are bad are also unconscious.'

To be honest, I was blown away at the wisdom of this statement even though I am his mum, and mothers are notoriously proud of their own children.

When you take things personally you add to the level of negative energy and are more likely to be unkind to someone else. Negative energy, as we know, is toxic and spreads quickly. To stop this negative chain reaction, keep calm, breathe deeply (by making your exhalations longer than your inhalations), and you will immediately activate your parasympathetic nervous system (see the Calmness Habit), which will create calmness. This allows you to remain conscious and not to react in an unconscious negative manner.

I hope that by now and after completing this book you believe you are generally a good person. If you are still carrying unhelpful beliefs from childhood or because of things you may have done but are not proud of, then these need to be addressed. Most of us have done things we later regret and perhaps we could have been kinder and more honest in certain situations. It is important to remember that this does not make you a bad person – good people make mistakes all the time. The crucial thing here is to cultivate honesty, kindness and compassion as this will allow you to live in greater harmony with yourself and with others.

The more open and positive you become, the more you seek out and attract like-minded, positive people. It truly is an upward spiral.

+ + +

Listening Is Love

CARL ROGERS, the eminent psychologist famous for his client-centred approach to therapy, believed that true healing comes from a positive relationship between the client and therapist; someone who actively listens to you can help the transformation from suffering to flourishing. The client returns to the state of the unconditioned child who feels valued not for what they do but simply as they are. Rogers highlights the importance of listening in the therapeutic process, 'We think we listen, but very rarely do we listen with real understanding, true empathy. Yet listening, of this very special kind, is one of the most potent forces for change that I know.'

The therapy room is not the only place where healing can occur. You can choose to be someone who genuinely listens from the heart without jumping in with advice or prejudging the situation. The answer is often within the person already waiting for the opportune moment to be revealed via the sympathetic listening of a friend or someone else. Verbalising pain usually eases it, and with the added ingredient of active listening a transformation can occur.

Heal While You Sleep

THE DETRIMENTAL EFFECT of lack of sleep on both our physical and mental health, as discussed in Part I, requires that we get a non-negotiable, eight-hour 'sleep opportunity' each night. Anything under seven hours per night is considered sleep deprivation and brain scans show a 60 per cent increase in the reactivity of the amygdala – the alarm bell of the brain and the one most activated when we feel anxious or stressed.[79] Keeping a regular sleep routine, that is going to bed and getting up at the same time each day, is pure gold for your body, mind and spirit whether you are working or on holiday.

If you have been consistently listening to the sleep time audio, the quality and length of your sleep will now be better and hence your humour and happiness levels will also be higher. I say this with confidence, as I am blessed enough to have seen thousands of my clients report significant increases in their overall wellbeing from improved sleep and from listening to *The Positive Habit* hypnotherapy audios.

Some of my clients have asked why they should continue to listen if they feel better and my response is always that this is exactly why they need to continue to listen, so that they continue to feel positive.

The Positive Habit is about persistence rather than perfection. Remember the growth mindset? Always choose to focus on the effort, not the result, and remember that the journey does not end, there is no destination, you are always learning, always loving.

The Pitfalls of Being a
Positive Person

IN ORDER TO MAINTAIN the six positive emotional habits that you have self-generated by following this book, it pays to be aware that there are a few common obstacles which I have seen many of my clients experience as they embrace positive change. And so I thank all my clients for their trust, courage and honesty in making this book possible. I am eternally grateful to each of them for their insights.

1. PERFECTION

If your routine goes off-kilter, regardless of whether it is sleep, diet, exercise or listening to your audios, start again, and again, and again. Remember, this is all part of habit-building. Perfectionism and high expectations of yourself and others produce equally high levels of anxiety and pressure. Eventually, the rewards from healthy behaviour start to far outweigh any perceived rewards from unhealthy ones; the effort is gone and the pleasures you seek lead to your happiness. For example, going for a run rather than a few pints will become an anticipated reward that you actually enjoy and which will serve you better. Hiccups are to be expected, it is your relationship to them that matters. There needs to be flexibility in your approach; being too strict with yourself will inevitably lead to the need to escape yourself and the old unwanted behaviours will find space to re-enter.

If you have a day when you are far from present, loving, calm, confident, grateful, hopeful and happy, if you feel the opposite, your mind races, you are irritable with those you love, your anxiety and stress levels are high, you doubt yourself, you take everything and everyone for granted, you feel hopeless and unhappy, that is okay too! I admit it doesn't sound too appealing and it is an extreme – you are more likely to have a day where you feel on edge and stressed – either way, the point is not to strive for perfection. The negative feelings you have are, as you know present for a reason, so be very gentle with yourself, the negative will pass in its own time.

Incredibly, Dr Jill Bolte Taylor, neuroanatomist and author of *My Stroke of Insight,* studied her own stroke as she was experiencing it. She discovered that negative emotions pass in 90 seconds, the period of time cortisol is released into the system. Find the courage to endure the negative feelings for one and a half minutes, then let them pass. This '90-second rule' is invaluable if you are gripped with stress or anxiety. When negative emotions and bad moods continue for hours and days, it is the negative thoughts that keep them alive.

Using techniques such as the four-second positive pause, the ARK technique and the courage to sit with negative emotions will help them pass sooner than you may have ever imagined, especially after a good night's sleep. If you overreact or you are irritable with people, apologise, own your behaviour, understand it, be kind to yourself and start again.

2. FEAR THAT IT WON'T LAST
When people start to feel better they are often so relieved they become suspicious, thinking it has a 'too good to be true' quality to it. After all, if you have been struggling with stress and anxiety for years it is understandable to question whether it is really possible to maintain this feeling. It can be like the first flush of

a new romance after being single for a long time – it is amazing, but can you really trust your new partner to stick around?

When and *if* you feel anxious and stressed, I cannot emphasise enough that this is *normal*, it is part of being human. It doesn't mean that you have 'failed' at being a positive person or that you are back to where you started. It is usually the opposite – you are aware, you are mindful and now you have the tools, the techniques and the capacity to deal with those emotions. You are strong.

People who seek perfection and fear that their positive shift won't last often forget to employ the most crucial part of the sustaining process which is to acknowledge *all* progress, no matter how small, for example, remaining calm when you lose your phone. At the end of each chapter there is an instruction to acknowledge progress and I urge you to continue to do this. If you manage to handle a situation better than you would have done, write it down in your journal or at least make a mental note to congratulate yourself on progress or it will all too easily unravel. Imagine a child at school who was struggling to focus and who decides to make an effort to concentrate, makes great strides forward and her work improves but neither her teachers or parents take any notice. Will she maintain her efforts? The child still needs external validation – you don't. Praise yourself often for each small step you take forward. It is an act of love and support to do so and, believe me, it will motivate you to continue.

3. CHANGE

The subconscious can be stubborn and will initially resist change regardless of whether it is positive or negative. Yet life is, by its nature, change – growing up and growing older means constant change, which can lead to feelings of vulnerability and fear. Your attitude to change is primary to your ability to flow with life. Focusing on the potentials in change rather than the problems will help you as you move through each of your life stages with acceptance and courage.

Love yourself in all the stages of your life.

As you change from a negative or neutral mindset to a more positive one you will need to be vigilant not to be triggered into old negative habits. Old associations fire old neural networks in your brain. Take time to look at the negative trigger list that you made on page 58. How many things still bother you? Which ones no longer bother or disturb you? When you experience any of the major life changes that we all experience, be mindful that these are the times when you will feel more vulnerable even if the changes are desired ones such as a new job or the birth of a baby. In times of loss you will also need to give yourself time and kindness to make the necessary transition (the Hope Habit).

4. OTHER PEOPLE

By transforming your mindset from negative or neutral to positive you are breaking an unspoken bond in how you communicate with others; the emotional patterns that formed the nature of your relationship previously are shifting. For example, if you are a social smoker and decide to stop, there will be people who encourage you to continue because you are changing the status quo, they feel you are not 'fun' any more and your quitting may cause them to have to examine their own behaviour. This might be obvious with behavioural habits, but it is also evident, albeit more subtly, in emotional ones. For example, if you have a partner who was used to providing emotional support that you now no longer need, they may unconsciously feel rejected and question their role now and whether you still need them. As you change, so must the relationship be redefined, and this can take time and patience. Above all, it is constructive to remember that your partner is probably acting out of unconscious habit and may feel threatened by change.

Families of origin can prove to be the most challenging because that is where many of your emotional habits were first established and as such the family are totally habituated to 'old', established patterns of behaviour. Like actors on a stage, each member has a role and if one 'cast' member decides that they no longer wish to play the same part that they have played since childhood the foundation, dynamic and habits of communication are threatened. For example, if you were the 'difficult' one who is now 'positive', the dynamics of how the group understands itself is no longer valid. Dysfunctional patterns of behaviour often emerge at Christmas or on family holidays when many families struggle to maintain the socially acceptable veneer of the 'perfect' family; resentment and tension that may have been building all year has the time and space to emerge. Such issues need to be dealt with as they arise, not through conflict but through courageous and polite mindfulness. Remember not to be triggered into unconscious reactions that replay the old patterns of behaviour.

At work, colleagues may be jealous or try to undermine you as you start to be more proactive, ambitious and assertive. Your boss, on the other hand, will likely welcome your positive mindset and it will help you to advance your career as your confidence and emotional resilience grow.

If you struggle with any of the relationships in your life, I suggest you re-read the Confidence Habit and use the colour of confidence technique. Do not get pulled in by other people's unconscious behaviour; breathe deeply. Your self-esteem will need all the support it can get to stay strong and focused.

If there is an issue with a family member and they are open, have an honest conversation with them. Replace the argument with conversation and conflict with peace and you will be amazed at how your relationship will improve.

If you have a partner who is happy to listen to the sleep time audio with you, they too will benefit and by doing so you will both grow closer together.

It should be noted that the people in your life do not intentionally want to curb your new enthusiasm; they might just be suspicious of the 'new' you, but with time, they will eventually not only adjust but start to mirror your positivity (via mirror neurons) and the contagious effects of positivity. Keep in mind that it is almost impossible not to smile if someone smiles at you.

You are an ambassador for positivity and an inspiration for others.

If you have children, rest assured, they will be thrilled with the positive you and will have no problem adapting to the change. Kids are naturally open to positive people. You are giving them what they desire more than anything: a happy parent. And happy parents tend to have happy children.

Flourishing in
an Uncertain World

APOLLO, the Greek God of music, light and prophecies, had many temples built in his honour. The ancient Greeks loved Apollo, not only for the joy his music brought but also for his oracles which gave them hope for the future. Apollo selected a high priestess to be his earthly oracle at Delphi and people came from all over Greece to look for certainty in an uncertain world.

Apollo told his oracle that she must tell people the truth about the future even if it was not good news. One day, the King of Lydia sought the advice of the oracle about a war he wanted to embark on against Persia and she assured him that if he went to battle he would win and take over the great empire. Instead, however, the opposite happened and the King lost his empire. So great was the faith of the people in Apollo that they did not fault the oracle or indeed Apollo but imagined that the king had gone against her advice, that she had told him the opposite.

The desperate wish to know what will happen in the future is a very human condition and is based on fear, which is used by insurance and pension companies to make millions every year. While the ancient Greeks looked to Apollo for certainty in the external world, the reality is that the only certainty you can rely on is internal and based on cultivating peaceful presence. The six steps on your ladder are built on this and using these habits will help protect you now and in the future. By replacing fear with love and presence you lose the need to 'know' what will happen.

Your actions matter, as does your measured and calm response to external situations. Having completed the book you now have the strength to face whatever the future may bring, good, bad or indifferent. You can live free from unnecessary fear both now in this moment and in all the ones that follow.

FEAR TO LOVE (5 MINUTES)

Use this exercise if you feel anxious or fearful. It is really useful if you are not sure why you feel afraid. In the exercise you speak directly to your own heart, which when you listen to it always has the answers you seek. Your heart always knows the truth. It will help you to transcend fear into love.

+ + +

Your Sacred Space

ULTIMATELY, in order to flourish in life, you need to create a space that always remains safe and sacred, a space to which you can retreat if life becomes difficult or fraught. This is like a temple of strength and courage that we have built together. Remember to treat yourself with love and care always, especially at times when you feel most vulnerable.

Observe your life as it unfolds: remain calm, poised and present.

We all suffer pain but having the knowledge that you can survive and overcome suffering makes it bearable as you no longer add to it.

I know what it's like to lose my sense of self and it is terrifying, debilitating and makes life a struggle that can at times be very hard to bear. Before I became a therapist, I was an actress for ten years. This was my *raison d'etre* and I was passionate about it almost to the point of obsession. While I had some high points, more often than not I was searching for work and thus lived in a constant state of striving. My sense of self completely depended on getting my next role and if there wasn't one, I didn't feel just not good enough, I felt entirely worthless. At the time, a lack of inner confidence, chronic anxiety and constant rejection took its toll.

In January 2007, I had my last ever audition in the Abbey Theatre for a play being directed by Hollywood director Sam Shepard. The part I was auditioning for had no lines and required me to be completely naked! When I 'failed' to get this mediocre part, coupled with a hangover from a very depressing play I had just been in, I knew that my once highly sought-after dream was slowly destroying me. When I was acting all I ever wanted was for my character to be happy, to overcome the misfortunes she endured, but she never did. Most drama is, after all, based on tragedy and there were no Hollywood endings in the plays I did.

The day I walked out of the doors of the Abbey from my final audition, I had no idea what I was going to do but I did know two things: first, I had the potential to be happier; and second, I was certain that I wanted to help people in a meaningful way. Today, my inner and outer values are aligned, I am living my life purpose and my years as a struggling actress, although behind me, are a part of what makes me, me. I'm grateful for all the lessons I've learned. When I was born, my dad, a poet, wrote this to celebrate my life.

After Birth – Rory Brennan

Today I saw my second born

From my wife's body gently torn,

The tiny image of outrage

At her eviction from the womb,

Called on to the world's cold stage,

From her warm dressing room.

You never asked to be born at all

But we made you human, vulnerable,

My love lay back in proud collapse,

her body's duty done –

A common miracle perhaps –

Was kissed and left alone.

Was I subconsciously influenced to be an actress by this poem? Or did my father instinctively know when he saw me? Either way the poem reflects the preciousness, joy and vulnerability of life.

And so I will end where I began, clearly stating that your life is a miracle. Go forth with love and do good in this world to yourself and to others. Equipped with your six positive habits, nothing is impossible and everything is possible.

IMAGINEERING

Imagine that you and I are back in the restful, light room where we first started our journey. We are giving each other our undivided attention, we are present and belong in this moment together. We have been through a lot side by side and there may have been moments when you felt it was too hard, too much effort and you may have wanted to run, to quit, to tell yourself you don't need help. But you didn't. You kept going and here you are, healthy, full of positive energy, at ease in your body and mind.

'Give a man a fish and you feed him for a day. Teach him how to fish and you feed him for a lifetime.'

The practical tools contained in The Positive Habit *will feed your soul for a lifetime.*

There is a feeling of trust and triumph between us and as we chat a ray of sun beams through the window. You feel calm, relaxed, content and proud of how far you have come. I ask you to think about your progress, to evaluate how you feel now. You tell me that you feel like yourself again. You feel positive and exciting things are now happening in your external world as a result of your inner contentment. I ask you if this feeling is worth maintaining. What do you say?

As the session comes to an end, we hug for at least 15 seconds, we both now know the science and our hearts connect. You know that I'm here always but as you leave, you feel like you are with the one person who can truly maintain this feeling – yourself. You have all that you will ever need right here in this moment. You know you are loved, you are calm, you are confident, you are grateful, you are hopeful, and you are happy. You are a positive person.

SUSTAINING YOUR SIX POSITIVE EMOTIONAL HABITS

+ Continue to listen to the morning and sleep time hypnotherapy audios for as long as you like but for at least **66 days.**

+ Continue to journal – see your journal as your sacred space to share, to learn, to vent, but most of all to acknowledge all your progress. If you want to continue to make progress, you must acknowledge what you have already achieved.

+ Ask yourself each day or with each new challenge which habit you need to focus on. For example, if you are in having trouble in a relationship, focus on the Love Habit. If you start a new job, focus on the Confidence Habit.

+ You have free, lifetime access to all the audios from this book, so find the ones that really work for you and use them often.

+ Use the four-second positive pause to break old negative emotional habits.

+ Take mindful moments throughout your day using the seven deep belly breaths technique.

+ Before you get out of bed each morning and before you go to sleep at night, list ten things you are grateful for, one for each finger.

+ Take time to read some of the material again that resonates with you.

+ Continue your research by reading some of the books in the *Further Reading* section.

+ Each day, write three things you are proud of.

+ Each day, say at dinner time, take turns to say three things you are grateful for.

- Choose one daily mindful practice from each chapter, every day, for example letting every second person out in traffic or hugging someone for 15 seconds.

- Look into a mirror each morning and say 'Good morning, I love you.'

- Consider following The Positive Habit online programme on www.thepositivehabit.com, which contains a further seven hypnotherapy audios to which you have six months' access.

AFFIRMATIONAL TOOTH BRUSHING

Maintain the habit of affirmational tooth brushing. You can use all the six habits as you brush, affirming 'I am loved, I am calm, I am confident, I am grateful, I am hopeful and I am happy.' Feel the emotion in your heart as you repeat them. You can also invent new ones for yourself as you progress and depending on which habit you need that day.

MINDFUL SHOWERING

Maintain the habit of mindful showering, let this be your sacred space each day, focus on the sensation of the water, cleansing your mind and body.

MEDITATIONS

- Morning ritual

- Sleep time hypnotherapy

- Fear to love exercise

DAY 1	DAY 2	DAY 3	DAY 4	DAY 5	DAY 6
○	○	○	○	○	○
DAY 7	DAY 8	DAY 9	DAY 10	DAY 11	DAY 12
○	○	○	○	○	○
DAY 13	DAY 14	DAY 15	DAY 16	DAY 17	DAY 18
○	○	○	○	○	○
DAY 19	DAY 20	DAY 21	DAY 22	DAY 23	DAY 24
○	○	○	○	○	○
DAY 25	DAY 26	DAY 27	DAY 28	DAY 29	DAY 30
○	○	○	○	○	○
DAY 31	DAY 32	DAY 33	DAY 34	DAY 35	DAY 36
○	○	○	○	○	○
DAY 37	DAY 38	DAY 39	DAY 40	DAY 41	DAY 42
○	○	○	○	○	○
DAY 43	DAY 44	DAY 45	DAY 46	DAY 47	DAY 48
○	○	○	○	○	○
DAY 49	DAY 50	DAY 51	DAY 52	DAY 53	DAY 54
○	○	○	○	○	○
DAY 55	DAY 56	DAY 57	DAY 58	DAY 59	DAY 60
○	○	○	○	○	○
DAY 61	DAY 62	DAY 63	DAY 64	DAY 65	DAY 66
○	○	○	○	○	○

NOTES

1   'Depression and Other Common Mental Disorders,' World Health Organisation, 2017. http://www.who.int/whr/2001/media_centre/press_release/en/

2   Remes, O., Brayne, C., van der Linde, R. and Lafortune, L. (2016) 'A systematic review of reviews on the prevalence of anxiety disorders in adult populations.' *Brain and Behavior* 6(7)

3   William James, *Talks to Teachers.* Cambridge: Harvard Press, 1889

4   'Habits: Why we do what we do.' *Harvard Business Review.* https://hbr.org/2012/06/habits-why-we-do-what-we-do

5   Interview with Niall Breslin, 29 May 2018, Dublin, Ireland

6   Daniel Goleman, *Emotional Intelligence: Why it can matter more than IQ.* London: Bloomsbury, 1996

7   The Dalai Lama and Howard C. Cutler, *The Art of Happiness.* New York: Riverhead, 1998

8   Interview with Miriam Kerrins Hussey, 18 June 2018, Dublin, Ireland

9   Shawn Achor, 'The happy secret to better work.' TED talk, 2011

10   James Clear, 'How long does it actually take to form a new habit?' *Huffington Post.* https://www.huffingtonpost.com/james-clear/forming-new-habits_b_5104807.html?guccounter=1

11   www.forastateofhappiness.com

12   Barbara Fredrickson, (2001) 'The role of positive emotions in positive psychology: the broaden and build theory of positive emotions.' *Am Psychol.* 56(3): 218–26

13   Eberhard Fuchs and Gabriele Flügge, 'Adult neuroplasticity: more than 40 years of research.' *Neural Plasticity,* Volume 2014

14   'How do neuroplasticity and neurogenesis rewire your brain?' *Psychology Today.* https://www.psychologytoday.com/intl/blog/the-athletes-way/201702/how-do-neuroplasticity-and-neurogenesis-rewire-your-brain?page=0

15   Ruby Wax, 'Adventures on the road.' http://www.rubywax.net/blog/adventures-on-the-road

16   'How you can make your brain smarter every day.' *Forbes.* https://www.forbes.com/sites/nextavenue/2013/08/06/how-you-can-make-your-brain-smarter-every-day/#f87370234efc

17   Martin Seligman, *Learned Optimism: How to Change your Mind and Your Life.* New York: Vintage Books, 2006

18   'Falling for this myth could give you cancer.' *Mercola.* https://articles.mercola.com/sites/articles/archive/2012/04/11/epigenetic-vs-determinism.aspx

19   Bruce Lipton, *The Biology of Belief.* London: Hay House, 2015

20   Oliver James, *Not in Your Genes.* London: Random House, 2017

21   Guo, Guang. (2005). 'Twin studies: What can they tell us about nature and nurture?' *Contexts* 4(3): 43–7

22   'Psychologist on a mission to give every child a Learning Chip.' *The Guardian.* https://www.theguardian.com/education/2014/feb/18/psychologist-robert-plomin-says-genes-crucial-education

23   Charles Duhigg, *The Power of Habit.* London: Random House, 2012

24   Matthew Walker, *Why We Sleep.* New York: Scribner, 2017

25   Lawrence, M., 'The unconscious experience.' *Am. J. Crit. Care.* 1995 May; 4(3): 227–32

26   'Awake under anesthesia.' *The New Yorker.* https://www.newyorker.com/books/page-turner/are-we-all-awake-during-anesthesia

27   Seye Kuyinu, *Good Morning: How To Hack Your Morning And Win The Rest Of Your Day.* Pressing, 2018

28   Interview with Ciara Cronin, 18 April 2018, Dublin, Ireland

29   'Sigmund Freud's theories.' *Simply Psychology.* https://www.simplypsychology.org/Sigmund-Freud.html

30   Yuval Noah Harari, *Sapiens – A Brief History of Mankind.* London: Harper Collins, 2015

31   'Overcoming the negativity bias.' http://www.rickhanson.net/overcoming-negativity-bias/

32   Cacioppo, J. T., Gardner, W. L. and Berntson, G. G. (1997). 'Beyond bipolar conceptualizations and measures: The case of attitudes and evaluative space.' *Personality and Social Psychology Review* 1, 3–25.

33   'Marriage and couples.' The Gottman Institute. https://www.gottman.com/about/research/couples/

34   'Attention spans, consumer insights.' Microsoft, Canada, 2015

35   Eckhart Tolle, *The Power of Now.* Vancouver: Namaste, 1997

36   Jon Kabat-Zinn, *Full Catastrophe Living.* London: Random House Publishing, 1990

37   'Deprivation in early childhood can affect mental health in adulthood.' King's College London. https://www.kcl.ac.uk/ioppn/news/records/2017/February/Deprivation-in-early-childhood-can-affect-mental-health-in-adulthood-news.aspx

38   'Adopted Romanian orphans "still suffering in adulthood".' *BBC News.* https://www.bbc.com/news/health-39055704

39   Interview with Ivor Browne, 2 May 2018

40   'The secret of happiness revealed by Harvard study.' *Forbes.* https://www.forbes.com/sites/georgebradt/2015/05/27/the-secret-of-happiness-revealed-by-harvard-study/#151e0e486786

41   Jeremy Holme, 'John Bowlby and attachment theory.' *Simply Psychology.* https://www.simplypsychology.org/attachment.html

42   Jordan B. Peterson, *12 Rules for Life, an Antidote to Chaos*. London: Allen Lane, 2018

43   Maslow, A. H. (1943). 'A theory of human motivation.' *Psychological Review*. 50(4): 370–96

44   Brené Brown, *Daring Greatly*. London: Penguin, 2015

45   Don Miguel Ruiz, *The Four Agreements*. California: Amber-Allen Publishing, 1997

46   Dr Barbara Fredrickson, *Love 2.0*. London: Penguin, 2014

47   'US Airways Flight 1549.' Wikipedia. https://en.wikipedia.org/wiki/US_Airways_Flight_1549

48   'No lyin': Hiker says opera scared off mountain.' *USA Today*. lionhttps://eu.usatoday.com/story/news/nation/2014/08/06/hiker-opera-scared-off-mountain-lion/13661809/

49   Kelly McGonigal, 'How to be good at stress.' TED. https://ideas.ted.com/how-to-be-good-at-stress/

50   Gayatri Devi, *The Calm Brain*. London: Penguin, 2013

51   'Chronic stress changes immune cell genes, leading to inflammation: study.' *Huffington Post*. https://www.huffingtonpost.com/2013/11/07/chronic-stress-health-inflammation-genes_n_4226420.html

52   Sam Harris, 'Waking up.' https://samharris.org/podcast

53   Carol Dweck, *Mindset: Changing The Way You Think to Fulfil Your Potential*. London: Little, Brown, 2017

54   Carol Dweck, 'The power of believing that you can improve.' Ted Talk, 2014

55   Ibid.

56   Amy Cuddy, *Presence: Bringing Your Boldest Self to Your Biggest Challenges*. London: Little, Brown, 2015

57   *Heartfulness Magazine*, www.heartfulnessmagazine.com

58   'What is gratitude and what is its role in positive psychology?' Positive Psychology Program. https://positivepsychologyprogram.com/gratitude-appreciation/

59   Emmons, R. A. and McCullough, M. E. (2003). 'Counting blessings versus burdens: an experimental investigation of gratitude and subjective well-being in daily life.' *Journal of Personality and Social Psychology* 84, 377–89

60   'In praise of gratitude.' *Harvard Health Publishing*. https://www.health.harvard.edu/newsletter_article/in-praise-of-gratitude

61   Jane Ransom, 'Discover the three keys of gratitude to unlock your happiest life!' TEDx, 2017

62   'Scientists calculate the probability of your existence, conclusions similar to Buddhism.' *Epoch Times*. www.theepochtimes.com/scientists-calculate-the-probability-of-your-existence_787114.html

63   'Invisible gorilla test shows how little we notice.' *Live Science*. https://www.livescience.com/6727-invisible-gorilla-test-shows-notice.html

64   Joe Dispenza, *You Are the Placebo*. London: Hay House, 2016

65   Shane Lopez, *Making Hope Happen*. New York: Simon & Schuster, 2014

66   Hamilton, J. P. et al. (2011). 'Default-mode and task-positive network activity in major depressive disorder: Implications for adaptive and maladaptive rumination.' *Biological Psychiatry* 70(4): 327–33.

67   Randy L. Buckner (2013). 'The brain's default network: origins and implications for the study of psychosis.' *Dialogues in Clinical Neuroscience* 15 (3): 351–8

68   Kross, E. et al. (2011) 'Social rejection shares somatosensory representations with physical pain.' *Proceedings of the National Academy of Sciences* 108(15): 6270–5

69   Nick Vujicic, 'Overcoming hopelessness.' TEDx Talk, 2016

70   'Core competencies of lifestyle medicine.' *JAMA* 304(2): 202–3.

71   Mokdad, A. H. et al. (2000) 'Actual causes of death in the United States.' *JAMA* 1(291): 1238–45.

72   Alain De Botton, *The Consolations of Philosophy*. London: Penguin, 2001

73   Interview with Rick Hanson, 16 April 2018

74   'Brain scans reveal the world happiest man: his secret is simple.' *BBN*. http://www.bbncommunity.com/brain-scans-reveal-the-world-happiest-man-his-secrets-is-simple/

75   Mihaly Csikszentmihalyi, *Flow: The Psychology of Optimal Experience*. New York: Harper Collins, 1990

76   'The science of laughter.' *Psychology Today*. https://www.psychologytoday.com/us/articles/200011/the-science-laughter

77   'Tanganyika laughter epidemic.' Wikipedia. https://en.wikipedia.org/wiki/Tanganyika_laughter_epidemic

78   'How to spot psychopaths.' *Live Science*. https://www.livescience.com/16585-psychopaths-speech-language.html

79   '"Sleep should be prescribed": what those late nights out could be costing you.' *The Guardian*. https://www.theguardian.com/lifeandstyle/2017/sep/24/why-lack-of-sleep-health-worst-enemy-matthew-walker-why-we-sleep

FURTHER READING

+ Abraham H. Maslow, 'A Theory of Human Motivation', *Psychological Review* 50(4): 370–96.

+ Amy Cuddy, *Presence: Bringing Your Boldest Self to Your Biggest Challenges*, Little, Brown, 2015.

+ Barack Obama, *The Audacity of Hope: Thoughts on Reclaiming the American Dream*, Vintage, 2008.

+ Barbara Fredrickson, *Positivity*, Harmony Books, 2009.

+ Brené Brown, *Daring Greatly: How the Courage to Be Vulnerable Transforms the Way We Live, Love, Parent, and Lead*, Avery, 2015.

+ Bruce Lipton, *The Biology of Belief*, Hay House, 2008.

+ Carol Dweck, *Mindset: The New Psychology of Success*, Ballantine, 2007.

+ Charles Duhigg, *The Power of Habit*, Random House, 2012.

+ Daniel Goleman, *Emotional Intelligence: Why it Can Matter More than IQ*, Bloomsbury, 1996.

+ Deepak Chopra, *The Seven Spiritual Laws of Success*, New World Library, 1994.

+ Don Miguel Ruiz, *The Four Agreements: Practical Guide to Personal Freedom*, Amber Allen, 2018.

+ Eckhart Tolle, *The Power of Now: A Guide to Spiritual Enlightenment*, New World Library, 1999.

+ Gayatri Devi, *A Calm Brain: How to Relax into a Stress-Free, High-Powered Life*, Plume, 2013.

+ Joe Dispenza, *You Are the Placebo: Making Your Mind Matter*, Hay House, 2014.

+ Jon Kabat Zinn, *Full Catastrophe Living: Using the Wisdom of Your Body to Face Stress, Pain and Illness*, Random House, 2013.

+ Jordan B. Peterson, *12 Rules For Life: An Antidote to Chaos*, Random House, 2018.

+ Mark Rowe, *A Prescription for Happiness: The Ten Commitments to a Happier, Healthier Life*, 2014.

+ Martin Seligman, *Learned Optimism: How to Change your Mind and Your Life*, Vintage, 2006.

+ Matthew Walker, *Why We Sleep: Unlocking the Power of Sleep and Dreams*, Scribner, 2017.

+ Mihaly Csikszentmihalyi, *Flow: The Psychology of Optimal Experience*, Harper, 2008.

+ Norman Doidge, *The Brain that Changes Itself*, Penguin, 2007.

+ Oliver James, *Not in Your Genes*, Vermillion, 2016.

+ Rick Hanson, *Hardwiring Happiness: The New Brain Science of Contentment, Calm and Confidence*, Harmony, 2013.

+ Ruby Wax, *How to Be Human*, Penguin, 2018.

+ Sam Harris, *The End of Faith: Religion, Terror, and the Future of Reason*, W.W. Norton, 2004.

+ Shane Lopez, *Making Hope Happen: Create the Future You Want for Yourself and Others*, Atria, 2014.

+ The Dalai Lama and Howard C. Cutler, *The Art of Happiness*, Riverhead Books, 1998.

+ Thich Nhat Hanh, *The Heart of the Buddha's Teaching*. Broadway Books, 1999.

+ Viktor Frankl, *Man's Search for Meaning*, Beacon Press, 2006.

+ Yuval Noah Harari, *Sapiens: A Brief History of Mankind*, Harper, 2014.

ACKNOWLEDGEMENTS

To the positive people in my life.

Thank you, the reader, for taking the time to read the book and follow the exercises. A book, even though it usually has one name on the cover, never truly has only one author, it takes the love, the support and input of many minds to create a book. Like a powerful piece of theatre it is a collaborative affair in which each person plays their vital role, including the audience, or in this case, you, the reader. What is a book without a reader?

To my clients, without you this book would not exist. Your courage, your honesty, your desire to be the best that you can be is the essence of this book. You have taught me a great deal about what it is to be human, to be vulnerable and I am so grateful to each and every brave soul who seeks my help – thank you.

Thank you with all my heart to my husband, Ciaran Hyde. Your role has been integral, your loyalty, love and the countless hours you have spent helping me on the text of this book mean the world to me. I couldn't do it without you.

My father, Rory Brennan, you are a walking fountain of wisdom and knowledge, your support and understanding has helped me more than you will ever know. I am grateful for each beat of your heart.

My mother, Fionnuala Brennan, I've watched you in awe as you navigated your way through life with fun, laughter, resilience and a loving presence that has influenced me and inspired me all my life.

Orla, my sister, your laughter lights my world. Your natural optimism has never failed to lift my soul and just being in your presence makes me happy.

Luca, my son. You are always my number-one priority. I am so proud of you. Your young heart is the kindest, funniest one I know. In memoriam, my grandmother Olive and Aunty Lally, your goodness and love of life lives on in my heart.

Síne Quinn, thank you for your help and faith in me, it has been my joy to know you literally ALL my life.

Aoife McElwain, thank you so much for your introduction to Sarah Liddy at Gill.

Sarah Liddy, my editor; thank you for taking a leap of faith with me, your professional guidance has been invaluable.

Graham Thew, who climbed into my subconscious and designed the cover of this book. When I saw it my heart lifted.

Sheila Armstrong for her clarity and help on the editing of the book.

Teresa Daly and Avril Cannon – the dynamic marketing duo at Gill – thank you.

Aisling Killoran, my supervisor, your incredible positive power has been the rock of my career.

Jane McDaid, from the tears of laughter to your brilliant business acumen I am very fortunate to have you as a friend. Thanks to all your amazing team at Thinkhouse.

Thanks to my circle of friends, Phoebe Crowe, Caoimhie Jordan, Linda Gambrill, Zara Griffith, Suzanne Lyndsay and Roisin Byrne, just thinking of you all makes me laugh and smile.

My heartfelt appreciation also goes to the following people for their input into the book: Jack Canfield, Liz Nugent, Ciara Cronin, Ivor Browne, Rick Hanson, Brian Pennie, Vicki Notaro, Dermot Whelan, Dave Moore, Dara O'Mahony, Niall Breslin, Gerry Hussey, Miriam Kerrins Hussey, Elsa Jones, Grainne Nugent, Miriam Richardson, Sarah Caden, Brendan O'Connor, Jean Callanan and Piera Sarasini.